A Critical Introduction to the Metaphysics of Modality

BLOOMSBURY CRITICAL INTRODUCTIONS TO CONTEMPORARY METAPHYSICS

Bloomsbury Critical Introductions to Contemporary Metaphysics introduces and advances the central topics within one of the most dynamic areas of contemporary philosophy.

Each critical introduction provides a comprehensive survey to an important metaphysical subject or question. Covering the historical, methodological and practical contexts, it identifies and explores the major approaches, theories and debates. Capturing the changes to the ways the discipline is being studied, the emphasis placed on the historical background allows connections to be made between contemporary issues and the wider history of modern philosophy.

Designed for use on contemporary metaphysics courses, these introductions are defined by clarity of argument and equipped with features to facilitate and encourage further study. The result is a series of essential introductions for upper-level undergraduates and postgraduates wishing to stay informed of the issues and arguments shaping twenty-first century metaphysics.

TITLES IN THE SERIES INCLUDE:

A Critical Introduction to the Metaphysics of Modality

ANDREA BORGHINI

Bloomsbury Academic
An imprint of Bloomsbury Publishing Plc

B L O O M S B U R Y
LONDON · OXFORD · NEW YORK · NEW DELHI · SYDNEY

Bloomsbury Academic

An imprint of Bloomsbury Publishing Plc

50 Bedford Square   1385 Broadway
London   New York
WC1B 3DP   NY 10018
UK   USA

www.bloomsbury.com

BLOOMSBURY and the Diana logo are trademarks of Bloomsbury Publishing Plc

First published 2016

British Library Cataloguing-in-Publication Data
A catalogue record for this book is available from the British Library.

ISBN: HB: 978-1-4725-2426-3
       PB: 978-1-4725-2526-0
       ePDF: 978-1-4725-3390-6
       ePub: 978-1-4725-2194-1

Library of Congress Cataloging-in-Publication Data
A catalog record for this book is available from the Library of Congress.

Series: Bloomsbury Critical Introductions to Contemporary Metaphysics

Cover image © Mmdi/Getty Images
Cover designer: Catherine Wood

Typeset by Fakenham Prepress Solutions, Fakenham, Norfolk NR21 8NN
Printed and bound in Great Britain

Contents

Acknowledgments

Writing of this book took place during a sabbatical leave granted by the College of the Holy Cross, and it was possible thanks also to a Publication and Research grant from the College of the Holy Cross, through which I could secure the impeccable assistance of Natalia Iacobelli in the early stages of the writing process. The book vastly develops, expands, and refines an earlier volume of mine, published in Italian by Carocci Editore, in 2009—*Che cos'è la possibilità* (Possibility: What Is It? (literal translation)). I thank the editorial staff of Carocci, and in particular Gianluca Mori, for allowing me to rework the ideas contained in that volume. Along the way I have benefited immensely from discussions of the themes considered here with numerous people. I wish to thank them all; among their great number is Adriano Angelucci, Sergio Bernini, Claudio Calosi, Andrea Cantini, Massimiliano Carrara, Elena Casetta, Annalisa Coliva, John Collins, John Divers, Maurizio Ferraris, Salvatore Florio, Laura Franklin-Hall, Pierluigi Graziani, Chris Haufe, Andrea Iacona, Philipp Keller, Vittorio Morato, Luca Morena, Luca Moretti, Stephen Mumford, Marco Nathan, Andrea Sauchelli, Giacomo Sillari, Matthew Slater, Giuliano Torrengo, Vera Tripodi, Sebastian Watzl, and Neil Williams. Thanks to Massimo Mugnai, who first acquainted me with the history of modality and contemporary theories of possibility, and who punctually followed my early research on the topic; and to Tommaso Tempesti for suggesting that I choose the topic for my Laurea thesis. I am much indebted to my colleague Carolyn Richardson, who provided superlative editorial assistance while reviewing the manuscript. I owe special gratitude to Achille Varzi for the continuous incitement and encouragement provided over the years. Finally, without Ave, Guido, Lisa, and Elena, not only the book you hold in your hands, but much more would not have been realized (of me and what is mine).

I dedicate this book to my grandfather Dario, his brother Guido, and their parents, Angiola and Angiolo: that our reflection on what can be will prompt us to teach more vividly that violence against innocent civilians cannot be.

Introduction:
Framing the debate

The introduction presents the main framework for the book and its structure. It starts by explaining the problem of possibility according to three main perspectives: semantic, epistemic, and metaphysical (§0.1.). The perspectives are closely entrenched and, for each modal theory, one of them shall be employed as a privileged point of departure (§0.2.). The first tool required for a discussion of modality is an appropriate vocabulary: some basic concepts and terms are presented (§0.3.). Next on the menu is an illustration of the key methodological and structural choices that characterize the book (§0.4.), followed by a map of the theories of possibility, through which the content of the volume is illustrated (§0.5.). Finally, the possibility of impossible scenarios is brought up, and its philosophical interest is discussed (§0.6).

But if there is a sense of reality, and no one will doubt that it has its justification for existing, then there must also be something we can call a sense of possibility. Whoever has it does not say, for instance: Here this or that has happened, will happen, must happen; but he invents: Here this or that might, could, or ought to happen. If he is told that something is the way it is, he will think: Well, it could probably just as well be otherwise. So the sense of possibility could be defined outright as the ability to conceive of everything there might be just as well, and to attach no more importance to what is than to what is not.

R. MUSIL, *THE MAN WITHOUT QUALITIES*, TRANS. B. PIKE AND S. WILKINS, KNOPF, 1995: I, 10–11

Why read a book on the metaphysics of possibility? At first one could argue that it is an abstruse topic reserved only for those with a strong philosophical disposition. Practical individuals are interested in who they are and what they do, what there is and what happens: "I am Italian"; "I have US $30,000 in the bank"; "Napoleon was defeated at Waterloo."

This is perhaps one of the most misleading observations that can be made regarding the topic, and it is so for at least three reasons.

> **Reason number one:** If we take a moment to reflect, we find possibility nestled in the most familiar of things: even in things that at first glance concern what there is and what happens. Being Italian means, among other things, that I *am able* to freely travel throughout the European community; having US $30,000 in the bank means, among other things, that I *am able* to buy certain goods; Napoleon's defeat at Waterloo is dramatic and meaningful precisely because Napoleon *could have* won. In that which is, and in that which happens, there are the seeds of what could be and will be, of what could happen and will happen. (As we will have a chance to see, some even claim that that which is and that which happens are what they are precisely because they contain these seeds.)

> **Reason number two:** If something is or happens, that means that it was possible for it to be or happen. Actuality, therefore, is but one of the faces of possibility. And, as we shall see in the next chapter, this has been a founding principle in theorizing modality since Aristotle, summarized in the Latin dictum: *ab esse ad posse valet consequentia* ("from the fact that something happens, it follows that it is possible").

> **Reason number three:** While the majority of possible things are not attemptable, possibilities play a primary role in our lives. We might consider the relevance of possibility in explaining our frames of mind and our judgments: we do not need to watch an atomic bomb explode in order to be scared of one, and we do not need to see a homicide in order to accuse someone of attempted homicide.

So, why read a book on possibility? Because we are immersed in it, much more than it might appear at first glance. In the remainder of this introduction, we shall first identify the main philosophical questions arising for any theorizing about possibility, thus explaining the problem of possibility according to three main perspectives: semantic, epistemic, and metaphysical (§0.1.). The perspectives are closely entrenched and, for each modal theory, one of them shall be employed as a privileged point of departure (§0.2.). The first tool required for a discussion of modality is an appropriate vocabulary: some basic concepts and terms are presented (§0.3.). Next on the menu will be an illustration of the key methodological and structural choices that characterize the book (§0.4.), followed by a map of the theories of possibility, through which the content of the volume is illustrated (§0.5.). Finally, we shall briefly consider the possibility of impossible scenarios (§0.6.).

§0.1. The three problems of possibility

This book will deal with the theme of possibility, beginning with its central philosophical problem, which will be denoted *The Problem of Possibility* (and, henceforth, abbreviated as PP):

PP: What does it take for a certain situation to be possible?

For instance, what does it take for it to be possible that tomorrow it will rain in Manhattan?

The PP is a more complex problem than it might appear to be at first. In order to tackle it, we will make use of three sub-problems related to possibility, which pertain to three distinct areas of research: semantics, epistemology, and metaphysics. Semantics studies the meaning of linguistic expressions, including the conditions under which an utterance is true or false. (For an introduction to semantics, see Soames (2010).) Epistemology concerns the modalities through which a subject acquires information about himself, what surrounds him, and whatever else the subject can conceptualize—for example, theoretical knowledge that does not concern spatio–temporal reality, or even fantastic imaginings. (For an introduction to epistemology, see Feldman (2002).) Metaphysics, finally, concerns entities themselves: whether they exist and what they are, as well as how this can be explained; what type of relationships can exist between them—for example, existential relationships, causal relationships, relationships of composition between part and whole; and what modes of classification there are. (For an introduction to metaphysics, see Loux (2006).)

The PP is therefore intimately tied to *The Semantic Problem of Possibility* (SPP), *The Epistemic Problem of Possibility* (EPP), and *The Metaphysical Problem of Possibility* (MPP):

SPP: What does it mean to say that a certain situation is possible?
EPP: How do we come to know that which is possible?
MPP: What sort of entity is a possible entity (of any given kind—a possible individual, property, state of affairs, or ...)?

The SPP, EPP, and MPP deserve special attention because possible situations play a key role in our lives. To cite three examples: *probability* is nothing but a type of possibility; therefore, when we are deciding how to invest our savings, what course of studies to undertake, or whether to approve the construction of a nuclear power plant in our neighborhood, we are also relying upon a certain representation of possibility. *Sentiments* make for another good case in point. Many of them, even the most visceral or uncontrollable emotions, concern possible situations: we find ourselves fearful of having an accident, or worried about the health of a loved one, despite the fact that these are only possibilities, not matters of fact. Finally, the ways in which *punishments and rewards* are accorded often rely upon what a person could have done or could do: we might think, for example, of a sentence given for attempted homicide or a promotion awarded for a person's fulfillment of her potential. Therefore, reflecting upon what possibility is is central to understanding ourselves, the universe, and the norms and values that influence us, and those around us.

The objective of this book is to examine the solutions of the PP that have been proposed, with special attention to their metaphysical underpinnings. To this end, the SPP, EPP, and MPP will be discussed from time to time. Before proceeding, we should consider the relationship between these three problems.

The contemporary debate on modality developed from an important contribution to the SPP, namely so-called possible-worlds semantics, which reached a mature state during the end of the 1950s and early 1960s. In possible-worlds semantics, the truth conditions of propositions—and, in particular, of propositions involving modal terms—are evaluated with respect to a class of possible worlds. A proposition involving a possibility operator is true at a world when true *at a possible world*, while a proposition involving a necessity operator is true at a world when true *at all possible worlds*. Thus, for instance, the proposition *Foffo the cat could have eaten milk and cookies* is true at our world if there is a possible world where Foffo does eat milk and cookies; on the other hand, the proposition *Foffo the cat is necessarily a cat* is true at our world when Foffo is a cat at every possible world. Equipped with this (apparently) simple semantic machinery, which can be modified in numerous important respects, philosophers were able to address many old philosophical questions concerning modality in a new guise. On the other hand, the machinery had a not-so-small issue that became increasingly worrisome over time: what is a possible world? This question, which will accompany us throughout the volume, sums up one of the central problems of metaphysics of the past fifty years.

The epistemic and metaphysical doubts concerning possible worlds reawakened a host of vexed issues surrounding modality, which are indeed also discussed independently of the specifics of possible-worlds semantics.

The difficulty with the EPP resides in the fact that the majority of possible entities are not actual: they are never materialized in our universe. Therefore, they are entities that we cannot experience directly. I can know that Foffo the cat is crossing the street because I am present at the scene; I can know that yesterday Foffo had milk and cookies because Elena, who was present at the scene, told me so; but how do I know that Foffo *could have* had milk and cookies again today, if instead he ate fish and potatoes? Neither I nor any other person has ever been present at that possible scene. Perhaps this possibility is purely an invention, a projection of our minds. Or maybe the knowledge is an induction, or an inference based on certain empirical data: we infer that Foffo could have eaten milk and cookies today based on the fact that he ate milk and cookies yesterday. Or perhaps it is a deduction, an inference based on purely logical reasoning: Foffo could have eaten milk and cookies today because nothing contradicts our thinking this. Thus, how do I know that Foffo could have eaten milk and cookies again today?

A strategy for unraveling the knot created by the EPP is to turn to the MPP for help. We must first clarify what type of objects possible entities are in order to have a point of departure for explaining how we can gain understanding of them. If possible entities are merely fictions (as the so-called *fictionalist* claims), like Hamlet, then we have an argument for claiming that they are the product of our imagination; if they are entities that are entirely similar to those we experience (as the modal realist maintains), then we might assert that we become familiar with them by way of induction, endorsing their existence by relying on a philosophical analysis.

Nevertheless, some philosophers seem to follow the opposite path: in order to resolve the MPP, they rely upon a certain solution of the EPP. This is the case with the agnostic theory, for example. In yet a different case, the fictionalist opts for a certain solution of the MPP based on the advantages of a certain solution of the SPP. Deciding which strategy to follow is a question of philosophical methodology, which the reader will find applied in a variety of ways throughout the course of this book.

§0.2. The sphere of discussion

In what follows, the reader will be introduced to the eight principal theories of possibility. The focus will be on the metaphysical outlook of each theory. However, in order to appreciate the metaphysical outlook of each view and to understand how it may be twisted or revised, the distinction between the SPP, EPP, and MPP must be kept in mind. We will highlight which of these three problems we are dealing with at any given point, and whether, and how, a proposed solution can apply to the other two. Thus, while the focus of this volume is on the metaphysical aspects of contemporary theories of modality, along the way the reader will find remarks that apply to epistemic and semantic aspects of these theories too.

Yet, the array of theories that will be surveyed certainly cannot be considered complete. The theoretical field of interest to us is restricted from two main standpoints. First, we will examine only theories belonging to the contemporary philosophical scene, confining for the most part the historical predecessors to Chapter 1 (more on this also in the following section). Second, from the standpoint of the philosophical community, we will discuss only the works of philosophers who—as they say—have an analytic approach to philosophy (see Chase and Reynolds (2010)).

By implementing this last restriction we do not intend in any way to embrace the view that the analytic approach is superior to others, much less the view that there is one approach that stands out as being analytic. Rather, we are simply advising the reader of the brute fact that the philosophical theories considered here were produced within a circle of philosophers belonging to a given philosophical milieu. Though the latter is not readily identifiable, two of its traits are plain. First, by and large, the theories were *initially* advanced by philosophers working in institutions in the United States, the United Kingdom, Australia, or New Zealand. Second, the articles and books that fuelled the debate were all originally published in *English*, with the exception of a few contributions in European languages, such as German (especially important for early stages of the debate) and Italian (one version of the new actualism, dispositionalism, was originally published in Italian).

The geographic and linguistic aspects alone, however, are not sufficient to pin down the content of the analytic approach to modality. As the label itself suggests, the approach relies crucially on philosophical analysis, which is often carried out by means of a formal language, such as quantified modal logic, along with a possible-worlds semantics. It is part of such an analysis to divide the philosophical problem of possibility into sub-problems and to define the different views on the market based on the semantic/epistemic/metaphysical treatments of modal expressions that they propose. This is indeed the approach endorsed in this book.

Finally, it is also important to clarify that several key figures involved in the debate were educated outside of the United States, the United Kingdom, Australia, and New Zealand, and that they were non-native English-language speakers. Moreover, the contemporary geographic distribution of academics contributing to the debate on modality is much different from the distribution of fifty years ago: it spans the five continents and dozens of countries, including Argentina, Austria, Belgium, Brazil, Canada, China, Czech Republic, Finland, France, Germany, Greece, Holland, Hungary, India, Israel, Italy,

Japan, Korea, Mexico, Norway, Poland, Portugal, South Africa, Spain, Sweden, Switzerland, Turkey, and United Arab Emirates.

§0.3. Methodology

At this point, we shall mention three ways in which the PP will *not* be discussed.

1 *This book will not deal with the PP by making use of a formal language.*

Relatively speaking, a language is natural if it can be used ordinarily and learned without a didactic aid: examples include English, French, Chinese, Swahili, Tagalog, and so on. By contrast, a formal language is a non-natural language whose alphabet and grammar are entirely different from those of English. For example, HTML-programming language is a formal language. Logical languages are formal languages as well.

Most of the considerations in the metaphysics of possibility (in analytic philosophy) were developed in connection with the growth of a field of logic known as *modal logic*: possible-worlds semantics is a chapter—by and large, a foundational one—in contemporary modal logic. Modal logic has provided a conceptual system of unparalleled rigor and precision, in which classic questions related to possibility—such as the question of free will—are reformulated and reconsidered. In other words, the development of modal logic has allowed the very concepts of "possible" and "necessary" to be analyzed in a new, more accurate language.

Some of the theories examined here are rooted in modal logic, particularly those that make reference to the concept of possible worlds. However, in this book the reader will not find formal expressions in possible-worlds semantics, for example, or formal expression of the modal skepticism of Willard van Orman Quine. Both topics will be dealt with, at the proper time, in the English language.

This decision has been made for reasons concerning space and complexity, and due to the conviction that the central philosophical questions can (and, at least at an introductory level, should) be discussed independently of their representation in a formal language. When formalisms are introduced, the discussion is often diverted from the original problem: the problem of possibility. The problem is embedded in daily life: it is expressed, in our case, in the English language; and it is our duty to give a response in the English language.

This is not meant to discourage the reader from studying logic, and in particular modal logic: as will be emphasized on multiple occasions, drawing upon a formal language produces a sharpness and clarity that are unknown in natural language. Logic remains an instrument that is to be used to clarify a philosophical question or sharpen a solution that has been devised, albeit in its preliminary stages. Here, however, we can rely upon decades of sharpening of modal logic: the problem and its solutions have been provided in both natural and formal languages. The main issue is which theory to choose, and our goal is to assess the metaphysical proposals on the market.

   2   *This book will not deal with the PP by undertaking an historical analysis of its solutions.*

We certainly are not the first to consider the PP, and there is much to be learned from those who have preceded us. Those who wish to gain a deeper understanding of the concept of possibility ought to study the classic texts by authors such as Aristotle and Leibniz. For this reason, indeed, we have reserved an entire chapter—Chapter 1—to discuss prominent philosophical results in modality. Yet possible-worlds semantics equips us with conceptual resources of unprecedented sophistication, leading to a debate that deserves to be discussed separately. More importantly, we seek to use the most appealing theoretical apparatus for dealing with modalities, since our priority is not historical development or accuracy but theoretical soundness. The main ideas and questions raised in the past centuries will be kept in the background, to guide us from time to time, especially—as we shall see in Chapters 7 and 8—in connection with some recent and important proposals concerning the nature of possibility and necessity.

   3   *This book will not deal with the PP by focusing on the classic themes and problems associated with possibility.*

The history of modality is by and large the history of theoretical apparatuses developed to address three key problems in ethics, metaphysics, and epistemology/philosophy of mind, namely: to show the compossibility of free agency in a predetermined world; to demarcate essential from accidental properties of individuals (e.g. to be able to separate what is essential from what is accidental to being human, or so-called natural kinds, such as electrons and stem cells); to distinguish between propositions that pick out their referents by description from those that—so to speak—embed their referents directly (e.g. "There is a fat cat on the couch" *vs.* "Foffo is on the couch"). Over time, the theoretical apparatuses dealing with these problems became increasingly systematic. Possible-worlds semantics is one of the latest tools to be able to address them, along with other cognate and remote (but no less important) problems. Our focus will be on the theories through which we can take on all these problems. For this reason the reader will find the problems discussed on multiple occasions (and further readings are suggested at the end of this Introduction), but without the systematic display they deserve.

Furthermore, it should be noted that we will be interested in what is possible *tout court*, while keeping the distinction between the various categories of possible situations in the background and pointing them out where most suitable. Nevertheless, such categories are highly relevant in certain areas. For example, a great deal of the literature on alethic modalities developed in conjunction with the literature on temporal modalities. The distinction between that which *was* possible, that which *is* possible, and that which *will be* possible is at the root of how we think about agency and responsibility, and serves to introduce the so-called problem of *future contingents*. According to this problem (addressed in Chapter 1), just as it seems intuitive (and in keeping with the linguistic details of most natural languages) that the present and the past are fixed, it is equally intuitive that the future is open. Thus, while it is a fixed truth that—say—Foffo had milk and cookies yesterday and that Foffo is having milk and cookies now, it is still open whether Foffo will be eating milk and cookies tomorrow—that is, both "Tomorrow Foffo will be eating milk and cookies" and "Tomorrow Foffo will not be eating milk and cookies" are possible futures at the moment; and yet, tomorrow only one of the two possible futures will be actualized, and the other will be regarded as a *counterfactual* situation, a situation that runs counter to the facts of the actuality. In short, intuitions suggest that there is only one past and only one present, but there are many futures. Needless to say, philosophers have challenged these intuitions on many counts, and to do so they had to resort not only to a theory of time but also to a theory of possibility. The theories we will discuss in the book can be (and have been) used to frame and solve the problem of future contingents in different ways; yet, it is not the aim of the book to discuss the details of such potential solutions.

Another relevant distinction among categories of possible situations is that between *nomic possibility* and *metaphysical possibility*. The former concerns the laws of nature, or the behaviors that seem to be inherent to spatio–temporal objects, while the latter concerns all of the non-contradictory ways objects can present themselves. The distinction is central to the philosophy of science: according to some authors (e.g. David Armstrong), what is nomically impossible is impossible *tout court*; others (e.g. David Lewis) contend that the realm of the possible is much wider than we can even imagine, extending far beyond what does not accord with the laws of nature. The distinction between nomic and metaphysical possibility will be considered in different chapters (especially Chapters 4, 5, and 8). Nonetheless, it is beyond the scope of this book to deal systematically with it.

§0.4. A bit of vocabulary

As in every field of intellectual research, philosophical reflection on possibility has assumed certain characteristic features as well as its own terminology. In addition to guiding the reader through the answers to the question regarding what is for something to be possible, we will also try to familiarize her with the distinctive terminology and concepts of the field.

To this end, the book will make extensive use of the expression "concept", which here refers roughly to that which can function as the subject of a cognitive act, or mental act, through which reality is understood. For an introductory and in-depth examination of the theme, see Carey (2009).

Moreover, in natural language we use an assortment of expressions to speak of that which is possible and necessary: "to be able to", "to have to", "to have the ability", "to have the opportunity", "possibly", "duly", "perhaps", "maybe", *and so on*. From a syntactic point of view, these are expressions that are applied to a sentence or to a part of a sentence (for example, the subject or the predicate). These are the adverbs, verbal modes, and enunciative *modal* operators classified in technical jargon as *alethic modalities* (or, simply, modalities).

The term "modality" comes from the fact that a modal expression characterizes *the mode of existence* of the entities that are referred to by the expressions to which it is applied. Let us take, for instance, the sentence "It is raining" along with the following variants: "Today: it is raining"; "In Manhattan: it is raining"; "I claim that: it is raining"; "It is (morally) good that: it is raining"; "Necessarily: it is raining"; "Possibly: it is raining". Each of these variants expresses a way of being of raining, that is to say, of the entity to which "It is raining" refers.

At this point, it becomes somewhat natural to classify the various modes into different categories, and consequently the modalities that express them. *Temporal modalities* ("today", "now", "in 1977", *et cetera*) specify the way of being in time of the entities which are referred to by the expressions to which they are applied. *Epistemic modalities* ("to believe that", "to know that", "to see that", *et cetera*), from the Greek επιστημη (*epistéme*), "knowledge", specify the way that the entities referred to by the expressions to which these modalities are applied are thought of. *Deontic modalities* ("it is good that", "it is wrong", "it should be encouraged", *et cetera*), from the Greek δεομ (*déon*), "obligation", specify the "way of being moral" of the entities referred to by the expressions to which they are applied. Finally, *alethic modalities*, from the Greek αληθεια (álétheia), "truth", specify the "way of being true" of the entities referred to by the expressions to which they are applied.

Possibility and necessity are alethic modalities. The modality of what is possible is used to express the fact that the existence of an entity can be realized; the modality of what is necessary is used to express the fact that, in any case, it will be realized.

Modality is one of the most fertile areas for philosophical reflection. It is so fertile that it forces us to create a restriction: our discussion will be limited to the alethic modalities. Henceforth, when we will speak of modalities, we will be referring to alethic modalities.

These limits notwithstanding, it is unlikely for a theory of possibility that makes contemporaneous use of all the alethic modal expressions to attain sufficient conceptual clarity. It has, therefore, become standard to make a choice that favors a restricted number of paradigmatic expressions of (alethic) modal discourse, to which all of the others can in some way be connected; such expressions are gathered within the following two groups:

1 "it is possible that" and "it is necessary that";

2 "necessarily", "possibly", "accidentally", "essentially", "impossibly", "contingently".

The modalities in group (i) are *enunciative operators*, that is, expressions that modify the meaning of an entire sentence, such as "It is possible that: tomorrow it will rain in Manhattan". The modalities in group (ii), on the other hand, are *adverbs*, expressions that modify the way of existence of certain entities, be they individuals, events, properties, relationships, or concepts; an example is the use of "necessarily" in: "Cheese is necessarily produced from milk". In one way or another, all of the theories presented here presuppose that the expressions in groups (i) and (ii) are paradigmatic: based on these we are able to shed light on many other (alethic) modal expressions in our ordinary language; the theoretical challenge, then, lies in revealing the meaning of the expressions gathered in (one of) these groups.

It would be equally useful to alert the reader to the following terminological choices that have been used in the text.

● *"Theory of possibility"/"Theory of modality"*: These expressions are used synonymously: a theory of possibility, just like a theory of modality, must explain not only the meaning of expressions such as "it is possible that" or "possibly", but also expressions such as "it is necessary that" or "necessarily".

● *"Ordinary language"/"Natural language"*: These expressions are also used as synonyms, to designate any language that can be learned without a didactic aid and used ordinarily. Languages used to formulate any formal logic are not to be understood as natural or ordinary.

- *"Situation"*: This expression stands for what is designated or described by a complete sentence, no matter its form: an action, an event, a state, or a relationship among these. In contemporary analytic philosophy, the expression "state of affairs" is often used rather than "situation". But because the former is now associated with specific metaphysical positions about which we wish to remain neutral, we have chosen to use the latter.

§0.5. Classification of theories and order of exposition

Most philosophers are inclined to consider their position to be distinct from those of others. And given that the philosophers who have dealt with possibility number well over eight (the number of theories we will discuss), it is very difficult to deliver an agreeable description of the debate in the chapters that follow. Texts that provide a comprehensive overview of the debate about the metaphysics of modality do vary to some extent with respect to the number of theories they discuss, and the names of the theories. This book is organized around eight main theories, that is, eight philosophical responses to the PP and its three sub-problems SPP, EPP, and MPP. The classification adopted strikes us as effective and easy to remember, and as carving the debate at three crucial joints. In the remainder of this section we will introduce the classification of the theories by illustrating the three philosophical problems that determine said crucial joints. For an illustration of the classification, see Figure 0.1. (As anticipated, Chapter 1, which is not in the diagram, deals with the history of work on modality.)

§0.5.1. A genuinely conceptual dispute?

The first joint dividing philosophers on matters of modality lies at the intersection between the cognitive and the non-cognitive. Do modal expressions really express concepts? Are we able to grasp these alleged concepts? The wide variety of modal expressions we find in most natural languages, the abundance of purposes they serve, and, most importantly, the opacity of their roles invite us to answer these questions in the negative. Indeed, some deny that alethic modalities express concepts: either because we are not able to truly understand what we speak of (**modal skepticism**), or because what is at stake are sentiments, not concepts (**modal expressivism**). Modal skepticism and modal expressivism will be taken up in Chapter 2.

The vast majority of philosophers, however, maintain that the task of a theory of possibility is precisely to explain certain concepts. Against the skeptics we can point out that modal expressions are constantly employed where conceptual rigor seems to be most desirable and logics dealing with them abound. Against the expressivists we can point out that modal expressions can be nested, to express subtleties that typically only concepts can exhibit; David Lewis offers a nice example (borrowed from a 1970 paper by J. Howard Sobel) in his book *Counterfactuals* (1973):

> If the USA threw its weapons into the sea tomorrow there would be war; but if the USA and the other nuclear powers all threw their weapons into the sea tomorrow there would be peace; but if they did so without sufficient precautions against polluting the world's fisheries there would be war; but if after doing so, they immediately offered generous reparations for the pollution there would be peace. (10)

Whether those and other rejoinders are sound, the expressivist position seems to defend an important intuition, which deserves to find room in a map of theories of possibility.

§0.5.2. A conceptual reduction?

The second joint in the debate on the metaphysics of modality divides those who maintain that alethic modalities cannot be analyzed in the terms of other concepts (**the modalists**) from those who maintain that they can. This is a recurring kind of distinction in analytic philosophy: analysis must have an end, but it is disputable where to draw the end line. Modalists—whose view will be discussed in Chapter 3—hold that there is no clearer way to explain what it means to say that Napoleon could have won at Waterloo than to say ... Napoleon could have won at Waterloo. To clarify, prominent modalists such as Graeme Forbes and Charles Chihara do believe that the variety of modal expressions can be captured in terms of two chief ones—that is, necessity and possibility; they also believe that the meaning of expressions aiming to convey the necessity or possibility of a situation is best captured by a formal language. Yet they deny that possible-worlds semantics permits us to infer the existence of possible worlds, regardless of what these may be taken to be. The meaning of necessity and possibility operators is not analyzable.

Others, however, have attempted to explain modal concepts. To the credit of modalism, the trend of analyzing modal concepts in terms of—say—possible worlds or dispositions is rather recent. Talk of possible worlds can be found far back in the history of philosophy, such as in the writings of Epicurus (341–270 BCE). But it was not until Leibniz (1646–1716) that the concept was used to systematically analyze propositions containing modal expressions. And again, until the 1960s, when possible-worlds semantics was more firmly established, modalism seemed the most prudent view. However, matters are now different: today most philosophers working on modality hold that modal expressions should be analyzed in terms of other concepts, possible worlds being chief among these. The widespread debate about the semantics, epistemology, and metaphysics of modality generated over the past fifty years may, indeed, be considered an attempt to fine-tune such alleged conceptual analysis.

§0.5.3. Possible worlds?

Among those who have attempted to explain modal concepts, some (modal realists, ersatzists, fictionalists, agnostics) make use of possible-worlds semantics. **Modal realism**, which will be taken up in Chapter 4, became prominent thanks to the writings of David Lewis, in particular the book *On the Plurality of Worlds* (1986), now a classic in contemporary metaphysics. According to Lewis, there is an infinity of worlds, each of which is as *real* or *concrete* as our world is. No two worlds overlap, though (parts of) worlds may resemble each other in virtue of their inhabitants sharing properties or taking part in the same events.

Lewis's view—which, in his own words, has often prompted an "incredulous stare"—was criticized left and right. The largest contingent of critics belongs under the label of "**ersatzism**", the subject of Chapter 5. The view owes its name to the German "*ersatz*", roughly translated as "surrogate". For ersatzists, possible worlds are surrogates of the actual world; unlike modal realists, they regard the actual world as having metaphysical priority over the other worlds. There are many versions of ersatzism, some of which can be traced back to Rudolf Carnap, Ludwig Wittgenstein, or even Leibniz. In *On the Plurality of Worlds*, Lewis raises some serious objections against this view, which he considers as the major rival on the market.

Shortly after the publication of Lewis's landmark book, Gideon Rosen, a colleague of his at Princeton, put forward a novel view, **modal fictionalism**, which will be discussed in Chapter 6 alongside the more recent **modal agnosticism**. There are a few variants of fictionalism, some of which have gained credence in recent years. All variants agree in the fundamental strategy, which can be divided into two stages: first, take the most conceptually powerful view on the market, modal realism, and pretend that it is true only for the sake of conceptual analysis; second, discard any ontological commitment of modal realism—it is merely a fiction. As we shall see, this strategy is difficult to pin down and probably lacks some of modal realism's theoretical virtues. **Modal agnosticism**, on the other hand, was first proposed by John Divers in a 2004 article, "Agnosticism About Other Worlds". As the name indicates, Divers suggests that we take possible-worlds semantics at face value, but remain agnostic as to the existence of possible worlds (regardless of what these may be taken to be). The details of this position are still evolving and under discussion; we will consider some objections in Chapter 6.

Finally, we come to those who reject possible worlds, but still aim to provide a conceptual reduction of modal expressions. These philosophers largely overlap with those whom Vetter (2011a) labels "new actualists", so we will borrow the term. New actualism will be analyzed in Chapter 7; it is the most recent position on the map and it is still under scrutiny and development. We will distinguish two main variants: the first (dispositionalism) relies on dispositions, entities' abilities to act a certain way if placed in certain conditions; the second (new essentialism) insists on the importance of preserving multiple, irreducible modal expressions—essence, metaphysical necessity, nomic necessity, and deontic necessity. Both positions have generated a considerable amount of interest in recent years, and lie at the core of prominent ongoing debates in modality. **Dispositionalism** was first suggested by Ellis (2001) and Molnar (2003), more explicitly defended first by Borghini (2003) and then by Borghini and Williams (2008), and later refined and developed in a number of works, including those of Contessa (2010, 2013), Mumford and Anjum (2011), and Vetter (2015). Although thinkers such as Aristotle recognized the importance of dispositions, the attempt to analyze the wide range of modal expressions in terms of dispositions is a bold one; and, as we shall see, it has been subject to some important criticisms. The **new essentialism** owes much to the works of Kit Fine (e.g. 2005). In some respects, Fine's position is akin to modalism (see for instance Melia (2003: Chapter 4)); this is because according to Fine there is a core of modal concepts that is ultimately irreducible, just as the modalist claims that necessity and possibility operators express irreducible concepts. However, Fine's work has also generated novel literature on such topics as *essences* and *grounds*, thus prompting new conceptual analyses of modal expressions. For this reason, new essentialism is classified alongside new actualism and not modalism.

While possibility and necessity are logically and hence theoretically entrenched, there are some questions pertaining to the truth of necessary statements that deserve to be discussed independently of specific theories of possibility. This is the task of Chapter 8, which will discuss **the varieties of necessity** (pragmatic, nomic, deontic, conventional, metaphysical, and essential); necessary truths concerning mathematical entities, such as geometrical figures and numbers, as well as truths concerning abstract entities such as sets; and, finally, *a priori* truths and the epistemic accessibility of modal truths.

§0.6. Impossibility

It is our intention to look carefully at certain theories of possibility. Yet—we might ask ourselves—what can be said about impossibility? Once we have a theory of possibility, will we also be able to account for that which is impossible? Yes and no. Once we establish an interpretation of alethic modalities, we will be able to tell where the boundary lies between that which is possible and that which is impossible. However, this does not mean that we will know how to treat the questions that emerge once impossible situations are taken into consideration: if two plus two were to equal three, then could I also go surfing this afternoon on twenty-seven different surfboards simultaneously? Or, could we admit a given impossibility without compromising the truth of the other things we think?

Since the contributions of Morgan (1973) and Yagisawa (1988), respectively addressing logical and metaphysical issues regarding impossible worlds, these and cognate questions have become increasingly prominent in the literature on modality. Impossible worlds have been particularly handy in explaining the behavior of agents who hold inconsistent beliefs, as well as in addressing the truth conditions of systems of propositions (e.g. legal systems) that contain contradictory claims. We shall come back to this topic in Chapter 8.

Study Questions

- What is a modality a mode of?
- What are alethic modalities?
- What other modalities, besides the alethic, are there?
- What is the problem of possibility?
- What are the three main sub-problems of possibility?
- What is possible-worlds semantics?
- What are the three main joints giving shape to the contemporary debate on alethic modality?
- What is an impossible world?

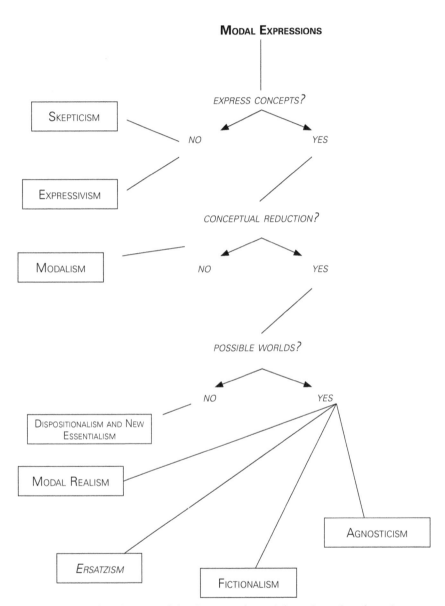

FIGURE 0.1 *Classification of the theories of possibility adopted in the volume*

FURTHER READING

For an **introduction to modal logic**, see Hughes and Cresswell (1968, 1984), Chellas (1980), Fitting and Mendelsohn (1998), Girle (2000), and Garson (2006). The last is particularly suggested for the more philosophically and less logically oriented.

On the **history of modalities**, see the classic by Kneale and Kneale (1962). For a reconstruction of the main moments in the development of possible-worlds semantics, see Copeland (2002) and Ballarin (2010); among the essential readings, see C. I. Lewis (1918), Wittgenstein (1921), C. I. Lewis and Langford (1932), Carnap (1946, 1947), Prior (1957), Kripke (1959, 1963), and Hintikka (1961, 1963).

For an overview of the debate regarding **modality and free will**, see Kane (2002). Among the most influential classic contemporary texts on this topic are Plantinga (1974b), Pike (1977), van Inwagen (1983), and Vihvelin (1988).

The debate on **essentialism** traverses the whole history of philosophy and is among the most assorted and vast; for a first approach, see Robertson (2013). The readers, edited respectively by Linsky (1974) and Loux (1979), are another useful starting point. The most significant contemporary texts on the topic include: Kripke (1980), Wiggins (1980), Sidelle (1989, 2002), Ellis (2001, 2002), Fine (2005), Mackie (2006), and Lowe (2006). For an introductory reading on **natural kinds**, see Bird (2009) and Bird and Tobin (2015). Beebee and Sabbarton-Leary (2010) and Campbell, O'Rourke, and Slater (2011) are updated collections of essays on metaphysical and semantic issues concerning natural kinds; among the recent monographic studies, see LaPorte (2009) and Khalidi (2013).

For a historical debate on **future contingents**, see the classic by Gaskin (1995), and the earlier classic work by Prior (1957). Hasle and Øhrstrøm (2011) provide an up-to-date framing of the debate.

For additional **introductory texts** on contemporary theories of possibility in analytic philosophy, see: Divers (2002), Melia (2003), Loux (2006: Chapter 5), and Pruss (2011). Also useful, although covering the debate only in part, is Sider (2003).

There are several **readers** collecting important writings about modality. Among these are: Linsky (1974); Loux (1979); Gendler and O'Leary Hawthorne (1992); and Hale and Hoffman (2010).

Finally, for an overview of the main issues relating to **impossible worlds**, see: Yagisawa (2010); Berto (2013a); and Jago (2014). See also the Further Reading section in Chapter 8 for additional bibliographical resources.

1

The metaphysics of modality: A historical overview

This chapter examines the key ideas and principal figures that, in the history of Western philosophy, have characterized and shaped the central theories of modality. It is divided into three main parts: Ancient (§1.1.), Medieval (§1.2.), and Early Modern (§1.3.). After considering the early ideas of Parmenides and Zeno (§1.1.1.), we examine the first author to have systematically studied modal concepts, Aristotle (§1.1.2.), and the first school to have done the same, the so-called Megarian School (§1.1.3.). The period in which reflection on modality flourished, however, is the Medieval, with the Arabic and Scholastic philosophical traditions (§1.2.1.). During the late Scholastic period, authors such as Ockham (§1.2.2.) and Buridan (§1.2.3.) enriched and refined the Aristotelian and Megarian teachings, setting the stage for the contemporary revival of reflection on modality. During the Early Modern period, modalities were used to put forward some bold metaphysical views, such as those of Descartes (§1.3.1.), Leibniz (§1.3.2.), Spinoza (§1.3.3.), and Hume (§1.3.4.). The concluding section (§1.4.) highlights the importance of nineteenth-century logic for the rise of quantified modal logic and possible-worlds semantics in the twentieth century (examined further in Chapters 2 and 3).

*****

The ability to reason using modal notions is characteristic of humans, and is certainly remarkable, arguably playing an important role in our evolution and setting us apart from other intelligent beings. Musil's famous passage on the sense of possibility, cited in the Introduction (see page 1), shows concisely the centrality of modal intuitions to human endeavors.

These intuitions often play an important role in assessing the palatability of a theoretical option and in getting it off the ground, and during our journey through the theories of possibility we shall have several occasions to appreciate this role. It is no surprise, then, that modality has been discussed since the earliest historical examples of philosophical speculation (see Gabbay and Woods (2004a)).

We shall begin our study of the metaphysics of modality with an excursus through the history of philosophy, examining the main authors and arguments that influenced Western theories of possibility and necessity. While the story we will tell starts with Ancient Western philosophy, it is important to note that its roots run much deeper into human history: in the work of key authors such as Parmenides and Aristotle, we can trace important influences from Ancient Indian philosophy and Jewish thought via the Babylonian, Egyptian, and Cretan civilizations (Gabbay and Woods 2004a). We shall not trace these connections, but rather stick to those texts and authors that more directly motivated the texts and also writers who take center stage in the chapters to come.

The discussion to follow has been organized around three main moments: Ancient (§1.1.), Medieval (§1.2.), and Early Modern (§1.3.). It goes without saying that there is an element of artificiality in this schema, and that the development of ideas about possibility and necessity follows not time, but variables such as place, school, cultural context, and individual genius. Our tour through this history will include only a few stops, and only for work that is so classic as to be essential to even an introductory treatment; and we shall give voice to the original texts as much as possible. The views of each author we examine have been the object of meticulous and extensive contemporary study, and often of complex controversies of interpretation; the reader can find ample suggestions for introductory presentations, monographic studies, and research articles in the Further Reading section at the end of this chapter. For each author, we shall provide—where possible—dates of birth and death as well as key locations where the author is known to have lived and been active.

§1.1. Modalities in Ancient philosophy

§1.1.1. Parmenides and Zeno

Parmenides (c. 515–450 BCE; Elea, Campania, Italy) is often considered to be the first significant figure in Western thought. Only about 160 fragmented lines of the original 3,000 lines of his philosophical poem *"On Nature"* are known to us, and yet based on these fragments, and also on the discussion of Parmenides's ideas in the work of other authors (such as Zeno and Diogenes Laertius), scholars have been able to agree about some of the central tenets of his philosophy.

In the second part of "On Nature", Parmenides lays out his chief metaphysical thesis: Being is all that there is, while not-being cannot be. Superficially, this may appear an uncontroversial claim; far from it, however, since Parmenides's thesis is a formulation of so-called *metaphysical monism*: there is only one thing, Being, which never changes and so never dies, which never came into existence, which has no boundaries and no detachable parts. Metaphysical monism contends not only that the entire universe is one simple entity, but—most importantly for our purposes—that this entity has some *necessary* features: it cannot go out of existence (it is eternal) and it cannot change. Parmenides may have defended, or have come close to defending, what we now call *necessitarianism*. This is composed of two theses: (i) the universe exists out of necessity, and (ii) it is necessarily the way it is. Metaphysical monism is an endorsement of (ii); however, whether Parmenides also endorsed (i) remains controversial (see Lewis (2009)). We shall encounter an instance of necessitarianism later on in this chapter when discussing the views of Baruch Spinoza (1632–77).

Possibility, as well, plays a role in Parmenides's philosophy. While true knowledge is recognizing the necessity of Being, false opinion is that which suggests the contingency of worldly affairs—such as that things could have been otherwise or that the future is open. It seems plausible that Parmenides's philosophy must be read as a reaction to Pythagorean science, which tried to explain worldly phenomena in terms of a multiplicity of opposing principles. Parmenides's method emphasized the importance of reason over the senses: philosophy becomes that way of life which goes beyond the surface of appearances and reveals, by means of the use of reason, the truth of seemingly incredible conclusions.

The Parmenidean reliance on reason is also at play in the work of his student (or young associate) Zeno of Elea (Campania, Italy), active during the fifth century BCE. Zeno is most famous for his ingenious paradoxes, having indeed introduced this genre of work in Western philosophy. It seems that the goal of Zeno's arguments was to lend credence to Parmenides's metaphysical monism. Confronting us with claims that at least *prima facie* contradict each other, the paradoxes force us to rethink the bounds of possibility and necessity. Zeno's paradoxes stand as excellent examples of the importance of modal reasoning to philosophizing. Relevant for our purposes is that they invite us to entertain some (seemingly) impossible scenarios; we shall come back to the importance of impossible scenarios for the metaphysics of modality at the end of Chapter 8.

Eight paradoxes have survived, although not all in their original formulation, They are typically divided into four groups: four paradoxes against motion; two paradoxes against plurality; the paradox of the millet seed; and the paradox of place. Let us briefly go through each of them.

§1.1.1.1. The four paradoxes of motion

While their original formulation is lost, we find these paradoxes discussed in the works of other philosophers, including Aristotle's *Physics*. The lack of textual evidence adds to the interpretive difficulty, as different readings of the paradoxes are hinted at by different formulations. Zeno's aim seems to have been to show the absurdity of Pythagorean science, which was *atomistic*—it explained worldly phenomena in terms of the interaction of atoms. The formulation of the paradoxes begins by raising a question: if atoms exist in space and time, are space and time either continuous (and hence infinitely divisible) or discrete? To this question we can provide four answers: that both space and time are continuous; that both are discrete; that space is continuous and time is discrete; that time is continuous and space is discrete. Each of the four answers is shown to be paradoxical.

1   When both space and time are discrete, we have the so-called *Paradox of the Stadium*.

2   When space is discrete and time continuous, we have the paradox of *Achilles and the Tortoise*.

3   When space is continuous and time discrete we have the *Bisection Paradox*.

4   When both space and time are continuous we have the *Paradox of the Arrow*.

The paradox of the stadium

Suppose that space and time are discrete. Imagine you have three logs of wood—A, B, and C—lying on the floor. Each log is three feet long. The logs are parallel to each other and are arranged in this manner: A is in the center of the room and is standing still; B is at the far left of the room and is moving right along its length; C is at the far right of the room and is moving left along its length. B and C, the two moving logs, travel at the same speed and start overlapping A at exactly the same time. There will thus be a moment when A, B, and C are all traversing each other, but they will do so at different speeds. In fact, in the time it takes for the front edge of B to pass one foot of A, the front edge of C will pass two feet of B (because both B and C are moving, and in opposite directions). Now, suppose we change the story in two apparently uncontroversial respects, by saying that each of A, B, and C occupy three units of the smallest unit of space, *and* that both B and C are moving at such a speed that they traverse the smallest unit of space in the smallest unit of time. Then, for B, it takes *half* the smallest unit of time to traverse a section of C that occupies the smallest unit of space; and, *vice versa*, for C, it takes *half* the smallest unit of time to traverse a section of B that occupies the smallest unit of space. But this is absurd, because the smallest unit is by definition indivisible. (The Paradox of the Stadium presents some particular interpretive dilemmas; the formulation provided here follows especially Siderits and O'Brien (1976).)

The paradox of Achilles and the Tortoise

Assume that space is discrete and time is continuous. Achilles is running after the tortoise and there are infinite units of time between the current moment and the point at which Achilles catches up (because we are supposing that time is continuous). In each unit of time, the tortoise must traverse at least one minimum unit of space, which means that the tortoise will traverse infinite minimum units of space, since there are infinite units of time. In order to reach the tortoise, Achilles must traverse each of the minimum units of space that the tortoise has traversed. But those units are infinite. Therefore, Achilles must travel an infinite distance to reach the tortoise, which is absurd.

The bisection paradox

Assume that space is continuous and time is discrete. Imagine a person walking from her bed to the restroom. Since time is discrete, she will take at least one minimum unit of time to cover each minimum unit of space. But there are infinite such units of space, so she will take an infinite time to reach the restroom, which is absurd.

The paradox of the arrow

Suppose that both time and space are continuous. Imagine an archer shooting an arrow. In each minimum unit of time, which is infinitely small, the arrow will cover a minimum unit of space, which is infinitely small: thus, in each minimum unit of time the arrow will be at rest. So, the arrow is at rest in every moment and is never moving, which is absurd.

§1.1.1.2. The two paradoxes of plurality

These paradoxes aim to prove that there cannot be a plurality of entities. The first paradox shows the absurdity of thinking that there are *finitely many* entities. Assume that the number of entities is finite; then, you must conclude that there are infinite entities, because between any two entities there have to be infinitely many dividing them. The second paradox of plurality deals with the absurdity of infinitely small and infinitely large entities. Suppose that the universe is inhabited by infinitely small entities (e.g. the points of a line); then, take one such infinitely small entity and add it to any plurality of entities: at the end of the process we will have the same number as we had at the start, because the added entity is infinitely small; that is, we added nothing. If, on the other hand, the universe is inhabited by entities that occupy space, then such entities will have infinite parts; hence, they will be unlimited—which is absurd.

§1.1.1.3. The millet paradox

This paradox focuses on the joint action of multiple entities. Suppose that there are multiple entities, say a good bunch of millet seeds; and suppose further that those seeds perform some joint action—say, they make a sound when dropped into an empty bucket. Then, each seed or each part of a seed (regardless how small) must make a sound too—which is absurd, since one tiny seed makes no sound.

§1.1.1.4. The paradox of place

This paradox focuses on the relationship between an entity—say, a chair—which occupies a place, and the place that is occupied by the chair, where the chair and the place are thought of as two distinct entities. If the chair has a place, then place itself—which is a separate entity from the chair—must have a place; but the place of a place must have a place too; and so on *ad infinitum*. Thus, nothing has a place, which is absurd.

Zeno's paradoxes stand as one of the clearest examples of the power of rational argumentation: without relying on any specific observation, Zeno rejects metaphysical pluralism. It is crucial for us to stress that the argumentative force of these paradoxes rests on our ability to imagine scenarios and to suppose that they genuinely represent our universe.

In the *Parmenides*, Plato states that Parmenides and Zeno paid a joint visit to Socrates in Athens around 450 BCE, and it seems plausible that Zeno had quarters in Athens for a time. The two philosophers from Elea may therefore have influenced Socrates and, through him, Plato and Aristotle. Certainly, the latter gave considerable attention to Zeno's paradoxes in the *Physics* and, for what concerns Plato, he touches upon problems related to modalities in a few places (e.g. the *Timaeus*, where we find a thorough discussion of necessity). But, on the basis of the textual evidence that we have, Aristotle's study of modalities reached far beyond the problems presented by Zeno's paradoxes and by other eminent colleagues, including Plato: Aristotle put forward the first articulated treatment of possibility and necessity in Western philosophy.

§1.1.2. Aristotle

Scholars of Aristotle have discussed at great length on his position with respect to modalities; a selection of significant publications can be found in the Further Reading section at the end of the chapter. In this section, we shall restrict our focus to two tasks: first, we will distinguish the different modalities that seem to emerge from Aristotle's writings, asserting that some important ones—logical possibility, synchronic possibilities, and conditionals—are missing; then, we will present and discuss in more depth the so-called problem of future contingents. But, first, let us note that another aspect of Aristotle's metaphysics often plays an important part in the contemporary debates on the metaphysics of modality: the theory of substances, and the related doctrine of essentialism. Since essentialism will be discussed at various stages in the chapters to come (especially Chapters 3, 7, and 8), we shall set this topic aside for now.

Necessities and possibilities

Aristotle (c. 384–322 BCE; Stagira and Athens, Greece) examines issues with possibility and necessity in many parts of his works, and most famously in the *De Interpretatione*, the *Prior Analytics*, and the *Metaphysics*. He considers four main topics: necessity; statistical or temporal frequency; diachronic possibility; powers or capacities. Let us review each of them in order.

Necessity
Aristotle distinguishes several senses of necessity in a particularly telling passage of the *Metaphysics*, book *Delta*, amidst the treatment of other fundamental notions such as "cause," "nature," and "element." Aristotle writes:

> We call 'necessary' (1) (a) that without which, as a condition, a thing cannot live; e.g. breathing and food are necessary for an animal; for it is incapable of existing without these; (b) the conditions without which good cannot be or come to be, or without which we cannot get rid or be freed of evil; e.g. drinking the medicine is necessary in order that we may be cured of disease, and a man's sailing to Aegina is necessary in order that he may get his money. (2) The compulsory and compulsion, i.e. that which impedes and tends to hinder, contrary to impulse and purpose. For the compulsory

is called necessary (whence the necessary is painful, as Evenus says: 'For every necessary thing is ever irksome'), and compulsion is a form of necessity, as Sophocles says: 'But force necessitates me to this act'. And necessity is held to be something that cannot be persuaded—and rightly, for it is contrary to the movement which accords with purpose and with reasoning. (3) We say that that which cannot be otherwise is necessarily as it is. And from this sense of 'necessary' all the others are somehow derived; for a thing is said to do or suffer what is necessary in the sense of compulsory, only when it cannot act according to its impulse because of the compelling forces—which implies that necessity is that because of which a thing cannot be otherwise; and similarly as regards the conditions of life and of good; for when in the one case good, in the other life and being, are not possible without certain conditions, these are necessary, and this kind of cause is a sort of necessity. Again, demonstration is a necessary thing because the conclusion cannot be otherwise, if there has been demonstration in the unqualified sense; and the causes of this necessity are the first premises, i.e. the fact that the propositions from which the syllogism proceeds cannot be otherwise.

    —Trans. W. D. Ross; available at *The Internet Classics Archive*: http:// classics.mit.edu/Aristotle/metaphysics.5.v.html

The passage identifies a general definition of necessity, then divides it into two kinds—conditional and absolute; conditional necessity is in turn divided into three kinds. The general definition, provided under point (3), is as follows: (N) Necessity is that which cannot be otherwise. Aristotle's idea, here, seems to come close to the contemporary logical notion of necessity, where a sentence *S* is regarded as necessary when it is not possible that its negation is true. This general definition supplies an umbrella under which to subsume two more specific notions of necessity. The distinction is drawn at the end of the passage, where Aristotle talks about the necessity of a geometrical demonstration. Geometry suggests a case of *absolute* or *intrinsic necessity*. In the case of geometry, the premises are necessary and their necessity is transmitted to the conclusion; if we agree that the nature of a triangle follows necessarily from its definition, then the sum of the angles of a triangle is necessarily 180 degrees in virtue of the necessary nature of the triangle. In deductive demonstrations (e.g. demonstrations in mathematics, geometry, and logic), the entities featured in the premises, in virtue of their necessary natures, secure the necessity of certain conclusions regarding them. On the other hand, many cases of necessity seem to involve a *conditional necessity*, such as the fact that eating is necessary for survival: if I have survived until now I must necessarily have eaten, but it is not necessary that I eat, and it is thus not necessary that I survive. Conditional necessity is divided into three kinds, identified at the beginning of the passage. First, there is (N1), the necessity of a *material condition* for the obtainment of some other condition; for instance, eating is necessary for survival. Second, there is (N2), the necessity of certain *courses of action* for achieving certain goals; for instance, I must take a medicine in order to heal. The difference with respect to (N1) is that, in (N2) the condition requires a will: someone must choose to act in a certain way and that choice is necessary for obtaining the relevant goal. Finally, there is (N3), the necessity of an action that is *constricted or forced*: for instance, where we have no choice but to surrender to our opponent.

In several passages, Aristotle reflects on the relationships between what is necessarily the case, what is possibly the case, and what is actually the case. Setting aside some controversial points of interpretation, Aristotle seems to accept and establish certain principles that eventually become core to the development of modal logic and modal metaphysics: (i) if something is necessarily the case, then it is actually the case; (ii) if something is actually the case, then it is possibly the case; in Medieval times, this principle will be summed up in the motto *ab esse ad posse valet consequentia* (it is allowed to infer possible existence from actual existence); (iii) by transitivity then, (i) and (ii) imply that what is necessarily the case is also possibly the case.

Despite this apparently settled net of relations between modal notions, we do not find in Aristotle a systematic and unitary treatment of modalities. The fragmented picture is most apparent when we examine Aristotle's treatment of possibility. Here we find at least three different notions: statistical or temporal frequency, diachronic possibility, and power or capacity.

Statistical or temporal frequency

Sometimes, possibility stands for that which *at some point in time* will be the case, and necessity for that which is the case *at all times*. For instance, because salt dissolves in water at all times in which we merge salt (and only salt) in water (and only water), we may conclude that necessarily salt dissolves in water. The relationship between salt and water, however, seems not to be a matter of conceptual necessity: arguably, there is nothing in the idea of salt that necessitates that it dissolves in water; and some may even think that we can easily imagine a scenario were salt does not dissolve in water. The notion of a statistical modality traverses the whole history of Western philosophy, and has been crucial at several points in time, including: Late Medieval philosophy (see Knuuttila (2013)); the dispute between Kant and Hume on the necessity of natural laws (see De Pierris and Friedman (2013)); and the contemporary debate on the relationship between natural, semantic, and metaphysical necessity (see Bird and Tobin (2015), Beebee and Sabbarton-Leary (2010), and Sidelle (2002)).

Diachronic possibility

The notion of diachronic possibility captures those scenarios that seem to change modal status as time goes by. Yesterday, Maria gave Luca some kulfi ice cream; Luca could have put the kulfi ice cream in the freezer, so that today it would have been still good to eat; alas, Luca forgot the ice cream on the kitchen counter, and the ice cream is irreparably spoiled now. So, yesterday it was the case that the ice cream was edible, and today that is no longer the case; more importantly, yesterday it *could have been* the case that Luca got to eat ice cream, but today it is *no longer possible* for Luca to eat ice cream.

There is a notion of necessity related to diachronicity too. If something must be the case *at some point in the future*, then we may say that it is diachronically necessary. For instance, to say that I am mortal is arguably to say that, necessarily, at some point in the future I will die. The diachronic notion is different from the statistical notion: to say that necessarily I will die is different from saying that, at every point in time, I will die (the latter is no longer the case after my death); and it is different from saying that, at every point in time, I must have died (it is obviously false now); and it is arguably different also from saying that, at every point in time, I must have died or will die (as I may be dying). So, the notion of possibility that is conjoined with a diachronic perspective reaches quite deep into the semantics of our modal talk; it is this notion that is at the root of a very difficult philosophical problem, the problem of future contingents. We shall turn to this problem in a moment, after examining the third notion of necessity—power or capacity.

Powers or capacities

The last notion of possibility we find in Aristotle is the one of power, sometimes also referred to as "capacity" or "disposition". Vipers' poison has the disposition or capacity to kill humans, in the absence of an antidote; humans have the power to think that things could have been otherwise; this key has the capacity to open that door. Powers do not establish a link at a specific point in time: under suitable conditions, it is correct to ascribe a certain power to a certain entity, even if that entity has never displayed the power. Maria has the capacity of saying ten times in a row the expression "Ten times in a row", even if she has never displayed it and—as is most likely—she never will. Note that there is a link between diachronic possibility and powers: some powers can be gained and lost with time, for they are tied to certain other abilities. Thus, while certain entities, such as ice cream, spoil forever, other entities can lose a certain capacity and then gain it back. For instance, when she used to train, Maria could run for 15 miles straight; now she cannot, but she plans on regaining that ability with two months of training. Aristotle's discussion of powers is quite important to the contemporary debate on the metaphysics of modality (see for instance Marmodoro (2015)). In Chapter 7, we shall return to powers, capacities, and dispositions, when discussing the so-called dispositional theory of possibility.

Aristotle's writings offer a wealth of ideas from which later theorists of the metaphysics of modality have drawn inspiration. At every point in the history of Western philosophy, Aristotle's ideas have been invoked and developed in different directions. Yet, for our purposes, it is worth noting that some notions of possibility that are important to the contemporary debate are absent from Aristotle's works. Three such notions shall be pointed out: logical possibility, synchronic possibility, and conditionals.

Logical possibility

Aristotle does not really entertain the idea that to be possible is *to be logically non-contradictory*. For instance, there seems to be nothing contradictory—one could argue—in Maria's being one-third human, one-third Alaskan salmon, and one-third oak tree. And yet, such a scenario is so far-fetched as to be possible in only the barest sense, such that the only way to consider it possible is to regard it as non-contradictory from a logical point of view. Aristotle seems not to consider possibilities of this sort as genuine. It will be the Megarian School that makes logical possibility a standard modality to bear in mind in philosophical theorizing.

Synchronic possibility

Maria gave the kulfi ice cream to Luca, but the ice cream spoiled. The possibility of the ice cream not spoiling thus remained non-actualized. From the point of view of many contemporary theories, non-actualized possibilities are still genuine possibilities; they comprise a large part of what we shall call "mere possibilities" (discussed further in Chapter 2). Aristotle seems to have little interest in mere possibilities, and perhaps he regarded them as non-genuine. It was Augustine of Hippo (AD 354–430) who brought the idea of synchronic possibility into Western philosophical discourse.

Conditionals

We have seen that Aristotle discusses conditional necessity. Also, some of the notions of possibility he entertains involve conditionals; for instance, a power is assigned to an entity based on the fact that, *if* the entity is in certain circumstances, *then* some other circumstances obtain (e.g. if a viper bites Maria in the absence of an antidote, then Maria will die). Nonetheless, Aristotle did not separately discuss conditional statements, and did not attempt to systematically analyze them. It was again the Megarian School, as we shall see, that first addressed the problem of assigning truth values to conditional sentences.

Future contingents

Through the notion of diachronic possibility—a notion of possibility that is entrenched with the perspective of temporal change—we can formulate the so-called problem of future contingents. In general, the problem deals with the question of whether there is an *open future* and whether, as time goes by, the number of options before us changes. Aristotle introduces the problem in the *De Interpretatione* 9, where we also find the famous example of a sea battle:

> Let me illustrate. A sea-fight must either take place tomorrow or not, but it is not necessary that it should take place tomorrow, neither is it necessary that it should not take place, yet it is necessary that it either should or should not take place tomorrow. Since propositions correspond with facts, it is evident that when in future events there is a real alternative, and a potentiality in contrary directions, the corresponding affirmation and denial have the same character.
> —Trans. E. M. Edghill; available at *The Internet Classics Archive*: http://classics.mit.edu/Aristotle/interpretation.1.1.html

The problem of future contingents relies upon the idea—intuitive during Aristotle's time and until modernity—that sentences can change in their truth value across time; so, our sentences regarding tomorrow's possible sea battle may change value as time goes by. The problem involves three crucial principles of logic, and shows that, in the case of future contingent proposi-tions, these principles do not square with one another. The principles are:

(B) *Bivalence*: Every sentence expressing a proposition is either true or false.

(EM) *Excluded Middle*: For every sentence *S* expressing a proposition, "*S* or *non-S*" is always true. (Hence, there is no intermediate truth-value for sentences.)

(NC) *Non-Contradiction*: For every sentence *S* expressing a proposition, it is always true that: "It is not the case that: *S* and *non-S*" is true. (Hence, it can never be the case that, at a same time, both *S* and *non-S* are true.)

In the case of the sea battle example, we intuitively accept that it is true that "either there will be a sea battle tomorrow or there won't be one" (so, the excluded middle holds); but, we intuitively deny that it is true that there will be a sea battle tomorrow, *and* we deny that it is true that there will not be a sea battle tomorrow (so, bivalence is given up); at the same time, we intuitively deny that both sentences are true (so, non-contradiction holds). However, denying bivalence cannot easily be squared with maintaining the excluded middle and non-contradiction, hence the quest for alternative explanations.

The problem of future contingents has occupied scholars for centuries and still, today, steers much controversial discussions (see Hasle and Øhrstrøm (2011)). It is also in an attempt to provide a clear framework for dealing with this problem that so-called temporal logics were developed in the late 1950s (see Prior (1957)); temporal logics influenced to a great extent the development of modal logic in the late 1950s and the early 1960s. We cannot examine the discussion of the problem in detail, but members of the Megarian School, who came up with a more refined analysis of future contingents, put forward what is known as the Master Argument, which shall occupy us in the next section.

§1.1.3. The Megarian School

The Megarian School (sometimes referred to as the Megaric School) was a philosophical movement first established by Euclides of Megara (c. 435–365 BCE; Megara, Greece), and most active between the fourth and third century BCE. Some of the members of the School—sometimes referred to as "dialecticians"—distinguished themselves by their work in logic, which was particularly fruitful in matters related to modalities. We shall focus on two figures who deserve special attention for having initiated some topics of philosophical conversation that are still alive today: Diodorus Cronus (died c. 284 BCE), and his student, Philo, for whom we have scant biographical information. While today we recognize the originality and importance of Diodorus and Philo, only fragments of their writings have survived; most of what we know of their ideas is due to later Roman philosophers, such as Sextus Empiricus (AD 160–210), and also Diogenes Laertius (third century AD), who wrote about them centuries after their death. Another key figure for the transmission of Diodorus's and Philo's ideas to Medieval scholars, and, therefore, all subsequent philosophers, is Severinus Boethius (AD 480–524); Boethius's work on logic and modalities is vast and articulated and deserves a separate treatment. Here, however, we shall confine ourselves to three central contributions of Diodorus and Philo, concerning conditionals, modalities, and the so-called Master Argument.

Conditionals

Philosophers within the Megarian School seem to have been the first among Ancient philosophers to accord a central role to *propositions*. Aristotelian logic took *terms* (in contemporary parlance: subject and predicate) as the key ingredients of logical analysis; for Diodorus and Philo, the fundamental units are instead *axiómatas*, which roughly correspond to what we now call propositions. These stand for the *content* of a sentence, so that different sentences can express the same proposition: for example, when we say that "It rains" and *Piove* convey the same content—that it is raining—in two languages, English and Italian. Unlike most contemporary authors working on propositions, however, Diodorus and Philo accept that propositions can change their truth value over time, so that the content of a sentence can be—say—true today, and yet false tomorrow.

The analyses of conditionals proposed by Diodorus and Philo crucially relied on their usage of propositions and inspired contemporary treatment of the issue. According to them (and to us), a conditional is a complex proposition formed by two simpler propositions—called respectively the antecedent and the consequent—that are related by an *"if ..., then ..."* relation. For instance, the sentence "If it rains, then I go surfing" expresses a complex proposition formed by the two propositions *It rains* and *I go surfing*, which are related by the *"if ..., then ..."* relation. By conceiving of conditionals in this way, Diodorus and Philo could appreciate their logical complexity and point out difficult questions that are still open for us. The central question being: When is it that a conditional proposition is true?

Conditionals are tricky because, in some instances, while we may know the truth conditions of each of the propositions composing a conditional, we may still not know whether the conditional is true or false. For instance, consider the sentence: "If it rains, then in one hour there are sixty minutes." The consequent of the conditional is true, since by definition there are sixty minutes in one hour; but is the conditional as a whole true? No matter whether it is raining or not, the problem seems to be that the antecedent and the consequent are not *relevantly* related.

Diodorus and Philo gave two different solutions to this problem. Diodorus's analysis was more complex, taking into consideration the *time* at which a proposition is true or false: he seems to have maintained that a conditional is true if *it is* not possible, and *it was* not possible, that its antecedent is true and its consequent false. By specifying the time at which a proposition is true, Diodorus aimed to devise stricter truth conditions for conditionals; the texts we have that recount Diodorus's position, however, do not offer sufficiently clear information to allow us to reconstruct its subtleties in a concise and uncontroversial manner. The solution he is aiming for, in any case, seems unable to address the problem of relevance expressed in the previous paragraph: for Diodorus the sentence "If it rains, then in one hour there are sixty minutes" seems to have expressed a true proposition.

Philo, on the other hand, proposed an analysis of conditionals that had much good fortune and is still endorsed in contemporary classical logic. According to Philo, a conditional is false just in case its antecedent is true and its consequent false; otherwise, it is true. Thus, for Philo, too, the sentence "If it rains, then in one hour there are sixty minutes" expresses a true proposition. But Philo's solution is straightforward: the truth of a conditional is evaluated in a simple way by taking into account the truth conditions of its antecedent and its consequent.

Conditionals form an important part of the contemporary debate on the metaphysics of modality. It is by means of conditionals that we express the possibility of many scenarios. To name just one notable instance, it is by means of a kind of conditional—so-called counterfactual conditional or *counterfactual*—that we express the possibility that matters could have been otherwise, as when we say that Napoleon could have won at Waterloo. Counterfactuals are quite relevant to the purposes of this volume: for example, they play a crucial role in our understanding of scientific laws, a central topic in the metaphysics of modality; and David Lewis, a key figure in the contemporary debates on the metaphysics of modality, offered the first articulated account of his modal realism (which we will take up in Chapter 3) in a book that dealt with counterfactuals (Lewis 1973).

Possibility and necessity in Diodorus and Philo

We cannot pass by the work that Diodorus Cronus and Philo did on modalities, though we won't have the space to analyze it. Again, an element of originality of their analyses is that they are carried forward in terms of propositions. But, most importantly, they provided us with two definitions of possibility that we do not find in Aristotle. (i) According to Diodorus, a proposition is possible just in case *it is true now or it will be true in the future.* This is a strict notion of possibility, which leaves no room for mere possibilities. Diodorus also offered a parallel notion of necessity that is also bound to time constraints: a proposition is necessary just in case *it is true now and it will never be false in the future.* (ii) Philo seems rather to have endorsed the logical notion of possibility as the absence of contradiction: a proposition is possible just in case, *by its own nature, it is capable of being true.* The expression "by its own nature" suggests that Philo is thinking that it is only a self-contradictory element that can render a proposition not possible. As we saw, the logical notion of possibility was missing in Aristotle. The merit of Philo's work is not only to have introduced logical possibility, but to have clearly defined necessity in terms of possibility: a scenario is necessary just in case it is not possible that it is not the case; and *vice versa:* a scenario is possible just in case it is not necessary that it is not the case; and he did all of this with propositions.

The influence of Diodorus Cronus and Philo on the contemporary development of modal logic and modal metaphysics can hardly be overestimated. Additional important contributions from Ancient philosophy were made by the Stoics: in particular, by Chrysippus (c. 279–206 BCE, Athens), who defined possibility in terms of the *absence of external conditions of impediment*. But it is especially through the works of Boethius that the legacy of Megarian and Stoic philosophers has reached us (see Bobzien (2011)).

The Master Argument

We have seen that Diodorus's work on modalities is particularly sensitive to the logical and philosophical conundrums of time: the definitions of modal notions he offered all take into account the fact that propositions can change their truth value over time. It is, therefore, not surprising that he put forward one of the most formidable problems concerning the philosophy of time, which is closely connected to the problem of future contingents discussed by Aristotle. Diodorus's problem can be expressed through the so-called Master Argument. In its simplest formulation, the argument asserts that the following three claims cannot all be true:

(M1) Every true proposition that is about the past is necessary.
(M2) A proposition that is possibly true cannot imply a proposition that is necessarily false.
(M3) There is a proposition that is possible, but that neither is nor will be true.

Diodorus argued that the problem rested in (M3). As a reader may recognize, in fact, (M3) violates Diodorus's definition possibility, according to which a proposition is possible just in case it is true now or it will be true in the future. This definition is highly controversial, however, because it suggests a strict notion of possibility. Alternatively, we could maintain that (M3) is true, but give up either (M1) or (M2). But since both (M1) and (M2) make substantial claims about propositions that are also superficially plausible, it becomes tricky to understand which of the two claims should be discharged.

Because of its centrality, the Master Argument has had several alternative formulations: most notable are the ones by Prior (1957), Lavenham (see Hasle and Øhrstrøm (2011)), and Gaskin (1995). During Medieval times, the argument gained centrality in connection with the problem of divine foreknowledge: if God *knows* the future—and thus facts about the future seem to be already determinately true or determinately false—is the future contingent or do we simply have an illusion of contingency? For instance, if God knows whether there will be a sea battle tomorrow, is it contingent that there will be a sea battle tomorrow? If facts about the future are not contingent, then are humans really free agents who are responsible for their actions?

§1.2. Modalities in Medieval philosophy

§1.2.1. The Arabic and Scholastic traditions

It is from the ideas of the Ancients—such as Aristotle, Diodorus, and Philo—that much of the contemporary debate in modal metaphysics takes root. But it would be an error to overlook the fact that those ideas were selected, transcribed, and often reformulated by philosophers that came later, and that, little by little, gave shape to the Western philosophical tradition. Today we read and discuss the ideas of Aristotle, Diodorus, and Philo *through the lenses* set by those philosophers. Among them, we find eminent figures of Late Antiquity, such as Boethius (c. 480–524, Rome). And we also find several Arabic philosophers who made a decisive contribution to the development of modal logic and metaphysics, such as Al-Fārābī (c. 872–950, Baghdad), Avicenna (c. 980–1037, Persia), Al-Ghazali (1058–1111, Khorasan, Iran), Averroes (1126–98, Córdoba), and Kātibī (died 1276, Persia). Finally, we find those philosophers who operated in the new university system that emerged throughout Europe in the eleventh and twelfth centuries, and that formed the so-called Scholastic tradition; this group includes figures such as Abelard (1079–1142, Paris), Kilwarby (c. 1215–79, Paris and Oxford), Aquinas (1225–74, Montecassino, Italy, and Paris), Scotus (c. 1266–1308, Oxford and Paris), and Gersonides (1288–1344, Avignon).

We cannot examine the details of the history of modal logic and metaphysics during this entire period; the reader will find ample suggestions for how to do so in the Further Reading section. Nonetheless, to convey a small sense of the relevance of the figures just listed, we shall point out just the innovative elements of two authors. One is Avicenna: he developed both a modal syllogistic (in the style of Aristotle) and a modal predicate logic (in the style of the Megarian School); most importantly, he understood each term, predicate, or proposition as standing for all of its possible applications, thus setting up a much more powerful theoretical framework than the one provided by the Ancient philosophers. The second author is Scotus, who forged a modal theory based on logical possibility and compossibility: a scenario is possible just in case existence is not in contradiction with it, though the scenario may not be compossible with others. Scotus's view comes close to the standard way of thinking about possibility in contemporary work. It also had a major influence over two central figures in our historical journey: Ockham and Buridan. Finally, we shall also remark that Arabic and Medieval authors greatly developed and enriched the Aristotelian theory of substances, including the associated doctrine of essentialism which will be discussed at various points in the remaining chapters (especially 3, 7, and 8).

Certain important ideas that characterize the contemporary debates on modalities in logic, semantics, and metaphysics have their origins in (and often were anticipated by) the works of William Ockham (c. 1287–1347, London and Munich) and John Buridan (c. 1295–1358, Paris). Needless to say, the ideas of these two philosophers developed in conversation and disagreement with their contemporaries. Still, because the views of Ockham and Buridan dominated the debates on modality in the fourteenth century, it is instructive to examine them.

§1.2.2. Ockham

Ockham was a prominent figure in England and continental Europe during the first half of the fourteenth century. He is best known for having defended a sophisticated and influential version of nominalism, which got him into trouble with the official representatives of the Church at the time (Ockham was a Franciscan friar, and, in the 1320s, he was called to defend his views both before his Franciscan province chapter in Bristol and before the Pope in Avignon). Looking at Ockham's nominalism will help us understand his contribution to modal logic and metaphysics. *Nominalism* is the metaphysical view according to which all there is to the world are particular entities. It stands in opposition to *realism*, the metaphysical view that there are both particular *and* universal entities. Consider for instance the sentence: "This one and that one are blue." For the Realist, the sentence is about two particular individuals ("this one" and "that one") and a universal ("blue"), which is common to both particulars; this strikes us as consistent with our most intuitive worldview. The Nominalist, instead, faces the challenge of explaining the truth of this sentence by means of particulars alone.

In order to deal with sentences such as "This one and that one are blue", Ockham devised an eliminativist strategy, which can be summarized in two steps (see also Read (forthcoming)). *First*, deny that universals are real; in our case, deny that "blue" is anything more than the creation of a human mind, so that when one attributes the color blue to some particular individual, one is simply describing a projection of one's mind. *Second*, deny that there is any object of thought—what some today call "concepts"—that is universal. When we use the word "blue" we are not employing the *same* concept over and over; rather, we are having a particular thought, which happens to be appropriately related to previous thoughts and uses. Each time we use the word "blue" to describe a particular, it is as if we are introducing a new name for that particular: hence the label "nominalism". The Medieval debate about nominalism and realism can readily be related to contemporary disputes in philosophy of mind, metaphysics, and semantics, standing as an example of Ockham's continuing significance in philosophy. Indeed, that very debate still occupies contemporary discussions in those fields.

The strategy Ockham embraced to argue for nominalism is recognizable also in the specific contribution he made to the analysis of modalities. First of all, Ockham pursues his analysis in terms of so-called *propositional dictums*, which correspond to the English "that" clause (e.g. *"That Ockham was smart,* everybody knows!") Second, Ockham distinguishes between two types of modal propositions: those having a divided sense and those having a composite sense. This distinction roughly corresponds to the contemporary distinction between *de re* and *de dicto*, which we shall discuss further in Chapter 2. Here are two examples:

Divided Modality: "Every philosopher necessarily likes Ockham."
Composite Modality: "Necessarily: every philosopher likes Ockham."

And here is how the two examples are analyzed in terms of Ockham's nominalist strategy:

Divided Modality: Every proposition where "likes Ockham"
                         is predicated of any specific philosopher is
                         necessary.
Composite Modality: Every proposition "Every philosopher likes
                         Ockham" is necessary.

Notice that the analyses refer to *every proposition* of a certain sort. This is because there is no single, universal proposition serving as the content of different sentences or utterances of the same sentence: that is, "Every philosopher likes Ockham" stands for a different proposition on every occasion on which it is uttered or entertained. The key point in Ockham's strategy is to reduce all modalities to attitudes that an agent takes toward propositions; the necessary (like any modality) is simply a way human beings regard propositions. For Ockham, indeed, there is no necessary being but God. Ockham's metaphysics of modalities is thus minimal, but such minimality is the outcome of a sophisticated semantics.

Our discussion of Ockham's analyses of modality should suffice to demonstrate how sophisticated the logical, semantic, and metaphysical theories of modality had become by the fourteenth century. With Buridan, we reach the most mature point of Medieval logic and metaphysics.

§1.2.3. Buridan

Buridan lived, studied, and taught in Paris. Like Ockham, he also defended nominalism; but, unlike Ockham, he did not get into trouble with the Church. Buridan's metaphysics is oriented by his views in semantics and logic. His theory of meaning was radical and ingenious. To start, he maintained that any term stands for a certain particular entity regardless of whether the proposition in which the terms appear is true or false. Hence, according to Buridan, the truth of a proposition does not depend on whether the terms in the proposition stand for (or pick out) something; rather, a proposition is true when the terms stand for entities that are in the appropriate relation. For instance, the sentence "This one is blue" is true when "This one" stands for the same entity as "blue". (Presumably, the sentence "This one and that one are blue" would be analyzed in terms of distinct identity statements, "This one is blue" and "That one is blue".)

With respect to propositions involving modalities, Buridan inherits the general strategy of Ockham, which used "that" clauses and distinguished between divided and composite modalities. But Buridan improved Ockham's approach in at least two respects. A first improvement is quantifying directly over "that" clauses, in the analysis of modal propositions. As such, the following two examples:

> *Divided Modality:*   "Every philosopher necessarily likes Buridan";
> *Composite Modality:*   "Necessarily: every philosopher likes Buridan"

... are analyzed by Buridan as follows:

> *Divided Modality:*   Every *that-likes-Buridan*, when predicated of any specific philosopher, is necessary.
> *Composite Modality:*   Every *that-every-philosopher-likes-Ockham* is necessary.

The second improvement is distinguishing three senses in which a proposition may be said to be necessary: conditional, temporal, and absolute. This move allows Buridan to concede the necessity of some propositions without giving up his nominalist conviction that there are no universal laws, no universal ties, but only particular relations.

Consider the sentence:

(W) "Necessarily: wisdom is a virtue."

Sentences such as (W) are problematic for the nominalist because they seem to be about universals, such as wisdom and virtue; thus, it is not clear how the nominalist may accept their truth without thereby affirming that there are universals. Instead of taking (W) at face value, Buridan maintains that (W) can be interpreted as making one of the three following claims:

Conditional: "If there is something that is wise, then that thing is virtuous."
Temporal: "If at some time there is wisdom, then it is a virtue."
Absolute: It is not possible that at any time: "Wisdom is not a virtue."

The conditional and temporal readings of (W) commit only to the existence of particulars—a particular entity that is wise, and a particular temporal instance of wisdom. And all it takes to falsify the third reading of (W) is an instance of a particular that happens to be wise and not virtuous.

Buridan and Ockham illustrate, perhaps to an extreme, a methodology that is still much in vogue among analytic metaphysicians: they settle on a certain metaphysics (nominalism), but do not employ metaphysical arguments to defend it, appealing to sophisticated and subtle semantic machinery instead. As we shall see, such a strategy is common in the contemporary debate on the metaphysics of modality. Contemporary scholars still have much to dig up and learn from the writings of the Arabic and Scholastic authors.

§1.3. Modalities in Early Modern philosophy

A few decades after Buridan's death, in the early 1360s, European society started a process of deep transformation, which led also to a change in how culture was produced and disseminated, and eventually resulted in Humanism and the Renaissance. By the early seventeenth century, European society, and European philosophy with it, was facing entirely new questions, and many protagonists of the philosophical debate were not academics, but rather laypeople. The logic and semantics of modalities were no longer of much concern; epistemology, metaphysics, and ethics took center stage. And yet the Early Modern period is especially rich in discussion of modalities. The most representative texts also happen to be quite accessible. For this reason, in what follows we shall exemplify some key ideas through the voices of their authors. Though the list of important figures is long, we will limit our survey to four: Descartes (1596–1650, France, Holland, and Sweden), Spinoza (1632–77, Holland), Leibniz (1646–1716, Germany and Central Europe), and Hume (1711–78, England and France).

§1.3.1. Descartes: Thought experiments and God's omnipotence

Descartes is canonically regarded as one of the first major Early Modern philosophers. Two aspects of his work contribute most distinctly to the debates on the metaphysics and epistemology of modality: his radical skeptical challenge and his conception of God's omnipotence. (A third important aspect is his analysis of free will, but since this volume will not directly tackle this issue, we shall leave it aside.)

At the end of the first of his *Meditations*, Descartes advances the hypothesis that there is an evil deceiver that is as powerful and ingenious as God, and who employs all its energies to deceive him with respect to what is true and false. This hypothesis is then used to show that one kind of self-knowledge (the so-called *cogito*) is infallible, and is, from an epistemic point of view, foundational; the centrality of self-knowledge, furthermore, is employed by Descartes to establish his metaphysics of God, the person, and every other substance.

From our perspective, the remarkable aspect of Descartes's argumentative strategy is the use of a *thought experiment*, where a seemingly impossible scenario is used to provide a fresh start in epistemology and metaphysics. Such a strategy did not go unnoticed by Descartes's contemporaries and remains controversial. Not only did Descartes have to defend himself from the charge of believing in the existence of an evil god, or that God is evil; more interestingly for us, Descartes had to justify his method: in what way can we gain philosophical insight from considering not simply a scenario that is false, but a scenario that is in all likelihood impossible? Here is what Descartes had to say in response:

> A philosopher would be no more surprised at such suppositions of falsity than he would be if, in order to straighten out a curved stick, we bent it round in the opposite direction. The philosopher knows that it is often useful to assume falsehoods instead of truths in this way in order to shed light on the truth.
>
> —*Fifth Replies*, AT 7:349–50, CSM 2:242

Descartes's reply is quite important to the theme of our book. He is indeed defending a strategy that is by now recognized as standard in many sciences. Not only do models and principles (in the natural, social, and humanistic sciences) typically rest on ideal scenarios; they often employ impossible or unlikely scenarios.

From an epistemological point of view, therefore, we seem to be justified in entertaining thoughts about the impossible; but what is the content of such thoughts? Do such impossible scenarios exist and, if so, in what sense? This is the root of the concern that, by using the hypothesis of the evil deceiver, Descartes was committing himself to the existence of an evil god. We shall discuss these and related questions at the end of Chapter 8.

The second aspect of Descartes's philosophy that deserves to be highlighted in this context is his conception of God's omnipotence. Descartes develops in an original way the thesis that God is the *only* necessary being. Since God is the only necessary being and God is omnipotent, then *any* other truth is contingent. Thus, Descartes maintains that ostensibly necessary truths, such as mathematical or geometrical truths, are contingent upon God's will:

> And even if God has willed that some truths should be necessary, this does not mean that he willed them necessarily; for it is one thing to will that they be necessary, and quite another to will this necessarily, or to be necessitated to will it.

In order to grasp the meaning of the position defended by Descartes we arguably must help ourselves—as he does, in the case of the evil deceiver—to certain impossible scenarios. To conceive of the contingency of mathematical or geometrical truths implies the ability to conceive of impossible scenarios. But can we really do that? Again, this is a question that runs deep into the contemporary debates on the metaphysics of modality and that Descartes's work vividly brings to light.

§1.3.2. *Spinoza's necessitarianism*

Spinoza's work is closely entangled with the metaphysics of modality and contains some radical and original views. We shall encounter it again in Chapter 2, when examining so-called modal expressivism. Here, we will confine ourselves to Spinoza's necessitarianism, a position that we encountered earlier when discussing the ideas of Parmenides and Zeno. As we stated at that point, necessitarianism rests on the acceptance of the two following claims: (i) the universe exists out of necessity; (ii) the universe is necessarily the way it is. Spinoza seems to have accepted both. Indeed, for him, God exists out of necessity, and God is necessarily the way God is. If to this we add that God is the only possible substance, then we have the result that God is the universe, which exists out of necessity and is necessarily the way it is.

Spinoza defended his necessitarianism by providing ample metaphysical details of his position. His view seems very different from the ones of

Parmenides and Zeno. The latter seem to have rejected all superficial impressions suggesting the existence of a multiplicity of entities; Spinoza, instead, has a place for every entity, including ordinary ones: they are all *in* God, as modes of existence of some of God's attributes (extension and thought). For instance, consider the naïve belief that there are a cup and a cell phone on the table. While Parmenides and Zeno would dismiss this belief as false because it postulates the existence of three entities, Spinoza would agree that there are three entities, but they are all modes of existence of one of God's attributes—extension.

Necessitarianism implies determinism, the view that no particular event could have been otherwise. In order to defend his view, Spinoza also puts forward an original account of causation as conceptual entailment. If God is the cause of the fact that the cup and the cell phone are on the table, this is because it follows from the concept of God that the cup and the cell phone are on the table. We shall see that Hume's position with respect to causation is at the other end of the spectrum with respect to Spinoza's: for Hume, the concept of the cup is in no way related to any other concept and, indeed, causation is not a real phenomenon. There is no need to enter into the details of Spinoza's view here; it suffices to point out that, in the contemporary debate on the modal status of scientific laws, Spinoza offers an original and important perspective.

§1.3.3. Leibniz: Possible worlds, theodicy, and super-essentialism

Leibniz is a central figure in the history of modality, if for no other reason than that he advanced a theory of modality in terms of possible worlds that greatly influenced the development of possible-worlds semantics in the twentieth century (see Chapters 2 and 3, and Menzel (2015)). Also connected to possible worlds is a second aspect of Leibniz's thought that we shall stress, that is, his theodicy, according to which we live in the best of all possible worlds. Finally, the third aspect of Leibniz's work that deserves to be examined is his doctrine of so-called super-essentialism. Let us look at each in turn.

§1.3.3.1. Possible worlds

Leibniz's views in metaphysics are presented over a vast array of writings; they are also tightly interwoven with each other, and the texts raise no small interpretive difficulties. We can provide not even an overview of the big picture here; more modestly, we shall limit ourselves to explaining the role of possible worlds in Leibniz's metaphysics. Leibniz may not have been the first philosopher to employ the notion of a possible world; however, he certainly is the first to have established it as central to philosophical discussions of modality. He seems to have begun using the expression "possible world" in the 1680s, using the idea to explain how his notion of a substance (e.g. a specific person or a specific organism) left room for contingency. The issue was not a minor one. For Leibniz, a substance is a *complete concept*: that is, at any given time, a substance is so determined that it contains all the properties that are true of it. So, while Leibniz was still alive, it was already true that this very book discusses Leibniz, and the complete concept of Leibniz contained this property (*viz.* the property that there is a book partly about Leibniz). In a famous letter to Arnauld of July 14, 1686, Leibniz explains how his metaphysics leaves room for contingency by appealing to possible worlds:

> I think there is an infinity of possible ways in which to create the world, according to the different designs which God could form, and that each possible world depends on certain principal designs or purposes of God which are distinctive of it, that is, certain primary free decrees (conceived *sub ratione possibilitatis*) or certain *laws* of the *general order* of this possible universe with which they are in accord and whose concept they determine, as they do also the concepts of all the individual substances which must enter into this same universe.
>
> —G II 51/L 333

One way to read Leibniz, which was made prominent by authors such as Carnap (1947), Mates (1972), and Adams (1974), is that possible worlds are ideas entertained by God. Each such idea is specified in all its details; it is a *complete* and *consistent* story about how the world could have been. In this sense, every world is fully determined. In the actual world, for example, Leibniz's destiny was already determined: this book had to discuss him; nonetheless, there is another world, which may be very similar to ours, where this book does not touch on Leibniz. Now, God chose to create the actual world over any of the others, but he might have done otherwise. The act of creation was the "law of the general order" by means of which this world— determined in all its details—came to be.

Leibniz's theory of possible worlds suggested a simple and intuitive analysis of modality that had not been seen before. According to it, a proposition is possible just in case it is true in at least one possible world; it is contingent just in case it is true in at least one possible world and false in at least one possible world; and it is necessary when it is true in all worlds.

It is unclear whether Leibniz's metaphysics is indeed compatible with the picture of possible worlds as complete and consistent stories (see Rudder

Beker (1985) for a criticism of such an interpretation). At any rate, Leibniz's suggestion has had a long career in the history of modality, and is of central importance today: it is at the core of the most popular modal semantics and of several alternative metaphysical theories of modality; moreover, the idea of possible worlds as complete and consistent stories is today a view called *linguistic ersatzism* (see Chapter 5).

§1.3.3.2. Theodicy

Possible worlds are employed by Leibniz also to answer a daunting question in ethics and theology: if God is infinitely powerful and infinitely good, how is it possible that there is evil in the world for which no human can be blamed? For instance, why is it that some people suffer—say, from random medical illnesses or geological disasters—without anyone being responsible for their suffering? Any attempt to answer this question is called a *theodicy*: that is, it is a justification of God's attributes in light of such forms of evil.

   Leibniz's solution is that God created the best of all possible worlds. There is no "innocent suffering", no gratuitous evil that takes place in our world, although this is not how things appear to us. We may fail to appreciate how any instance of evil is connected to some good because of the infinite complexity of the universe. But, God, who understands the complexity, chose for the best. In the *Candide*, Voltaire ridicules Leibniz's solution. Doubts about its soundness notwithstanding, the solution is an excellent example of the relationship between the metaphysics of modality, ethics, and the philosophy of religion.

§1.3.3.3. Super-essentialism

Before moving on, it is important to mention another notion that comes out of Leibniz's philosophy and that is of importance to contemporary metaphysics of modality: the so-called super-essentialism. We shall return to essentialism in Chapters 3, 7, and 8 but, in brief, an essence is any property that belongs to an individual *unconditionally* (at all times and in all possible scenarios). Some analyze such unconditionality in modal terms, suggesting that essential properties belong to an individual out of (metaphysical or natural) necessity; others, instead, analyze the unconditionality in terms of identity: an essence is a property that *defines* an individual. Leibniz's theory of substances— according to which substances are complete concepts—suggests a radical form of essentialism, super-essentialism: *all the properties of an individual belong to it unconditionally.* That is, at all times and in all possible scenarios, an individual (a substance, in Leibniz's terminology) never changes its properties.

§1.3.4. *Hume on separability*

The fourth and last Early Modern author we shall discuss is Hume. His views on possibility and necessity stand in stark contrast with those of Spinoza, and have greatly influenced contemporary discussions on the epistemology and the metaphysics of modality. For instance, it is difficult to understand the work of a prominent contemporary author in the field, David Lewis, without reading Hume's work. Moreover, Hume's views on possibility and necessity are crucial to appreciating Kant's metaphysics.

The key modal notion for Hume is *separability*. For him, each individual is separable from any other, and so is each event. While Leibniz maintained that the concept of an individual was so rich as to contain all of its properties, Hume strips down the concept of an individual to its bare minimum—that which we perceive of it:

> From the first appearance of an object, we can never conjecture what effect will result from it. But were the power or energy of any cause discoverable by the mind, we could foresee the effect, even without experience; and might, at first, pronounce with certainty concerning it, by the mere dint of thought and reasoning.
>
> —EHU 7.1.7; SBN 63

Since individual entities and events are separable, there is no contradiction in thinking that any individual (or any event) can be combined in any way with any other (as long as, indeed, no contradiction ensues). Thus, there is *no necessary connection* in nature between individuals, which may be justified on the basis of our definition of said individuals:

> It has been observ'd already, that in no single instance the ultimate connexion of any objects is discoverable, either by our senses or reason, and that we can never penetrate so far into the essence and construction of bodies, as to perceive the principle on which their mutual influence depends.
>
> —T 2.3.1.4; SBN 400

As we have seen, the notion of the possible as that which is non-contradictory can be traced back to Philo, and it was not until Scotus that this notion received more systematic treatment. However, Scotus was a realist, who worked with a rich notion of the individual (or substance). So, Hume is typically a "modal hero" to the empiricists working with the notion of possibility as non-contradiction. His legacy, furthermore, includes another really important idea: that conceivability is a reliable guide to possibility:

The mind can always *conceive* any effect to follow from any cause, and indeed any event to follow upon another: Whatever we can *conceive* is possible, at least in a metaphysical sense.

—T Abstract 11; SBN 650

Hume's ability to couch original ideas about the metaphysics of modality in a simple and direct style is exemplary. Whether he is right is still a widely debated issue, which we shall confront a few times in the rest of the volume (for instance, Chapters 3 and 6).

§1.4. Towards quantified modal logic and possible-worlds semantics

It would be unfair to say that modalities were not studied in nineteenth-century Western philosophy; we find them discussed, for instance, in such masterpieces as Hegel's *Science of Logic* (1812–17) and Mill's *A System of Logic* (1843). Yet, modalities did not take center-stage in this period either: key disputes do not center around the understanding of modalities and there is arguably little originality in the ways they are understood.

Still, nineteenth-century developments in logic quietly sowed the seeds of a new era in the study of modalities. The innovations of Mill's *A System of Logic* and Boole's *An Investigation of the Laws of Thought* (1854) culminated in the seminal works of Frege and Russell, preparing the ground for a new logic and semantics of modality. It would be C. I. Lewis (1918) who first developed Quantified Modal Logic, in connection with which possible-worlds semantics made its appearance at the end of the 1950s. The details of this story will be discussed in Chapters 2 and 3.

The study of modalities over the history of Western philosophy has neither been guided by a fixed set of questions nor required a fixed set of philosophical skills. As we have seen, modalities have been approached from the viewpoints of logic, semantics, metaphysics, ethics, and epistemology. Also, because modalities are connected with so many branches of philosophy, their study can be particularly fruitful. In the rest of this volume, we shall concentrate on the metaphysical details of the contemporary debate about modalities, leaving aside the difficulties confronting those who want to provide an adequate logical or semantic treatment. Nonetheless, questions of semantics, logic, and epistemology will surface from time to time, and will accompany us in our journey.

Study Questions

- What is Parmenides's metaphysical monism?
- What is necessitarianism?
- What was the goal of Zeno's paradoxes?
- What are Zeno's four paradoxes of motion?
- What are Zeno's two paradoxes of plurality?
- What is Zeno's millet paradox?
- What is Zeno's paradox of place?
- How does Aristotle define general necessity?
- What is the distinction between conditional and absolute necessity in Aristotle?
- What are the three varieties of conditional necessity, according to Aristotle?
- What are the three senses of possibility introduced by Aristotle?
- What are the three senses of possibility that Aristotle fails to sort out?
- What is the problem of future contingents?
- What are the three main contributions of the Megarian School to modal discourse?
- What is the Master Argument?
- What is the distinction between divided and composite modalities?
- What are the three senses of necessity discussed by Buridan?
- What is the controversial modal aspect of Descartes's thought experiments?
- What are the elements of originality in Descartes's conception of God's omnipotence?
- What is Spinoza's necessitarianism?
- What is a possible world, according to Leibniz?
- What is Leibniz's theodicy?
- What is Leibnizian super-essentialism?
- What is separability, for Hume, and why is it important for discussing modality?

FURTHER READING

For a comprehensive overview of the main moments in the **history of modal logic**, the classic by Kneale and Kneale (1962) is still a good starting point. Other useful readings include: Knuuttila (1998); Gabbay and Woods (2004a, 2004b, 2006, 2008a, 2008b); and Bobzien (2014).

For an overview of **Parmenides**'s philosophy, including a discussion of his metaphysical monism along with its implications for modality, see Palmer (2009: Chapters 1–4, 2012a). As for the study of **Zeno**, good starting points are Palmer (2009: Chapter 5, 2012b) and Huggett (2010).

▶

To place **Aristotle's view on modalities** in the broader contexts of his metaphysics and logic see, respectively, Cohen (2014) and Smith (2014). Many are the monographic studies on Aristotle's views on modality, including Hintikka (1973), Waterloo (1982), van Rijen (1989), Patterson (1995), and Rini (2010). Among the recent articles on the subject are Denyer and Makin (2000), Malink (2006), and Marmodoro (2015).

On **future contingents** in Aristotle and the Megarian School, see the classic by Gaskin (1995). For a history of the debates on future contingents in Late Antiquity, see Mignucci (1989); for a history of the debates during the Medieval period, see Normore (1982) and Knuuttila (2014); for a history of the problem of future contingents in connection with divine foreknowledge, see Craig (1988); and for an up-to-date framing of the debate, see Hasle and Øhrstrøm (2011). Prior (1957) is a contemporary classic on the subject.

For an introduction to the key figures of the **Megarian School,** and their views on modality, see Bobzien (1998, 2011).

The key moments of the **Medieval debates on modality** are surveyed in Dutilh Novaes and Read (forthcoming), Lagerlund (2000), Thom (2003), and Knuuttila (2008, 2013). For a comparison of Arabic and Medieval views on modality, see Kukkonen (2000, 2005) and Knuuttila and Kukkonen (2011). Also useful to consult are Rescher et al. (1974) and Dutilh Novaes (2007). On the developments of logic in the fourteenth century, see Read (forthcoming); for an overview of **Ockham**'s philosophy, see Spade (1999) and Spade and Panaccio (2011). As for **Buridan**, good starting points are Klima (2009) and Zupko (2014).

For the connection between Medieval and **Early Modern** views on modality, see Friedman and Nielsen (2003). For a discussion of modalities in **Descartes**'s thought, see Curley (1984), Normore (1991), Bennet (1994), and Cunning (2014). For a comparison between Descartes's and Leibniz's views on modality, consult Wee (2006). For **Spinoza**'s view on necessity, see: Curley and Walski (1999); Miller (2001); Garrett (2001); Koistinen (2003); Martin (2010); and Chignell; also useful is Lin (2012). For **Leibniz**'s contribution to the development of the history of modality, a good starting point is Look (2013); still useful to consult is the classic by Mates (1986). Among the articles on the subject are: Blumenfeld (1973); Fitch (1979); Mondadori (1985); Wilson (2000); Jauernig (2008); Lin (2012); and Newlands (2013). For a discussion of **Hume**'s ideas on necessary connections, starting points are Strawson (1989, 2000) and Craig (2002), but see also Garrett (1985) and Kail (2003). For a discussion of Hume's ideas on liberty and necessity, see Bricke (2011).

On the development of logic in the **Modern period**, see Gabbay and Woods (2006, 2008b, 2009). For the modern origins of possible-worlds semantics and modal logic, see Ballarin (2010) and the Further Reading section of Chapter 3.

2

Modal skepticism and modal expressivism

In this chapter, we consider the opinions of those who regard modalities as expressing no clear conceptual content (modal skeptics) or no content at all (modal expressivists). We will begin our analysis by examining what perhaps cannot strictly be called a theory, but rather an attitude toward the topic at hand. The attitude in question is skepticism, and we will see three versions of it: the first is more attentive to certain difficulties in providing a semantics and logic of modality, and Willard van Orman Quine was its most renowned proponent (§2.1.); the second is more attentive to certain difficulties regarding the epistemology of modality, and Peter van Inwagen was its most renowned proponent (§2.2.); and the third is the more naïve and radical approach, but is, nonetheless, relevant to our discussion (§2.3.). Afterward (§2.4.), we will take up modal expressivism, according to which alethic modalities express sentiments of speakers in much the way that the expressions "woohoo!" and "boo!" express sentiments of, respectively, approbation and disapprobation on the part of a speaker. Modal expressivism is an appealing approach to modalities, and it is especially useful to test one's own views; it suffers from two major problems, which we will address.

§2.1. Modal skepticism: Preliminary remarks

Skepticism is a philosophical attitude rooted in doubting. Philosophers who endorse skepticism, or take its challenges very seriously, can be found in every age and place. Among the chief figures are Arcesilaus, Carneades, Aenesidemus, Sextus Empiricus, Michel de Montaigne, René Descartes, David Hume, George E. Moore, Ludwig Wittgenstein, and Hilary

Putnam. Skeptical doubting is peculiar, and should be distinguished from a different form of doubting. If Giovanni tells you that today is the 6th and you firmly believe that it is the 7th, you will doubt Giovanni's words because you strongly believe *you have the truth otherwise*. This is not skeptical doubting. Consider instead a different scenario. Giovanni tells you he believes that President Obama is a KGB spy; you do not have any way to disprove him, but you are not confident that his source is reliable. In this case, you do not believe you have the truth otherwise: more modestly, you *refuse to commit to either the truth or the falsity* of Giovanni's claim. You are now raising a skeptical doubt towards that claim, flagged by your *suspension of judgment*.

Skeptical doubts can be differentiated based on their targets. For instance, if you doubt that someone *knows* that such and such is the case, your doubt goes under the umbrella of *epistemic skepticism*. If instead you doubt that something exists, as when you doubt that God exists or that there is a ghost in the house, your doubt goes under the umbrella of *ontological skepticism*. The most famous formulations of skepticism are of the epistemic variety. Particularly famous was the skeptical method developed by Arcesilaus of Pitane, the philosopher who took the directorship of Plato's Academy about seventy years after his death, in 272 BCE. Arcesilaus's skepticism, which goes under the name of "Academic Skepticism", applies across the board, to any sort of target. It is so radical that it cannot even be formulated. Without entering into details that are unnecessary here, the gist of the position is this: for any claim *A*, including the present one, neither affirm *A* nor affirm its contrary; and do not even affirm or deny that you are neither affirming nor denying it. Of course, as anticipated, this cannot be taken as *the* formulation of Academic Skepticism: first of all because, if it were, there would be a proposition *A* (the formulation) that the Academic skeptic accepts; second, because the formulation is clearly contradictory.

The three kinds of modal skepticism to be considered in this chapter all propose that we suspend judgment with respect to (some of) our modal opinions. They differ in the extent of the modal opinions that allegedly should be doubted and in their motivations for doubting. Quinian modal skepticism is a form of *semantic* doubting, because it advocates suspending judgment on whether we can adequately analyze the meaning of certain modal sentences (so-called *de re* modal sentences). Van Inwagen's modal skepticism is of the *epistemic* variety, because it advocates suspending judgment regarding the truth of certain far-fetched scenarios (e.g. the scenario where I have a mind but not a body). Radical skepticism, finally, embraces the full spectrum of our modal talk: it advocates the suspension of judgment with respect to it all.

§2.2. Quinian modal skepticism

If you were to ask an analytic philosopher to explain what skepticism is in relation to modality, he would speak to you of the position long-defended by Quine, one of the most influential philosophers in the United States in the second half of the last century. Quine first put forward his modal skepticism in a series of writings published in the late 1940s and early 1950s (1947, 1953a, 1953b), going on to refine the view for the subsequent fifty years (cf. especially Quine (1974, 1976) and Barrett and Gibson (1990)). The main lesson, drawn from these writings, is still a matter of debate (for some recent contributions, see Fine (2005, Chapters 2 and 3), Divers (2007), and Keskinen (2012)). Details aside, it is safe to say that Quine's skepticism is far from being as radical as the Academic skepticism of Arcesilaus, and is of a *semantic* variety: it concerns the meaning of certain types of modal sentences. Quine's target was very specific and, in order to be appreciated, his modal skepticism requires a bit of introductory discussion.

Quine's polemical targets were certain sentences of quantified modal logic (QML), as developed in particular by his Harvard colleague Clarence Irving Lewis. QML is the cradle of possible-worlds semantics and it is for this reason that Quine's skepticism has been much debated: it struck at the core of the most significant conceptual apparatus ever developed to analyze modalities (for an overview of the modern origins of modal logic, see Ballarin (2010)). At the syntactic level, QML uses the formal languages of predicate (or propositional) logic, adding two operators, named after their shapes: one operator for necessity—the so-called "*box*"—and the other for possibility—the so-called "*diamond.*" At the semantic level, the standard version of QML introduces one additional key element: a set of possible worlds, at which (or: *in which*, depending on one's views; see e.g. Williamson (2002)) the truth of a sentence is determined. The set of possible worlds is crucial to clarifying the truth conditions of modal sentences of increasing complexity. The analyses of sentences involving only one of the two operators are, respectively, as follows: "It is necessary that: 'p' is true when, and only when, 'p' is true at all possible worlds"; "It is possible that: 'p' is true when, and only when, 'p' is true at at least one possible world." Starting with these two analyses, analyses of sentences involving multiple operators could then be provided.

So far, so good. As we know from the Introduction, many have quarreled over the metaphysical status of possible worlds, but this was not until after QML was established as a key conceptual tool for discussing modalities, in the 1970s. Quine's concerns are, rather, about the semantic details of the theory. In particular, for Quine it is suitable to attempt to make an analysis of certain *de dicto* modalities, but not of *de re* modalities. In order to outline his position, we must therefore look into the classic distinction between *de dicto* and *de re* in its connection with the topic at hand. Let us consider the following sentence:

1 Foffo the cat eats fish and potatoes.

Next, let us distinguish three ways in which (1) can be involved in other sentences. First, we sometimes find ourselves in a situation in which we wish to say something with regards to (1). For instance, we might find Foffo's meal surprising, and so we might say:

2 It is surprising that: Foffo the cat eats fish and potatoes.

Those who assert (2) are not trying to add any detail *to the situation* described in (1); on the contrary, they are assuming (1) and expressing a certain frame of mind with regard to that situation. Similarly, in other cases, instead of a frame of mind, we find ourselves expressing an attitude toward the situation, or even a certain relationship between the situation being considered and another. For example, we might say:

3 Norberto believes that: Foffo the cat eats fish and potatoes.

4 What Rosalba said calls into question that: Foffo the cat eats fish and potatoes.

Let us keep in mind for a moment this first of three types of sentence, in which a situation is related to a frame of mind, an attitude, or another situation.

Second, at other times, we find ourselves wanting to add certain details to the entire situation described in (1); for instance, we might say that:

5 Voraciously: Foffo the cat eats fish and potatoes.

Statement (5) does not express a frame of mind or attitude of the person who makes it; nor does it express a relationship between situations; rather, it modifies the situation described in (1) by adding a detail: it is now specified that the meal took place in a certain way.

Third, at yet other times, we find ourselves wanting to add a detail that does not concern the entire situation, but only some of its components. For example, we might say:

6 Foffo the *young cat* eats fish and potatoes,

or:

7 Foffo the cat eats *fresh fish* and *warm potatoes*.

Quine (1953a) points out that these three ways in which a sentence can be modified are also detectable when we consider modal terms—or, at least, when we try to interpret their meaning. Let us consider the following three sentences:

8 It is possible that: Foffo the cat eats fish and potatoes.

9 Possibly: Foffo the cat eats fish and potatoes.

10 Foffo the cat is able to eat fish and potatoes.

Sentence (8) appears to be analogous to (2), (3), and (4) insofar as it expresses a frame of mind of the speaker with regards to (1); (9) appears to be analogous to (5), insofar as it adds a detail to the description of the entire situation in (1); finally, (10) appears to be analogous to (6) and (7), insofar as it adds a detail to Foffo, the cat, one of the components of the situation in (1).

Traditionally, sentences such as (2), (3), (4), and (8) are considered to be *de dicto*: in them we say something about other sentences, without modifying the situation that these sentences describe. Sentences such as (5), (6), (7), (9), and (10) are considered to be *de re*: in them we modify the state of things (*res*, in Latin); and "things" may refer to entire situations, as in (5) and (9), or components of situations, as in (6), (7), and (10) (see Campbell (1964), Quine (1953a), and (1953b)).

Incidentally, it is this last use of modal terms—illustrated in (10)—upon which rest the doctrines of essence and capacity, or (as it has been called) disposition, which we encountered in Chapter 1 and which will be discussed again in Chapters 7 and 8. If we say that Giovanni knows how to drive a car, or that he essentially belongs to the species *Homo sapiens*, we are attributing a capacity and an essence, respectively, to Giovanni. This occurs through the application of a modal term to one of the parts of the sentences: an operation that is understood as a modification of the "thing" to which that part of the sentence refers.

Getting back to our topic, the theory defended by Quine is that the only legitimate use of modal terms is that illustrated in (8); sentences (9) and (10), by contrast, use modalities in an equivocal manner. To frame Quine's skepticism within the present volume, recall the problem of possibility (PP), presented in the Introduction, along with its three sub-problems (SPP, EPP, and MPP):

PP: What does it take for a certain situation to be possible?
SPP: What does it mean to say that a certain situation is possible?
EPP: How do we come to know that which is possible?
MPP: What sort of entity is a possible entity (of any given kind—an individual, property, state of affairs, or …)?

Quine's view is that PP cannot be raised with respect to *de re* modalities. Because sentences containing *de re* modalities—and, thus, the propositions these sentences express—contain equivocal terms, which cannot be assigned a clear semantic function, we ought to refrain from employing such sentences to express our (philosophical) opinions.

As for *de dicto* modalities, Quine's solution lies in interpreting them as the attitudes of the speakers toward the actual sentences. Such interpretation is typically referred to as *meta-linguistic*, because it holds that modal claims are assertions, in the language of the speaker, concerning claims of another language—referred to as the object language. Thus, for instance, in (8) the phrase "It is possible that" conveys the speaker's attitude, while "Foffo the cat eats fish and potatoes" belongs to the object language and is the target of the speaker's attitude. Consequently, for Quine a sentence containing a *de dicto* modality will not express a possible situation, but rather the perspective of the speaker toward a (non-modal) situation. As he summarized it, "necessity resides in the way we talk about things, not in the things we talk about" (1953a: 174). Incidentally, as we shall see, this motto is also largely supported by expressivism.

The philosophical significance of Quine's skepticism toward *de re* modalities and his interpretation of *de dicto* modalities must not be underestimated. They flew in the face of QML, the semantics fine-tuned by C. I. Lewis, which would later be used to develop the possible-worlds semantics that is at the core of this volume. Thus, if Quine is right, possible-worlds semantics has no solid footing. But is he right?

To substantiate his theory, Quine appeals to considerations from both metaphysics and the logical analysis of sentences. Let us first consider the former. Put simply, if attributed to situations or components of them, modalities can be very complex entities to explain. In particular, sentences such as (9) and (10) force us to buy into *Aristotelian essentialism*, which Quine regarded as highly suspicious. In the words of Quine, Aristotelian essentialism holds that:

> some of the attributes of a thing (quite independently of the language in which the thing is referred to, if at all) may be essential to the thing, and others accidental. E.g. a man, or talking animal, or featherless biped (for they are in fact all the same *things*), is essentially rational and accidentally two-legged and talkative, not merely qua man but qua itself.
>
> —Quine (1953a: 175–6)

Aristotelian essentialism would, thus, force us to pinpoint, for each thing, what is essential to it and what is accidental. For instance, we would have to take a stance on whether Foffo is essentially furry or not, or whether his genetic makeup is essential to him. But these are hard questions, to which we should not presume that there are answers that are valid regardless of how we approach them. To reiterate the point from a more familiar stance, consider Napoleon. We all have heard of him and his deeds, but it is another matter to be able to draw the line between what he did and what we believe he could have done. Suppose we were to agree that he could have won at Waterloo; how might we explain this attribution? And, how might we distinguish it from false attributions of possibility? For example, could Napoleon have been a fisherman living in Ajaccio, France, in the eighteenth and nineteenth centuries? Or, could he have been a tomato growing in Pisa in May, 1977? Precisely in order to avoid troublesome questions of this nature, which have pestered Aristotelian essentialism for centuries, suggesting the need for an alternative, Quine refuses to regard assertions of the form of (9) and (10) as meaningful.

The criticism arising from Aristotelian essentialism is connected to Quine's other reasons to distrust *de re* modalities, namely those concerning the logical analysis of sentences. This is because essentialism is *implied* by the logical analysis proposed by those who accept *de re* modalities:

> My logical point about essentialism was that he who accepts quantification into modal contexts as making good sense should not balk at essentialism [...]. If you are going to take the one you must take the other. That was not an argument against essentialism. But it happens further that I do not myself make sense of essentialism, or of metaphysical necessity.
> —Barrett and Gibson (1990: 244)

We have just seen Quine's reasons to reject essentialism. His reference to "quantification into modal contexts" is what we have to explain next. In quantified modal logic, such quantification is of two varieties, corresponding to sentences of the sort of either (9) or (10). First, we have quantification over possible worlds (whatever these are taken to be), because necessity and possibility are interpreted as expressing truth at (or "in", depending on one's views), respectively, all worlds or some world. Thus, the sentence:

11 Necessarily, Foffo is furry

is analyzed as:

12 At all possible worlds, Foffo is furry.

While the sentence:

13 Possibly, Foffo is wet

is analyzed as:

14   At some world, Foffo is wet.

The second type of quantification concerns sentences where the modality modifies a specific thing, as in (10). Thus, the sentence:

15   Foffo is essentially furry

is analyzed as predicating of Foffo the following:

16   There is an x such that, essentially, x is furry.

Now, in quantified modal logic "essentially" is standardly regarded as equivalent to "necessarily" (see Chapter 8 for a challenge to this interpretation), thus (16) is analyzed as:

17   There is an x such that, necessarily, x is furry.

Sentences such as (17) are the main target of Quine's criticism. According to him, because we have multiple ways of picturing any x (i.e. any *thing*), the truth conditions of sentences like (17) will vary as our representation of x varies. So, consider two descriptions of Foffo—the "x" in question in (17)—such that both pick out Foffo, but one does so necessarily and the other accidentally. If in (17) x is described as "Foffo the cat", (17) turns out (at least intuitively) to be true; but, if x is described as "Laura's favorite pet", (17) turns out not to be true, because Laura's favorite pet is furry (it is indeed Foffo), but Laura happens to like cats only accidentally—she could have developed a taste for lizards instead. The only way to avoid this problem is to buy into essentialism, but we have seen that Quine does not want to do that.

Thus, according to Quine, by trying to take at face value *de re* modalities, quantified modal logic is forced to adopt essentialism in order to remain able to assign a fixed truth value to certain sentences. But essentialism is problematic. Thus, we should not buy into quantified modal logic: "Necessity does not properly apply to the fulfillment of conditions by *objects* [...] apart from special ways of specifying them" (Quine 1953b: 151). Now, Quine acknowledges that certain assertions that are apparently *de re*, such as (9), can be reinterpreted as *de dicto* assertions and can therefore be recognized as legitimate in some way. Nevertheless, this type of *de re* assertion proves to be conceptually muddled; how are we to explain, for instance, the meaning of the following sentence: "Possibly: necessarily: possibly: Napoleon loses at Waterloo"?

To date, Quinian skepticism continues to play an important role in the philosophical debate, as demonstrated by the recent works of Boghossian (2009), Burgess (1997), and Neale (2000). Furthermore, it is crucial for understanding the development of the debate on modality which we will consider in the remainder of this book. After all, it was the desire to reject the skepticism of their professor that drove Saul Kripke and David Lewis, Quine's students, each to formulate a semantics of *de re* modal expressions and a theory of possible worlds, all of which have since structured the debate.

Needless to say, many philosophers did not buy Quine's modal skepticism. A particularly convincing line of reply in recent years has come from John Divers (2007) (but see also Fine (2005: Chapters 2 and 3) for another reply to Quinian skepticism). Divers considers the status of Quine's criticism of quantified modal logic after the works of David Lewis, that is, after the "return of metaphysics" in analytic philosophy and, more specifically, in the debates regarding alethic modality. To Divers, Quine equivocates between semantic and metaphysical issues. Clearly, in the example discussed above, how we come to describe "*x*" matters to the truth conditions of (17); and, clearly, there is more than one way of describing *x*. Yet, this is not to say that *x*, in itself, does not have necessary and accidental properties that belong to it no matter how we describe it. The fact that we can describe the world in many ways, and that what holds necessarily or possibly based on those descriptions therefore varies, does not make the world itself inconstant and dependent upon our descriptions. To put it in terms that are proper to this volume, Divers criticizes Quine for conflating the SPP and the MPP. To agree with Divers we have to endorse a good deal of metaphysics; but, as we will see in later chapters (especially 4 and 5), there are multiple ways of rejecting Quine's modal skepticism, and gaining the conceptual benefits of quantified modal logic, while refraining from committing to a wild metaphysics.

§2.3. Van Inwagen's modal skepticism

A second variety of modal skepticism was put forward by Peter van Inwagen (1998), in an article titled "Modal Epistemology". While the article generated considerably less discussion than Quine's writings, it is, nonetheless, instructive to discuss it because it defends a different sort of skepticism regarding propositions involving modalities, namely *epistemic* skepticism. Van Inwagen considers arguments that have been at the center of heated disputes in the history of philosophy, such as the following three (18–20; 21–3; 24–6):

18 It is possible for there to be a being that has all perfections essentially.

19 Necessary existence is a perfection.

20 *Therefore*, There is a perfect being.

21   It is possible that I exist and nothing material exists.

22   Whatever is material is essentially material.

23   *Therefore*, I am not a material thing.

24   It is possible that there exists a vast amount of suffering for which there is no explanation.

25   If there exists an omniscient, omnipotent, and morally perfect being, there cannot also exist a vast amount of suffering for which there is no explanation.

26   *Therefore*, It is impossible for there to be a necessarily existent being that is essentially omniscient, omnipotent, and morally perfect.

Van Inwagen calls these *possibility arguments* because their first premise—(18), (21), and (24)—claims that a certain situation is possible. A striking feature of possibility arguments is that their logical structure seems sound; and yet, many regard them as not valid. Moreover, it is extremely rare for someone who is inclined to deny the validity of the argument to change her mind at a later point. According to van Inwagen, arguments of this sort suggest that our opinions regarding the truth of certain propositions involving modalities rest on questionable grounds and we would do better to take a skeptical stance towards them. This is because they describe far-fetched scenarios about which we cannot have any opinion that we can suitably justify. Here is a passage where van Inwagen expresses his view:

> My own view is that we often do know modal propositions, ones that are of use to us in everyday life and in science and even in philosophy, but do not and cannot know (at least by the exercise of our own unaided powers) modal propositions like the crucial modal premises of our three possibility arguments. I have called this position "modal skepticism". This name was perhaps ill-chosen, since, as I have said, I think that we do know a lot of modal propositions [...] It should be remembered, however, that there has been another sort of skeptic: someone who contends that the world contains a great deal of institutionalized pretense to knowledge of remote matters concerning which knowledge is in fact not possible. (Montaigne was a skeptic in this sense, as were, perhaps, Sextus and Cicero.) It is in this sense of the word that I am a modal "skeptic."
>
> —van Inwagen (1998: 69)

Van Inwagen's skepticism challenges modal discourse at a crucial link in the chain—that between possibility and imagination. Is imagination a reliable guide to possibility? And, what does it take to *imagine* a possible scenario, really? The discussion on this topic is vast and still ongoing. David Lewis (1986) famously rejects that conceivability can be a reliable guide to possibility. A 1993 article by Stephen Yablo—"Is Conceivability a Guide to Possibility?"—reopened the debate. The article's merit lies in the fact that it asks what the constraints would be on our conception of conceivability in order for it to play a suitable role as a guide to possibility. For instance, there are many scenarios that are too complex for us to be able to conceive (e.g. those involving a transfinite number of entities); or scenarios that are on the verge of being contradictory (e.g. the scenario under which Goldbach's conjecture is false); or scenarios that are too iffy for us to take a stance (e.g. those indicated by van Inwagen). While we cannot enter into the details of the debate, which tackles epistemic issues, it is important to recognize that there are many propositions involving modalities (including *de re* modal propositions) whose truth conditions we cannot establish, even if we believe that the sentences expressing them are meaningful.

§2.4. Radical modal skepticism

We come now to the third type of skepticism, which is significantly more naïve and—all things considered—radical than Quine's and van Inwagen's, in that it encompasses the full spectrum of modal talk. For this reason, we will name it *radical modal skepticism*. Although it would be doubtful to attribute it to any particular author, nonetheless radical modal skepticism represents a position that, from time to time, can act as an antagonist or as an ally in philosophical disputes. More generally, to fully understand the theoretical force of radical modal skepticism helps us comprehend the nature of each theory of possibility. For this reason, it is very important to consider it in some detail.

Let us begin with a simple consideration. The majority of sentences that concern possible situations deal with what can be termed *mere possibilities*: situations about which there neither are, have been, nor will be any concrete facts in our world. For instance, take the following sentence:

27 There could have been more stars than there are.

There are no facts or events in our world that indicate with certainty that there could have been more stars than there are. How, then, are we to judge the truth or falsehood of this affirmation? Why must we claim that, through a theory, the truth conditions of (27) can be explained? Indeed, how are we to make sense of the proposition expressed by (27)? Sentence (27) certainly makes some sense in English, but so does the proposition:

28 Tomatoes fly only in February.

There are no facts in our world indicating whether tomatoes fly only in February, so we are at a loss when trying to assign a truth value to (28).

Of course, these doubts can be extended to all other mere possibilities, suggesting that only modal talk concerning actuality is meaningful. If we concede this much, however, we probably can no longer plausibly maintain that the PP (or, subordinately, the SPP, EPP, and MPP) has an answer. In recent years, Huw Price (cf. 2004) has suggested that the problem posed by mere possibilities be included in the list of what he calls *placement problems*. The list includes all the cases that are hard to explain for those who are empirically minded and believe that there is only the actual world. In the case of our subject, how can such thinkers accommodate modal truths? Where are they to locate the so-called truthmakers (i.e. the entities that would make-true) for such truths? The radical modal skeptic interrupts the debate with an easy and yet drastic solution: it would be better simply to exercise a radically skeptical attitude towards modal talk.

It is very important to realize that radical modal skepticism does not cast into doubt only abstruse cases. When she was stopped by the police, Giulia was driving with a blood alcohol level that was higher than the limit allowed by law; as a result, she will incur certain penal and administrative sanctions. Yet— we might ask ourselves—what considerations justify such sanctions? One crucial role pertains to certain *merely possible* events: driving with a blood alcohol level that is higher than a given value makes the possibility of having an accident (and, more importantly, an accident that involves people other than Giulia) much more probable. Here a skeptical attitude, which sometimes stirs within us, will set in: how can we incriminate Giulia on the basis of a possible event that never occurred? How are we to know that Giulia *could* cause an accident when she has a certain blood alcohol level, if she has never been involved in one? Certainly, others have been involved in many accidents with that same blood alcohol level, but not Giulia. And every person is different.

Little by little, we begin to see where the radical modal skeptic points her finger: the difference between that which is and that which could have been. This is effectively summarized at the beginning of chapter XV of Niccolò Machiavelli's *The Prince* (1513):

> And many have imagined republics and principalities that have never been seen or known to exist in truth; for it is so far from how one lives to how one should live that he who lets go of what is done for what should be done learns his ruin rather than his preservation.
>
> —Chapter 15: 61

While Machiavelli's objective was not to raise a general objection to the theories of possibility, his position regarding the theory of effective government adequately summarizes the radical skeptic's crucial point. We would be crazy to believe that we can justify not only our theories but also our life practices on the basis of that which could have been, but which we know was not, is not, and will not be. That which we cannot experience, we cannot judge or, much less, rely upon.

The doubts raised by the radical modal skeptic involve the semantic, epistemic, and metaphysical planes. With respect to the first, radical modal skepticism can be taken to imply positions of increasing radicalness. In its milder interpretation, radical modal skepticism argues of merely possible scenarios that we cannot *verify* that their truth conditions are met, because we can never witness them; nonetheless, we can tell what these truth conditions are; thus, the propositions expressed by sentences about merely possible situations are meaningful because we can understand what it would take to verify them. Under a bolder interpretation, radical modal skepticism claims that we cannot *specify* the truth conditions of sentences about merely possible scenarios, since these sentences are really about entities that are mysterious to us; thus, the question arises whether we even grasp the meaning of the propositions expressed by these sentences.

As for the epistemic plane, it should be noted that radical modal skepticism delves even deeper than skeptical attitudes adopted in other contexts, such as the one that deals with inductive reasoning. The problem with inductive reasoning is to make sense of an alleged link between past and actual events, on one hand, and predictions of future events, on the other. If the future is yet to come, then what *will* be seems much like what *could* be or—from after the fact—what *could have been*, as opposed to what *is* or *has been*. (Incidentally, this is the reason why temporal and modal semantics have been developed alongside each other and are often still discussed jointly.) Nevertheless, there is a crucial difference: predictions can be confirmed; of that which is merely possible, though, we cannot have any sort of confirmation. For this reason, we cannot attempt to justify a theory of possibility on the basis of certain empirical correlations and their degree of confirmation, as some do in the case of predictions. Thus, radical modal skepticism strikes deeper than skepticism about induction and constitutes one of the chief epistemic challenges to any theoretical project in modality. The conclusion is that "no metaphysical account which renders it impossible to give a plausible episte-mological theory is to be countenanced" (1985: 217), as Graeme Forbes observes in his classic volume on modality.

As for the metaphysical plane, the suspension of judgment with respect to propositions involving modalities, and in particular with respect to merely possible propositions, is an ally of anti-realist approaches to modality. Our talk of possibility, as it turns out, may regard no real entity. Indeed, many philoso-phers who endorse or have endorsed some radical form of anti-realism, or who look or have looked at metaphysics with little sympathy, will subscribe, if not to the letter, at least to the spirit of radical modal skepticism. Mere possibilities belong to the category of scenario that philosophers are better off not discussing, never mind using as a basis for their theories.

There is a single way to respond to the radical modal skeptic: by asserting that there are certain characteristics of our universe that can be understood independently of experience, and that possibility is among these characteristics. The only position that escapes this response is modal expressivism, another radical but *sui generis* approach to modality. The rest of us, facing the full force of the radical modal skeptic's challenge, must appeal to that one available response. This points toward the connection between that which is possible and that which is actual, illustrating that the link cannot be found in an empirical fact or the past, present, or future. The only response open to theorists of possibility is to assert that the missing link (or links) is a semantic, epistemic, or metaphysical fact whose validity must be understood and accepted to some extent independently of experience.

First, we must clarify the expression "independently of experience". Let us consider the following sentence:

29 The sum of the angles of a triangle is 180 degrees.

When we say that (29) is independent of experience, we are qualifying the way it can be learned. Without entering into superfluous detail, we will say that a sentence is known *independently of experience* when there are at least two ways (and typically many more than two) of learning the sentence that are independent of one another. For example, Giovanni learned (29) through a personal demonstration on May 10, 1996 in Pisa; Rebecca learned it from her elementary school teacher on June 12, 1987 in Philadelphia; Piero just learned it by reading a book at home in Athens. In each of these cases, the same proposition expressed by the sentence (29) is learned. And the modes of learning are all independent of each other: in order for Giovanni's attempt to be valid, he does not have to be privy to what the person who took him through the personal demonstration knows. By contrast, the following statement requires a very specific observation in order to be learned:

30 On April 27, 2008, at three o'clock in the afternoon, Dario Fo wears a green shirt.

Certainly, Dario Fo himself can tell us how he is dressed, but our knowledge depends on someone's observation of the situation. There is no way to become privy to (30) independently of the specific observation of the situation depicted in (30) (with the exception of those who have divinatory powers).

Two qualifications are in order. First, independence of experience has been regarded by some authors (e.g. Kitcher (1980, 2000)) as the hallmark of so-called *a priori* knowledge. To the extent that this conjecture is correct, then, we are suggesting that there is a core of modal epistemology that necessarily relies on *a priori* knowledge because it cannot rest on the bare observation of actual situations. Analogously, Humean skepticism toward inductive reasoning pointed out that the bare observation of present events, or recollection of past ones, cannot provide knowledge of a logically *entailed* future event, indicating that there is a core of inductive reasoning that cannot be justified *a posteriori*. Second, our suggestion is not that a broadly empiricist account of modal knowledge cannot be provided (we will see some notable examples in Chapter 3, on modalism, and Chapter 7, on the new actualism). Rather, we are suggesting that a radically empiricist project, in which knowledge of actual facts alone can justify knowledge of modal facts (and thus of mere possibilities as well), seems destined to fail. Incidentally, the last point may help explain why the most recent accounts of modal epistemology (including Peacocke (1999), Chalmers (2002), Williamson (2007b), and Lowe (2012)) all have a rationalist bent. However, as said, we shall not rule out too quickly accounts that are more empiricist in spirit, such as that by Bueno and Shalkowski (2015).

Let us recapitulate. In order to respond to the radical modal skeptic, we must assert that certain aspects of possibility are learned *a priori*. Naturally, the radical modal skeptic will argue that it is irrational to trust *a priori* knowledge, and that it would be best to suspend our judgment regarding sentences on possibility. Such is the key challenge that this radical form of skepticism leaves us with. It is a challenge that must be taken seriously and that affects each of the theories to be considered in the rest of the volume. Most of those who have written about modality regard the radical skeptic's position as blind to an important characteristic of human knowers: some aspects of reality are undoubtedly known *a priori*; and possibility, which is omnipresent to us, is one of these. We cannot suspend our judgment of possibility because we would at the same time be suspending our judgment of reality. This is all fine: but what further response can we provide to the radical modal skeptic's challenge? Several answers will be considered in the following chapters. Now, we shall proceed to see the position of those who maintain that modal talk simply expresses emotions and who, for this reason, do not feel the full force of the radical modal skeptic's challenge.

§2.5. Modal expressivism

The first response to the skeptic we will consider is *modal expressivism*. The expressivist position has been supported in various philosophical fields and it is not particularly well-known as a modal theory. Perhaps the most fruitful field of application for expressivism is meta-ethics, the branch of philosophy that sets out to provide a definition of the concepts "right", "wrong", "good", and "bad". The expressivist position is particularly significant in aesthetics, as well. Among the classic texts in which expressivism of one kind or another can be found, we might mention Spinoza (1677, esp. Appendix to Part I) and Hume (1739–40). The authors who have most pursued this position in recent times are Simon Blackburn (see especially (1984, 1993, 1998)), Alan Gibbard (see especially (1990, 2003)), and Shroeder (2010, 2008a, 2008b). We should also keep in mind the past formulations by Ayer (1936: Chapter 6) and Wittgenstein (1953).

Expressivism is a peculiar theory of modality, in that it shares with radical modal skepticism a strong anti-realist bent. The core claim of modal expressivism is a denial that modal expressions bear cognitive content: they are, rather, ways to express non-cognitive attitudes of speakers. We shall refer to these attitudes as *sentiments*, interpreting the term broadly as referring to all non-cognitive mental states.

Providing an adequate definition of *non-cognitive* can be complex; to date, there is good reason to suspect that the distinction is not as clear as it has appeared in the past (see, for example, Boghossian (1995)). In any event, roughly speaking, non-cognitive states are those that lead us to act, rather than to understand, a situation. If I believe that Giovanna was wrong, this means (at least, roughly) that I possess a representation of a situation in which she appears; yet it is not due to this that I will act one way instead of another. If I wish to punish Giovanna, though, my wish suggests a way in which I might act towards her—I might refuse to forgive her. Beliefs are cognitive mental states, insofar as they essentially consist of understanding a situation; desires, on the other hand, are non-cognitive mental states, insofar as they are essentially not tied to a representation, but to an action.

In the most recent and sophisticated versions of expressivism, sentiments are understood against the background of social convention (cf. Gibbard (1990, 2003)). Thus, the claim that a certain action is wrong is to be understood as the speaker's expression of conformity to a normative convention regarding the action. The crucial feature of the account is that the expression of conformity is a non-cognitive attitude: although beliefs or intentions can to some extent influence it, ultimately such expression is rooted in a sentiment.

Analogously, modal expressivism takes sentences containing modalities to express the speaker's conformity to a certain conventional way of regarding the non-modal content of the sentence. For example, the sentence:

31 It is possible that: Foffo will play with the carpet in the afternoon

will express the conformity, on the part of whoever endorses it, to all the conventions typical of possibility (e.g. to leave open that in the future (31) will be true, or to prepare for (31) to be the case, and so on).

By slightly modifying Quine's motto, the expressivist theory could be summarized as claiming that "necessity resides in the frame of mind with which we relate to things, not in the things to which we relate". A succinct definition of the position, to be carried forward in the remainder of this volume, is thus the following:

EXP: The sentence of natural language: "It is possible that: *s*" expresses a certain (conventionally codified) sentiment, on behalf of the person who asserts it, toward *s*.

The first and chief upshot of modal expressivism is that modal talk cannot be charged with truth or falsity. Truth and falsity are based on situations, not on sentiments; and the expressivist argues that sentences featuring modal terms express sentiments, not beliefs. The expressivist, therefore, would deny that the SPP, the EPP, and the MPP pose a problem. There is certainly a captivating side to the expressivist proposal: explaining what it *means* to say that a certain situation that is possible or necessary is an arduous task; oftentimes, we are under the impression that there is no meaning in modal expressions, and that they express an attitude of the speaker toward what he is saying. Evidence of this is found in the number of times we use the term "necessary", relativized to the contexts of use: that which is necessary for the mathematician; that which is necessary for a soccer player; or for a student; or for Piero; or for Lulù, the dog; and so forth. The same can be said for the use of the term "possible". How are we to believe that there is one single meaning to modal expressions? More importantly, how are we to believe that modal expressions involve any meaning at all?

Two additional features of the modal expressivist theory deserve to be highlighted. The first is that, unlike all other modal theories, the expressivist has no need to reduce the complex variety of modal talk to the two standard modalities of possibility and necessity. It is indeed plausible to conjecture that there will be conventions associated with "It is possible that" distinct from those associated with "It may be the case that" or "Perhaps" or "It is likely that". This is no small theoretical advantage, as keeping faith with the pragmatic nuances of the variety of modal expressions is a daunting task for basically all other modal theories on the market. Of course, such a feature comes at the cost of giving up a cognitivist analysis of modality, and thus giving up also the conceptual subtleties allowed by quantified modal logic.

The second feature is more delicate. Modal expressivism both can and must offer an analysis of modal talk such that the non-cognitive attitude is clearly demarcated from the cognitive component. For example, according to expressivism, when we say "There could have been more stars than there are" we are expressing a certain (conventionally codified) sentiment towards the following non-modal sentence:

32   The number of stars is greater than the actual number.

In a way, therefore, modal expressivism is committed to interpreting all modal talk in terms of *de dicto* modalities. This is because modal expressions are all ways of speaking about a certain situation, and in particular they are all ways of expressing certain sentiments regarding such situations (as when one says "This ice cream is yummy!" or "Your behavior is disgusting!"). Contrary to the Quinian skeptic, the expressivist would consider legitimate sentences such as that illustrated in (10) ('Foffo the cat is able to eat fish and potatoes'); however, the expressivist would interpret these sentences as *de re*: that is to say, as expressions of frames of mind addressed specifically to one of the "things" (*res*) that belong to the situation expressed by the sentence. It is nonetheless a challenge for modal expressivism to provide plausible analyses for every sentence embedding some modality. For instance, it is not straightforward to analyze claims embedding a predicate that itself involves a modality, as in:

33   Clara is likeable.

It may prove equally difficult to analyze long and convoluted sentences containing modal expressions, such as the famous example by Sobel cited in Lewis (1973: 10):

34   If the USA threw its weapons into the sea tomorrow there would be war; but if the USA and the other nuclear powers all threw their weapons into the sea tomorrow there would be peace; but if they did so without sufficient precautions against polluting the world's fisheries there would be war; but if after doing so, they immediately offered generous reparations for the pollution there would be peace.

While the debate on expressivism in ethics is lively, very few are the recent contributions to modal expressivism. Nonetheless, the ideas put forth with regard to ethics may be used in coming years to provide an adequate level of sophistication to modal expressivism as well.

Before considering some of the problems of modal expressivism, a variant of this view deserves to be mentioned. It is the so-called *modal normativism* put forward by Amie Thomasson (2010); on this topic, see also Sidelle (2009). Modal normativism shares with modal expressivism the denial of the idea that claims involving modality are descriptive claims that can be true or false. The two views, however, depart on the analysis of the non-descriptive content: while for the modal expressivist such content should be analyzed in terms of specific sentiments, for the modal normativist "modal assertions serve a normative (rather than descriptive) function of conveying constitutive rules for using the terms" (Thomasson 2010: fn. 6). The chief philosophical task for the modal normativist is therefore to specify the norms that are at play in the constitutive rules of our modal expressions. These norms should not be spelled out in terms of a logical framework such as the one provided by QML. Rather, the goal is to clarify the rule which constitutes the foundation for our use of modal expressions: that is, for each modal expression we should specify when one is *allowed* to use it. For example, consider once again (8) ("It is possible that: Foffo the cat eats fish and potatoes"): while a modal expressivist reads (8) as conveying a certain non-cognitive attitude on the part of who endorses it, a modal normativist analyses (8) in terms of the circumstances under which a speaker is taken to reasonably claim, or an agent is taken to reasonably believe, that Foffo the cat eats fish and potatoes.

§2.6. Two problems for modal expressivism

There are two principal criticisms of modal expressivism. The first concerns sentiments; more specifically, we might ask ourselves: what sentiments are we speaking of? The extant literature does not offer thorough answers on this point. Still, we may attempt to clarify the matter for ourselves, starting from the two paradigmatic cases of necessity and possibility.

Presumably, the sentiment associated with necessity is to be revealed in the absolute steadfastness with which one accepts the sentence in question. If we believe that, necessarily, the sum of two plus two is four, this means that we would be willing to make a lofty bet on the truth of the sentence, or that we are ready to fervently defend the truth of the sentence from those who claim that the sum is five. The sentiment associated with possibility, on the other hand, leads to a break: if we believe a certain situation to be possible, we would also be willing to entertain the thought that things might be or have been otherwise.

Nevertheless, bringing sentiments into play when dealing with possibility arouses certain perplexities. In fact, a given sentence can be the object of varying sentiments, depending on the occasion. Let us consider, for example, how sentiments vary in relation to how likely we believe it is that the sentence will be confirmed. We will assign the sentences that are considered necessary the same likelihood (or the value 1.0, which indicates certainty) and, therefore, we can reasonably expect a similar frame of mind; but when we consider the sentences that are held to be possible, we will have values that span the entire range of probability, from greater than 0 to 1.0 (because, after all, that which is necessary is also possible). Let us take the following sentences:

35   It is possible that you are reading this sentence.

36   It is possible that a recipe for happiness will be discovered by next April.

37   It is possible that next year I will win New Year's raffle.

38   It is possible that the sum of two plus two is four.

It appears difficult to claim that there is *one*, univocal sentiment that is associated with these sentences. And, besides, this would not be sufficient: in order for the modal expressivist theory to be correct, the sentiment must be specific to *all and only* sentences concerning possibility.

Earlier, we had mentioned that modal expressivist theory might be more appealing than the cognitivist approach to modality: the objection might be made against the latter that a single meaning of expressions such as "possible" and "necessary" does not exist. However, this criticism raises a similar problem for the modal expressivist: it does not seem plausible to assert that there is one sentiment expressed by all and only sentences that refer to a possibility.

In reality, the modal expressivist is worse off than the cognitivist about modality. Here we might introduce the second criticism, which can initially be expressed circumstantially and later generalized. Relationships of implication between meanings can be constructed with relative ease. For example, if certain dietary elements are necessary for all soccer players, then they will also be necessary for Giovanni, who is a soccer player; or, if it is *logically* necessary that a whole be greater than each of its parts, then it will also be *physically*, *biologically*, *geometrically* necessary. Yet, on the other hand, it has been verified that it is difficult to find ties between sentiments. We might infer that a person who likes apples also likes apple juice; if she likes to travel, then she would most probably like to receive an airplane ticket to Marrakech as a gift; but, unfortunately, this is often not the case.

The question of inferences raises a more general problem for the expressivist theory—one that concerns all forms of expressivism (see the discussion of this point in Hale (1993)). There are certain inferences among modal sentences that are considered valid by the vast majority of human beings. Let us take, for example, the following argument:

39 *a* is a triangle.

40 It is necessary that: if *x* is a triangle, then *x* has three sides.

41 *Therefore*, It is necessary that: *a* has three sides.

The validity of this argument appears rather simple to demonstrate. Nevertheless, an expressivist encounters serious difficulties when explaining why the argument is valid. In fact, in order to do so, a theory of implication between modal sentiments is required: yet, as we have seen, there is good reason to believe that this sort of theory cannot be provided.

Moreover: a proponent of the cognitivist approach would point out that she can also explain the validity of inferences that are far more complex than the one just seen, on the grounds of the meanings attributed to the two principal modal concepts: "necessary" and "possible". Let us consider, for example, the following argument:

42 *a* is a triangle.

43 It is necessary that: *a* is identical to *b*.

44 It is necessary that: if *x* is a triangle, then *x* has three sides.

45 For every triangle *x*, it is possible that: *x* is isosceles.

46 *Therefore*, It is necessary that: *b* has three sides, and it is possible that: *b* is isosceles.

A cognitivist can explain the validity of this argument by resorting to logic; but not an expressivist. The expressivist would retort at this point that the concept of validity cannot be applied to arguments containing modal expressions. Or, more specifically: we cannot apply the concept of validity implicit in the criticism raised, which concerns the relationship between a series of propositions that guarantees the truth of the conclusion, upon the acceptance of its premises. This is because expressivism denies that there is truth or falsity when it comes to sentences involving modalities.

However, this does not mean that the expressivist is unable to explain the acceptance of an argument that contains modal terms. At least two explanations can be conceived. According to the first, the acceptance of an argument is explained through the use of a certain sentiment with regard to the conclusion of the argument itself, or, the sentences (41) and (46) in the two previous examples. The second explanation introduces an expressivist definition of validity as a sentiment we express when we consider *the relationship* between a series of sentences; that is to say: we can have sentiments not only with regard to single sentences, but also certain relationships between sentences.

Yet the temptation remains to believe that necessity and possibility involve something more than mere sentiments. Sentiments are not the only thing— we might believe—that make us quit smoking in the face of health effects or that lead us to punish or praise a person based on what he could have done. There's something more: an actual argument founded on the understanding of certain modal concepts. And it is not an argument that we have made up through the introduction of a constitutive rule, as the modal normativist would have it. It is just these modal concepts that we often find combined with the representation of a situation, and that express what we call possibility and necessity. The following chapters will be devoted to the theories that aspire to explain these presumed concepts.

Study Questions

- What is the main target of Quinian modal skepticism?
- What is the distinction between *de dicto* and *de re* sentences?
- Why are *de re* modal sentences problematic for Quine?
- What is quantified modal logic?
- What is the main target of van Inwagen's modal skepticism?
- What is the main challenge posed by radical modal skepticism?
- What is the definition of modal expressivism?
- Name three distinguishing features of modal expressivism.
- What are the main problems for modal expressivism?
- What is modal normativism?

FURTHER READING

The distinction between **de dicto and de re** attitudes, propositions, and sentences plays a key role in several philosophical fields. For the applications to modality, see especially: Quine (1953a, 1953b); Campbell (1964); Lewis (1979, 1986: Chapter 4); Fine (1974, 1994); and Burgess (1997).

Among the views examined in this chapter, **Quinian skepticism** is the most debated. For an overview of the position from the point of view of the debate on modality, see Haack (1978: Chapter 10), Forbes (1985: 216–17), and Melia (2003: Chapter 3). See Hylton (2007) for an overview that places Quine's skepticism within the context of his other work. Quine's position is most famously outlined in his work of 1953a but, for a more comprehensive picture, it is important to look at other writings as well, including those of 1947, 1953b, 1974, 1976, and also Quine's contributions to Barrett and Gibson (1990), in particular his replies to Ruth Barcan Marcus. Critical appraisals of Quine's position abound and, to a certain extent, all the theories discussed in Chapters 3–7 of this volume can be regarded as rejoinders to Quine. For a reconstruction of Quine's view, see Divers (2007) and Keskinen (2010, 2012). Among the most recent articles directly discussing Quine's position, see Burgess (1997), Neale (2000), and Ray (2000). Classic articles that gave shape to the debate include: Smullyan (1948); Føllesdal (1961); Parsons (1967, 1969); the essays collected in Linsky (1974); van Fraassen (1977); and the essays collected in Marcus (1993: especially 14 and 15). For a reconstruction of the main moments that characterize the **modern origins of modal logic**, see Ballarin (2010).

Van Inwagen's modal skepticism is outlined in his work of 1998. For a recent defense of the position, see Hawke (2011). Van Inwagen's position should be read against the background of the broader debate on the relationship between conceivability and possibility; some important readings in this regard are: Yablo (1993, 2001), Sosa (2000), Geirsson (2005, 2014), Kung (2010, 2011), Roca-Royes (2011), and Ichikawa and Jarvis (2012).

Radical modal skepticism cannot be attributed *strictu sensu* to any particular author. For a formulation of the placement problem, also with respect to modality, see Price (2004). On the *a priori*, see Casullo (2003) and Russell (2014). For a relatively recent and influential collection of papers, see Boghossian and Peacocke (2000). For some recent work on the epistemology of modality, see Peacocke (1999), Chalmers (2002), Williamson (2007b), Lowe (2012), and Bueno and Shalkowski (2015).

For a short introduction to **modal expressivism**, see Melia (2003: Chapter 1). For an overview of the expressivist position with a special focus on its applications in ethics, see Shroeder (2010) and van Roojen (2014). For a defense of expressivism in ethics, which might be employed also to elucidate modal expressivism, see Shroeder (2008a, 2008b) and, especially, Gibbard (1990, 2003). Modal expressivism was notoriously endorsed by Blackburn in a series of writings, including his works of 1971, 1984, 1993, and 1998. Among the important precursors of the position are: Spinoza (1677: Appendix to Part I); Hume (1739–40); Ayer (1936: Chapter 6); Wittgenstein (1953) and the related discussion in Wright (1980: Chapters 19–23). For some recent articles, see especially Hale (1993), Sidelle (2009), and Thomasson (2010).

3

Modalism

A general characterization of modalism is first provided. Modalism accepts that modal statements can be true or false and, moreover, that the formal language of QML is well-suited to express them; however, modalism refuses to provide a semantics that further analyzes the modal operators of necessity and possibility, such as a possible-worlds semantics (§3.1.). Next, two problems for modalism are discussed: one related to the expression, within the modalist framework, of certain types of sentences involving modalities; the other concerning the relationship between the formal language adopted by modalists and natural language (§3.2.). Three more recent variants of modalism are then considered, concerned with—respectively—the semantics, metaphysics, and epistemology of the theory. The semantic variant was proposed by Charles Chihara: it brings together the modalist credo that modal concepts cannot be analyzed and the use of possible worlds to provide truth conditions for modal sentences of QML (§3.3.). The metaphysical variant is inspired by Jonathan Lowe's proposal that modal knowledge rests on our knowledge of essences (§3.4.) The epistemic variant, which aims to make empiricism possible for modalists, was put forward by Bueno and Shalkowski (§3.5.). The chapter ends with a look beyond modalism, by means of which we introduce the notion of possible-worlds semantics for QML as providing a conceptual analysis of modal expressions (§3.6.).

* * * * *

§3.1. At the roots of modalism

Based on what has been discussed in the previous chapter, from here on out we will analyze the positions of those who: (i) accept the challenge posed by the radical modal skeptic to show that modal expressions (including *de re* expressions) express something; and (ii) dismiss the hypothesis that modal expressions express sentiments.

The next area of dispute concerns the analysis of the modal concepts presumably expressed by modal terms. In other words: is it possible to undertake an analysis of modal concepts? The so-called *modalists* claim that it is not; proponents of possible worlds (modal realists, ersatzists, fiction-alists, and agnostics) and dispositionalists claim that it is. In this chapter, we will focus on the modalists. Lastly, we will be introduced to the concept of possible world, which will appear frequently in the remainder of the book.

Modalism takes its name from the acceptance of modality as a brute fact. That is to say: the modal concepts "possible" and "necessary" express the possibility or necessity of a situation. Period. While it may seem trivial, this position merits further consideration. In order to explain it, we will turn to a well-known metaphor in contemporary metaphysics: the universal catalogue. Let us suppose that we are to compile a catalogue of the universe, in which we will include everything—every last thing—that exists. We will include Napoleon and the Battle of Waterloo; the Colosseum; Tasmania; rhythm and blues; cider; and so on. At some point, we will have to consider that which is possible: should we include it in the catalog, and, if so, how? The modal skeptic would advocate doubting that modal scenarios can be included; the expressionist would include the sentiments expressed by modal terms; and the modalist? She would include … modal facts: the possible victory of Napoleon at Waterloo; the possible end of the world on December 31, 1999; the necessary fact that the sum of two plus two is four; and so forth. Therefore, the modalist's solution to the PP is the following:

> M: The sentence in natural language: "It is possible that: *s*" expresses the existence of a modal fact of our world: the fact that it is possible that *s*.

Let us consider, for example, the following sentence:

1   Today, in Pisa, Foffo the cat could have eaten milk and cookies.

According to the modalist, (1) expresses a fact of our world, which is compa-rable to the fact that there are three apples on this table: the fact that today, in Pisa, Foffo the cat could have eaten milk and cookies.

Despite the simplicity of the theory, modalism is the result of serious reflection on modal concepts and the analysis that can be made of them through a formal theory. Precursors to modalism can be found among Ancient, Medieval, and Modern philosophers, including Aristotle. But it is with the advent of quantified modal logic (QML) that modalism as such can be identified as a theory on the market. While modalism need not be expressed by means of the language of QML, it typically is. In other words, modalists typically do not set out to apply the principle M directly to the terms and modal concepts of ordinary language, but to the well-formed formulas of QML, in particular those formulas where the symbols expressing necessity (i.e. the box: "□") and possibility (i.e. the diamond: "◇") appear.

As noted in the Introduction, the modalist's choice to work with a formal language is a common one among the theories discussed in this book. Not only modalism, but modal realism, ersatzism, fictionalism, and agnosticism prefer to treat questions of the metaphysics of possibility through a language in which the meaning of expressions has been established in an unequivocal manner. One of the motivating reasons behind this choice is the ease with which a notion of truth and one of validity, applicable also to modal sentences, can be established through an artificial and unequivocal language. As seen earlier, the expressionist must accept that judgments regarding what is possible or necessary are all, to some extent, equivocal. It is not easy to understand what sentiments can be used to define possibility or necessity; nor is it a simple task to identify what relationships exist between sentiments. The use of an artificial and unequivocal language eliminates these problems.

The core idea for a modalist is to endorse the syntax of QML, but reject the semantic account appealing to possible worlds. A sentence such as:

2 It is necessary that: Foffo is a cat

is not true because, at every world, "Foffo is a cat" is true; rather, it is a brute fact of the actual world that (2) is true. Analogously, the sentence:

3 It is possible that: Foffo has milk and cookies

is true not because, in at least one world, Foffo has milk and cookies; rather, it is a brute fact of the actual world that (3) is true. If this is the case, however, modalists must be able to tell a story—in particular, a metaphysical story—regarding actual primitive modalities. That is, although resorting to the language of QML eliminates ambiguities and helps solve one of the three core questions presented in the Introduction, the two other questions remain—even more urgently—open. Recall the questions:

SPP: What does it mean to say that a certain situation is possible?
EPP: How do we come to know that which is possible?
MPP: What sort of entity is a possible entity (of any given kind—a possible individual, property, state of affairs, or ...)?

For the modalist, the answer to the SPP is trivial. To say, for example, that it is necessary that Foffo is a cat is to say that it is necessary that Foffo is a cat; this is because the necessity of such a scenario is a brute fact. Yet, can the modalist provide suitable answers to the EPP and MPP? This is the central question to be addressed in this chapter.

An early modalist proposal is found in the postscript to Prior and Fine (1977). The first to defend modalism in a systematic manner was Graeme Forbes (1985, 1989), and his work remains fundamental for those interested in this theory. We will come back to Fine's view in Chapters 7 and 8. For the time being, in order to pinpoint two problems for modalism, we shall assume the perspective of Forbes (§3.2.). Afterwards, we shall consider three important alternative versions of modalism, focusing respectively on its semantic, metaphysical, and epistemic aspects. In §3.3., we will consider the variant proposed by Charles Chihara (1998), according to which the semantics of modalism can make use of possible worlds, thus enjoying their conceptual benefits, while denying that necessity and possibility can be *analyzed* in terms of possible worlds. In §3.4., we will consider the variant suggested by Jonathan Lowe (2012), which introduces the metaphysical category of essences in order to provide a suitable interpretation for the operators of necessity and possibility. Finally, in §3.5., we will discuss the proposal of Octavio Bueno and Scott Shalkowski (2015, 2013, 2009), whose ambition is to put forward a modalist view with an empiricist outlook. The chapter will end (§3.6.) with a look ahead to theories that, unlike modalism, endorse a semantics for QML based on possible worlds.

§3.2. Two problems for modalism

In Forbes's classic rendition, modalism rests on three choices: (i) enriching the language of first-order logic with the two operators for necessity and possibility; (ii) maintaining—unlike modal skepticism and expressivism—that sentences containing these operators do have a truth value; but also (iii) holding that it is a matter of brute fact whether a sentence is *necessarily* or *possibly* true or false. Declining to provide an analysis of modal expressions (in QML), the modalist avoids the metaphysical and epistemic troubles of possible worlds, which we will discuss in the next three chapters; on the other hand, modalism runs into objections. We will examine two main ones. The first regards the expressive power of the theory, the second the relationship between, on one hand, the two modal primitives countenanced by the language of the theory and, on the other, the issues in natural language that the theory is supposed to address. Let us consider them in order.

In numerous works (1992, 2003, 2005), Joseph Melia has pointed out that the modalist finds it difficult to translate certain sentences into the artificial language of the theory. Consider, for example, the following sentence:

4   There could have been more stars than there are.

Sentence (4) makes a comparison between the stars of this world and those of a possible world. More generally, (4) makes a comparison between two situations: actuality and a possible way that actuality might have been. Because the modalist does not allow for there to be more than one world, it is not clear how she can express a comparison between actuality and what might actually have been. The problem had already been discussed in Forbes (1989). There, Forbes sets out to enrich the language of the theory with terms that carry out the same function as a possible world. That is, he introduces a term A_n for every world W_n, where the term's function is to relativize the interpretation of a sentence (or one of its parts) to a certain context. Thus, Forbes can relativize a part of (4)—the part that concerns the number of stars in our world—to the actual "actuality", and the other part—the part that concerns the possible number of stars—to another "actuality". The strategy is effective from a formal point of view; but authors such as Melia argue that the meaning of the "actuality" expressions is obscure unless it is interpreted in the spirit of possible-worlds semantics, jeopardizing the modalism of the theory.

Other paradigmatically challenging sentences are those referring to multiple possibilities. Let us consider the following:

5   There are three possible ways to secure a contract.

How is a modalist to explain the connection between the three possible ways of securing a contract? The translation would say that there are (only) three actualities, in each of which there is a way to secure a contract. Or, that the three possibilities are each relativized to a different actuality. But, it's hard to see what the actualities mean without appeal to a metaphysics of possible worlds. Once again, the strategy of relativizing different actualities produces a result that is satisfying from a formal perspective, but troubling from a metaphysical and epistemic point of view.

Fortunately, Melia offers another way of interpreting (4) and (5). This form of interpretation differs from Forbes's in proposing a dissociation between the artificial language and the world it speaks of. In order to explain the meaning of (4) and (5), it is not necessary to provide a paraphrase of them in the artificial language of the modalist theory or to make an explicit reference to the relationships between the various situations (the three possibilities in (5) and the actual and possible number of stars in (4)). A simple list of the situations will suffice; for comparison, a metaphysical explanation (expressed in ordinary, not artificial, language) is provided. Consequently, (4) would be interpreted in the following manner (and it should be imagined that the inter-pretation can be expressed in formal language as well):

6.1 In the actual world, there are x number of stars;

6.2 it is possible that: the number of stars is greater than x.

Statements (6.1) and (6.2) are both easily expressible in formal language: the former does not contain any modal terms; the latter is a simple modal sentence. The relationship between the two sentences must be explained in a supplementary manner by means of natural language (e.g. by pointing out that it is the very same entities and kinds of entities, *viz.* stars, that are under scrutiny).

And (5) would be interpreted in the following way (again, it should be imagined that the interpretation can be expressed in formal language):

7.1 It is possible that: the contract is secured in manner A;

7.2 it is possible that: the contract is secured in manner B;

7.3 it is possible that: the contract is secured in manner C.

Statements (7.1), (7.2), and (7.3) are all expressible in formal language: they are nothing but three simple sentences, each expressing a possible fact.

The solution proposed by Melia closely follows a methodology supported primarily by David Armstrong, according to which an artificial language can be useful, but cannot completely substitute for natural language when facing a philosophical problem. (See, for example, Armstrong (1997) and (1978).) In the contemporary debate on possible worlds, this is certainly one of the most profound points of discussion. Further ahead, in Chapters 4–6, we will analyze the four theories that oppose Armstrong's methodology; not until the final chapter, when we discuss dispositionalism, will we see a theory that is inspired by it.

We shall now consider the second criticism aimed at modalism, which concerns the relationship between the formal language in which the theory as interpreted by Forbes is molded and the three problems of possibility—the SPP, EPP, and MPP.

There are entire books that discuss the metaphysics of possibility through the almost exclusive use of an artificial, unequivocal language. Yet the problem lies in being able to connect the expressions of such a language with those of ordinary language. For example, as illustrated earlier, the language used by Forbes makes use of the following two symbols: "□" and "◇". These symbols are meant to capture to some extent the meaning of the concepts of necessity and possibility as expressed in natural language. If they were not, Forbes would not claim to have resolved the problem of possibility, but simply that he had provided us with a new language. Still, many disagree with Forbes. Some—whose positions we will soon examine—believe that the two symbols must be analyzed further. Others believe, more simply, that Forbes's work does not actually address the three central questions introduced at the beginning of this book. Let us take a brief moment to see why.

Fundamentally, there are two reasons to doubt that the symbols "□" and "◇", together with a series of rules concerning their correct use, capture what we mean when we talk about possibility and necessity. The first is that Forbes, like the other modalists, does not provide a precise model for translating from the artificial language of the theory into ordinary language. Forbes claims that modal facts are among the facts of our world. But, seeing as his language only offers us two symbols to express these facts, it becomes difficult to interpret certain sentences in natural language, such as:

8 Perhaps Ubaldo could have and should have eaten less ice cream last night.

The point is not that we lack a model for translating (8) into the language of Forbes's theory (although this sort of objection can be made for sentences with distinct characteristics, as we will soon discover), but that Forbes's theory does not jibe with the way we speak of possibility. According to Forbes's theory we must interpret (8) as the expression of three facts: that Ubaldo ate ice cream; that he could have eaten a smaller portion than the one he did; that he should have eaten a smaller portion than the one he did. Yet many will read (8) as the expression of a single fact: that Ubaldo ate ice cream—a fact with which a certain possibility and certain obligations are associated. Perhaps, then, modalism does not yield a metaphysics of modality; it is unable to provide an interpretation of our modal expressions that would explain what makes sentences containing such expressions either true or false. And, in this sense, modalism does not solve the MPP.

The second reason for doubting the explanatory power of the symbols "□" and "◇" lies in what is customarily referred to as their brute character. It could be argued that the modalist does not give us a theory of possibility since he does not believe he must explain the meaning of modal expressions. As we shall see in the following chapters, a theory of modality is not required to provide a *definition* of the principal modal concepts (possibility and necessity):

that is to say, it is not necessary to find concepts that can completely replace modal concepts, as is the case, for instance, when we define the water molecule in terms of two atoms of hydrogen and one of oxygen arranged in a certain way. Nevertheless, a theory must at least *explain* the principal modal concepts by means of some kind of *philosophical analysis*: that is, it must demonstrate how the relevant concepts are tied to other concepts that are familiar to us. The modalist denies the need for any definition or explanation; the only requirement is to identify the modal concepts through certain symbols of a formal language that avoid the equivocality of ordinary language expressions. To many, this is an utterly unsatisfactory solution that trivializes both the EPP and the PP.

§3.3. Modalism with possible worlds

Over the past two decades, some important variants of modalism have been put forward. They can be grouped together insofar as they share the core idea that facts about modality are brute; however, they also differ in important respects. The first variant we will consider was proposed by Charles Chihara; it focuses on the semantic aspect of modality.

Chihara sets out his position primarily in the volume *The Worlds of Possibility* (1998), which is divided in two parts. In the first, Chihara criticizes four main views. Three of them appeal to possible-worlds semantics; they are the views of David Lewis, Alvin Plantinga, and Gideon Rosen, which we will discuss respectively in Chapters 4, 5, and 6. The fourth view is Forbes's modalism.

Lewis's and Plantinga's theories can be regarded as realist theories of possible worlds, in that they read possible-worlds semantics as talking about *real entities*, namely, possible worlds. On the other hand, Rosen's and Forbes's theories are anti-realist. That said, they are anti-realist for different reasons, which is important to specify in order to understand why Chihara's view falls in the modalist camp. Rosen is a fictionalist about possible worlds: he regards the conceptual analysis of modality in terms of possible worlds as well-suited to the ends of modal theorizing, but he rejects the metaphysical commitment to worlds by arguing that possible-worlds semantics is a useful fiction; possible worlds are *no more real than* the world of Shakespeare's *Othello*. Just as the play is a story that deeply moves and enthuses us without being about any real thing in the world, so possible worlds have the theoretical virtue of explaining modal scenarios without being about any real thing (more on fictionalism in Chapter 6). Forbes is an anti-realist in quite a different sense. Forbes takes modal expressions in the language of QML to be about brute modal facts. While Rosen endorses the analysis of modality by means of possible-worlds semantics, but attempts to stay away from its dubious metaphysical implications, Forbes provides no analysis of modality at all.

Chihara's position, which he sets out in the second part of his volume, resembles Forbes's more than Rosen's. Chihara, in fact, denies that it is possible to provide a conceptual analysis of modal expressions in QML, much less of those in natural language. For this reason, Chihara's can be regarded as a modalist position. On the other hand, Chihara maintains that modalism is compatible with the acceptance of possible-worlds semantics. This is because a schema can be provided that takes us from possible-worlds semantics to a semantic theory that does away with possible worlds. Chihara goes into great detail to spell out and defend his view. The core idea exploits a standard trait of semantics for non-modal sentences: it is relatively standard to evaluate the truth of a non-modal sentence according to an *interpretation* of its terms, which specifies what the terms are about; thus, for any given sentence, there will be a set of admissible interpretations for its terms. For instance, consider the sentence:

9 Foffo is happy.

There will be an interpretation according to which (9) is about Foffo, the cat; another interpretation according to which (9) is about a certain Foffo living in Paris; another still, according to which (9) is about a certain Foffo living in Lima; and so on. In the case in point, that is, each interpretation will provide a different value for "Foffo", so that the truth of (9) may vary depending on the interpretation. Chihara's suggestion is to regard possible-worlds semantics as analogous to truth-under-an-interpretation, where the actual world plays the role "Foffo" plays in (9), being reinterpreted as (or: substituted by) one world or another, depending on the scenario. Thus, in the sentence:

10 It is possible that: Foffo is happy

the actual world is substituted by a possible world such that, at that world, "Foffo is happy" is true. The semantic machinery of possible worlds turns out to be an exercise of substituting other worlds for the actual world, and evaluating sentences in accordance with such substitution. No conceptual reduction is really achieved with the addition of possible worlds: we have simply made the semantic operation of substitution more familiar and easy to follow.

Chihara's proposal is the outcome of a thorough study of the semantics of modality; and it is ingenious. It definitely puts on the map a non-realist account of modality that seems to satisfy Forbes's desiderata without falling prey to the conceptual shortcomings of Forbes's view. On the other hand, as pointed out by Sider (2001), Chihara overlooks important metaphysical and epistemic desiderata for a theory of modality. To be fair, Chihara does not seem to be concerned with those desiderata and it is still an open question whether his proposal could be adequately supplemented to meet them. Any modal theory should at least provide an indication of how sentences within the formal language of the theory are linked to sentences of natural language; it should also explain how the meaning of those sentences is grasped by agents; and it should, finally, explain what those sentences are about. Thus, until Chihara's view answers these demands, we cannot deem it a satisfactory account of modality.

§3.4. Modalism and essentialism

Metaphysical and epistemic aspects of modalism are at the core of our next two modalist proposals. Modalism has been regarded by many as metaphysically suspicious because it introduces brute modal facts, without any story of what grounds such facts. In a 2012 article by Jonathan Lowe—"What Is the Source of Our Knowledge of Modal Truths?"—we find the inspiration for providing adequate metaphysical foundations to the modalist project. Lowe's proposal is to find such a foundation in the modal entities known as *essences*, which—according to him—we have independent reasons for admitting into our metaphysics. Once the existence of essences is recognized, we gain access to a suitable epistemic account of our modal knowledge.

Before considering Lowe's proposal in more detail, it is important to dispel a potential source of taxonomic confusion. Lowe's project—as he himself claims (e.g. 2012: 934)—was inspired by Kit Fine's work on essences. Fine's view, though, is more generally considered as part of the so-called New Actualism, which will be discussed in Chapter 7. This is because—unlike the modalists—Fine argues that the two operators of necessity and possibility fall short of providing adequate conceptual richness to a theory of modality; instead, he advocates the adoption of a variety of "necessity operators", among them an operator for essential dependence. Thus, Lowe's project can be regarded as belonging to modalism only to the extent that essences are invoked to provide the metaphysical foundation for a QML language equipped with the two classic box and diamond operators (expressing, respectively, the concepts of necessity and possibility). For this reason, we will rather say that Lowe *inspired*—rather than *endorsed*—a certain metaphysical foundation for modalism.

Lowe sums up his view as follows:

Put simply, the theory is this. Metaphysical modalities are grounded in essence. That is, all truths about what is metaphysically necessary or possible are either straightforwardly essential truths or else obtain in virtue of the essences of things. An essence is what is expressed by a real definition. And it is part of our essence as rational, thinking beings that we can at least sometimes understand a real definition—which is just a special kind of proposition—and thereby grasp the essences of at least some things. Hence, we can know at least sometimes that something is metaphysically necessary or possible: we can have some knowledge of metaphysical modality. (2012: 947)

There are (at least) three major theoretical claims summed up in this passage. The first concerns the metaphysical foundation of modality, which is found in essences. The second is a doctrine of essences as real definitions. The third is the view that our own essence as thinking beings entails that we are able to understand at least some real essences. Let us look at each of those claims, in order.

Modalists such as Forbes and Chihara saw modalism as a form of anti-realist theory of modality, that is, a theory with no additional metaphysical commitments other than the commitment to the existence of the two modal concepts utilized in QML. The modalist variant inspired by Lowe's proposal, by contrast, sets out to find truthmakers for modal sentences of QML. Of course, such truthmakers will have to belong to the actual world, as there is no other world. Lowe, moreover, suggests that the truthmakers are concrete, spatio-temporal entities. They are essences. Because it sees our modal claims as being about concrete, spatio-temporal entities, the modalist variant under consideration is a hardcore realist view.

Secondly, Lowe's account of essences departs from classic accounts (e.g. Kripke (1980)) based on possible worlds. The latter explicates essences in terms of essential properties. Essential properties are those that belong to an individual in every possible world at which the individual exists. The essence of an individual is therefore defined as the totality of its essential properties. Kit Fine criticizes this view because it is not sufficiently fine-grained. For instance, arguably all of us have the essential property of living in a world such that "2 + 2 = 4" is true at that world; or, Foffo, the cat, has the essential property of belonging to the set that has Foffo as its sole member; but, intuitively, such properties should not be part of (respectively) our essences or Foffo's essence.

To avoid the pitfalls of the classic view, Lowe (taking his cue from Fine and classic texts such as John Locke's *Essay on Human Understanding*) proposes to regard essences in terms of *real definitions* of a thing:

> A real definition of an entity, E, is to be understood as a proposition which tells us, in the most perspicuous fashion, what E is—or, more broadly, since we do not want to restrict ourselves solely to the essences of actually existing things, what E is or would be. (2012: 935)

The key feature of the view that essences are real definitions is that it makes essences identical with the entities they define. Foffo's essence *is* Foffo and not—as the account of essences in terms of possible worlds has it—a cluster of Foffo's properties. An essence, in other words, is nothing over and above the individual that it defines. This is a quite nice result for the modalist variant under consideration: Lowe's suggestion, it turns out, commits the modalist simply to the existence of individuals. Thus, for instance, once we have Foffo, we also have Foffo's essence and, thus, we will have sufficient metaphysical foundation for all the modal claims regarding Foffo.

At this point, our reader may suspect that Lowe has done some metaphysical juggling. How is it possible that the actual Foffo provides the foundation for all modal claims about Foffo, without buying into the existence of any further entity? How can it be that Foffo, who ate fish and potatoes today—that very Foffo—is the foundation for the contention that Foffo could have had milk and cookies instead? Foffo did not have milk and cookies, so there is nothing in the actual Foffo that entitles us to conclude that he could have had a different meal.

Lowe's rejoinder to this objection rests on the third of his claims in the foregoing passage: that our own essence as rational, thinking beings entails that we are able to understand at least some real essences. This is the core of Lowe's proposal in modal epistemology. It is a rationalist contention, for Lowe holds that we need not experience—say—Foffo having cookies and milk in order to understand that such a situation is possible for Foffo; as long as we grasp Foffo's essence, we also grasp that possibility.

> Given that all metaphysical modality is grounded in essence, we can have knowledge of metaphysical modality, provided we can have knowledge of essence. Can we? Most assuredly we can. [...] Knowing an entity's essence is simply knowing what that entity is. And at least in the case of some entities, we must be able to know what they are, because otherwise it would be hard to see how we could know anything at all about them. How, for example, could I know that a certain ellipse had a certain eccentricity, if I did not know what an ellipse is? (2012: 944)

Thus, according to Lowe, in order to know that Foffo could have milk and cookies, we do not even need to *see*, or somehow be acquainted with, Foffo. All it takes to have that knowledge is to know that Foffo is a cat.

Lowe's proposal rests on two controversial bases: a rationalist perspective on knowledge and a view of real definition that hardly seems extendable to all entities (e.g. what is the real definition of bucatini all'amatriciana?). Nonetheless, Lowe's work inspires a plausible story for a modalist and realist theory of modality, a story that deserves being placed on the map of the theories of modality.

§3.5. Modalism and empiricism

Finally, we come to the third modalist proposal. Its distinctive trait is to be geared towards philosophers of an empiricist bent. *Empiricism* is the view that sensory experience is a necessary requirement for knowledge; nothing can be known, that is, unless it is first experienced through the senses. The problem of possibility is especially daunting for an empiricist because, as we noted in Chapter 2 when discussing radical modal skepticism, by definition we cannot experience *mere possibilities* (those scenarios that could have happened, but did not). What is a modalist who is also an empiricist going to say about our knowledge of mere possibilities? And what grounds such possibilities in actuality?

Bueno and Shalkowski's main contention is that modal knowledge rests on judgments of similarity and the observation of constant regularities:

> In both the well-defined and the less well-defined cases, judgments about a particular case are made against a background of similar cases, constant regularities, and the like so that we can have warranted judgments about particular outcomes based on track records for similar cases. (2015: 688)

We are now far from Lowe's rationalist proposal, where knowledge of Foffo's possible meal was derived from our *a priori* understanding of Foffo's real essence. Bueno and Shalkowski, rather, suggest that we know that Foffo could have had milk and cookies because we have seen other cats like Foffo eating such meals, or because cats regularly have milk and cookies. Conceivability plays no role here: what matters is actual observation.

In order to argue for their main claim, Bueno and Shalkowski set out to provide a "geneaology of modal knowledge"—that is, to explain how modal knowledge is developed from particular observations. They begin with how simple possibility claims (such as the one regarding Foffo) are known starting from actuality claims. Then they consider dispositional claims (e.g. "Foffo's cage is fragile"), necessity claims, and probability claims. Their project is quite ambitious because, arguably, it is unclear how all our modal knowledge can be grounded in the observation of actual events. We shall come back to this issue in Chapter 7, when discussing dispositionalism. Despite the challenges faced by their proposal, Bueno and Shalkowski have secured an epistemic foundation for the anti-realist modalist, which had been missing since the works of Forbes.

§3.6. Possible worlds

At this point, before going on to discuss the theories that endorse a conceptual analysis of modal concepts, it will be helpful to introduce the notion of so-called possible worlds. As we have seen, the typical modalist expresses the core of the theory in the formal language of QML, equipped with two symbols—"□" and "◇"—that express the concepts of necessity and possibility, respectively, of ordinary language. Nevertheless, the modalist proposal has proven to many to be unsatisfactory, especially because it is unable to explain the two principal modal concepts.

The modalist choice to use the formal language of QML while analyzing claims containing the box and diamond as being about the actual world is far from standard. In fact, since at least the 1950s, a semantics for QML based on possible worlds has been predominant. In Chapters 4, 5, and 6, we will see a number of different metaphysical positions advanced to back up such a semantics. Each of these positions is problematic and, today, more than fifty years later, views that do away with worlds are coming back (and will be discussed in Chapter 7). But if, despite the difficulties, the metaphysics of possible worlds has been pursued for at least half a century, this is because it rests on a formidably nuanced and conceptually powerful semantics. Thus, before moving forward with our discussion, some remarks on *possible-worlds semantics* are in order.

While it was in its embryonic stages in the works of Wittgenstein (1921) and Carnap (1946, 1947), *possible-worlds semantics* underwent a significant evolution starting at the end of the 1950s with the works of the young Kripke (1959, 1963) and Hintikka (1961, 1963; see also the reconstruction of Copeland (2002)). Possible-worlds semantics is a theory of the meaning of modal expressions, expressed in a formal language, in which certain terms are referred to as "possible worlds". Intuitively, a possible world is a thorough and consistent scenario, a way in which our world could have existed, though there could be worlds that are so different that they have not a thing to do with our own. Simply put, the theory sets out to evaluate the truth and falsity of every situation expressed by a modal sentence of natural language according to the following schema (where s stands for any sentence):

(P) The sentence in natural language: "It is possible that: *s*" is true if and
   only if the sentence in the language of the possible-worlds theory:
   "There is a possible world *w* in which: *s*" is true;

(N) The sentence in natural language: "It is necessary that: *s*" is true if
   and only if the sentence in the language of the possible-worlds theory:
   "In every possible world *w*: *s*" is true.

In other words, possible worlds represent all of the possible scenarios that
we can imagine. If we say (in English) that a situation is possible, in the
language of the possible-worlds theorist we are saying that there is a world
(a scenario) in which that situation is realized; if we say (in English) that a
situation is necessary, in the language of the possible-worlds theorist we are
saying that, in all worlds (all scenarios) that we can imagine, that situation is
realized. For possible-worlds semantics, thus, every English sentence talks
about a world—either the actual world, or some of the possible worlds. For a
systematic formal presentation, see Girle (2000, 2003). Also useful is Garson
(2006).

   The apparatus of possible-worlds semantics is standardly completed with
the addition of a relation among worlds, the so-called *relation of accessibility*,
defined for each world. (The semantic theory introduced by David Lewis and
discussed in Chapter 4, counterpart theory, is a notable exception to this rule:
in counterpart theory the key relation is not accessibility among worlds but
qualitative similarity among worlds.) Each world, that is, is assigned a set of
worlds, which are accessible from it: intuitively, this is the set of worlds that
define the full spectrum of possibilities that hold at that world. There are no
constraints on how the relation of accessibility is defined. The set of accessible worlds may be empty—those will be the worlds at which nothing is
possible. Or it may contain only the world for which the accessibility relation
is defined—those will be the worlds at which that which actually happens,
necessarily happens. Or, it may contain all the possible worlds whatsoever:
those are the worlds at which that which is possible coincides with the
maximum extent of possibility. Typically, each world will have access to a set
of worlds in which some characteristic is fixed, such as the set of worlds
that contain the same laws of nature, and that is smaller than the total set of
possible worlds.

   By means of this simple semantic apparatus, possible-worlds semantics
manages to express conceptual nuances that extend far beyond our linguistic
intuitions. For instance, consider the following sentence:

11 It is possible that: it is necessary that: it is possible that: Foffo the cat
   speaks English.

While (11) is conceptually tortuous in English, possible-worlds semantics delivers a straightforward machinery to check its truth conditions:

12   There is at least one world W_x accessible from the actual world and such that, for any world W_y accessible from W_x, there is at least a world W_z accessible from W_x such that, at W_z: Foffo the cat speaks English.

Of course, (12) is still conceptually tortuous, but checking the truth value of (11) now becomes a matter of doing the proper calculation in terms of what's true at certain possible worlds. Possible-worlds semantics turns modal discourse, as a variety, into a discourse about possible worlds and accessibility relations among these worlds, a discourse that can easily be implemented and checked by a machine. Indeed, possible-worlds semantics has undergone immense growth in its fifty years of life; it has been revised, enriched and fine-tuned in countless ways to give rigorous and straightforward expression to an incredible spectrum of topics, including: mathematical claims (e.g. theorems and proofs); claims in the natural sciences (e.g. laws and principles); medical claims (e.g. epidemics and predictions); the behavior of agents in game theory and economics; ethical principles; political principles; engineering systems; and more. Today, we can claim that the conceptual machinery of possible-worlds semantics enabled an analysis of the various modal expressions, and of their conceptual ties, that is much more profound than the analyses provided by any other society or civilization up until this point.

Nevertheless, the problem encountered with modalism presented itself again with possible-worlds semantics: how are the terms that express modality in QML to be interpreted in natural language? In other words: what are these possible worlds the theorist of possible-worlds semantics speaks of? Joseph Melia nicely sums up the problem:

Many philosophers have been impressed by possible-worlds semantics. Possible-worlds semantics has shed light upon a wide range of modal notions, has helped us understand counterfactuals and answered questions about the validity and soundness of modal logics. But many philosophers have been depressed by possible worlds themselves. Impressive though its scope and explanatory power be, Lewis's theory that merely possible worlds are concrete objects like our own simply defies belief, and the ersatzer's theories are not particularly palatable to those with a taste for desert landscapes. But without accepting some form of possible worlds into our ontology how can we regard possible-worlds semantics as anything more than a formal game? And if the semantics is nothing more than a formal game then how could it shed any light upon our modal notions?
—Melia 2000: 333

The criticism of the semantic notion of possible worlds deserves particular attention. Certainly QML, as developed by theorists of possible-worlds semantics, has tremendous conceptual potential. Yet the key philosophical problems that interest us here concern our everyday behavior; furthermore, those problems are rooted in the language and concepts that we use daily, not in the language of particular specialists. When we ask what the meaning of modal expressions is, or what a possible entity is, or how we are to know that a certain situation is possible, we ask in English, in Finnish, or in Tagalog; and the answer must be in that language, not in a formal language.

Some (not the majority) consider this criticism to be misplaced. After all, the main topics of medical, technological, or engineering research concern our everyday behavior and are rooted in ordinary language, and yet we have gained great benefits from the development of specialized languages (including formal languages) for the consideration of these themes. Who, as a layman, can sit through a specialized seminar on cardiology or electronic engineering and truly understand what is being discussed? Why, then, should philosophers be required to express their theories in ordinary language? Or, why should they care about the metaphysical or epistemological implications of their theories, so long as those theories serve to provide rigorous analyses of certain ways of speaking?

It could be replied that, in order to carry out their work, a doctor or an engineer might find it sufficient to use ordinary language when writing a medical prescription or when explaining how to use a certain piece of machinery. The rest of their work is conducted outside language—in actual treatment of patients or dealing with machinery. The case of philosophical research seems to be different: is the philosopher's pill not made of words? How can we expect a philosophical theory to resolve a problem if it does not offer an answer in the language in which the problem was raised? As Sider (2001: 91) points out, among the goals of a theory of modality there is also providing "an account of quantification over possibilities in everyday language, for example 'there are five ways to win this chess match'."

At this point, the dispute shifts towards the purpose of philosophy: perhaps philosophy does not attempt to resolve the problems of ordinary humans, but only of those who are willing to venture into the formal languages of philosophers and who are able to perceive the solutions offered through them. The question extends beyond the themes of this book but, having read up until this point, perhaps the matter is worth pondering. A good start is provided in Hendricks and Symons (2005).

And yet, implicitly or explicitly, the majority of analytic philosophers who have concerned themselves with possibility have accepted the challenge: to explain in their own language the meaning of what is known in formal language as possible worlds. We shall take this up in the following three chapters by examining four (types of) theories of possible worlds. It should be kept in mind that the term is nothing more than a figurehead: just as the term "God" has been identified with all that there is, with the supernatural, with history, and with a specific person—to offer a few examples—the term "possible world" has been identified with a potentially infinite number of entities.

What, then, is a possible world?

Study Questions

- What is the relationship between modalism and QML?
- What is the core thesis of modalism?
- What are the two main objections to Forbes's modalism?
- What is the distinctive trait of Chihara's modalism?
- What are the three distinctive theses of Lowe's modal account?
- What is an essence, according to accounts based on possible worlds?
- What is an essence, according to Lowe?
- How do we know the essences of individuals, according to Lowe?
- What is the distinctive trait of Bueno and Shalkowski's modalism?
- What is possible-worlds semantics?

FURTHER READING

For an **overview** of modalism that stresses the semantic issues of the theory, see Melia (2003: Chapter 4). For an **early version** of the view, see the postscript to Prior and Fine (1977). A **classic** exposition is found in Forbes (1985, 1989). Chihara's variant is amply developed in Chihara (1998). For Lowe's essentialist proposal, see Lowe (2012); for an introduction to theories of essence, see Robertson and Atkins (2013). For Bueno and Shalkowski's position, see Shalkowski (1994) and Bueno and Shalkowski (2009, 2013, 2015). Among the writings that set out to discuss specific versions of modalism, see: Sidelle (1989), Melia (1992), Forbes (1992), and Melia (2005).

For an overview of the issues surrounding the relationship between **logic and metaphysics**, a good starting point is Hendricks and Symons (2005); see also Zalta (2010).

For a historical overview of **possible-worlds semantics**, see Ballarin (2010) and Copeland (2002). For an introductory treatment of the topic, see Menzel (2015). A systematic presentation of the semantics is offered in a large number of volumes and handbooks, among them, Girle (2003). Among the classic texts that gave shape to this branch of logic and formal semantics are C. I. Lewis (1918), Wittgenstein (1921), C. I. Lewis and Langford (1932), Carnap (1946, 1947), Prior (1957), Kripke (1959, 1963), and Hintikka (1961, 1963).

4

Modal realism

Modal realism is the most bizarre contemporary take on modal metaphysics and one of the most debated. It is associated with the name of David Lewis and it was a pivotal contribution to the field, reviving interest in metaphysics among analytic philosophers. First, a general characterization of modal realism is provided (§4.1.). Then, its core metaphysical (§4.2.), semantic (§4.3.), and epistemic (§4.4.) tenets are presented. Five theoretical virtues of modal realism are then considered (§4.5.). Finally, we consider a major objection to the modal realist project, according to which the theory's effort to reduce modalities to the existence of individuals (in worlds) fails on two counts (§4.6.).

* * * * *

Sometimes referred to as "extreme realism" or "concretism" (see Divers (2002), Melia (2003: Chapter 5) and van Inwagen (1986)), modal realism is the theory of possibility conspicuously associated with the name of David Lewis. Sketched in the article "Anselm and Actuality" (1970), its first formulation is in *Counterfactuals*, published in 1973. But Lewis's views were fully developed in *On the Plurality of Worlds*. The latter volume, published in 1986, is one of the most influential studies in analytic metaphysics of the past fifty years; it is focused on the metaphysics of modality and has thus contributed decisively to the legitimacy of this field of metaphysics. The importance of Lewis's work on modality can hardly be overestimated; since 1986 the debate on the metaphysics of modality and cognate issues has been one of the liveliest in analytic metaphysics and has paved the way for other theories of possibility, such as modal fictionalism, which we will discuss in Chapter 6. And yet, the view defended by Lewis is patently bizarre, so much so that he himself claimed (1986) that modal realism produced an "incredulous stare" in the person who first heard about it.

To date, only a handful of philosophers have openly endorsed modal realism, a recent and notable case being Yagisawa (2010). Our challenge in this chapter is to understand why a philosopher as brilliant as David Lewis defended such a bizarre view, and whether it was worth it. We begin with an outline of modal realism (§4.1.), followed by an exposition of its core metaphysical (§4.2.), semantic (§4.3.), and epistemic (§4.4.) tenets. Five theoretical virtues of modal realism are then considered in §4.5. Finally, in §4.6., we consider a major objection to the modal realist project, according to which the theory's effort to reduce modalities to the existence of individuals (in worlds) fails on two counts.

§4.1. The realist program

Modal realism literally follows the advice, given by Robert Musil and cited at the outset of the Introduction, "to attach no more importance to what is than to what is not". To Lewis, possible scenarios and the possible entities they involve exist in exactly the same sense that we would say that you and I, the Amazonian forest, and the Eiffel tower exist. According to Lewis, there are infinite worlds, as *real* or *concrete* as we would be willing to say that our world is real or concrete. Such a simple and bold conjecture invites a wide variety of philosophical objections, yet solves in an elegant manner the three sub-problems of possibility.

Lewis's theory is a brilliant exercise in philosophical analysis. The argument for modal realism is presented as resting on the fruitfulness of the hypothesis that there is an infinity of worlds as real as our own. In an often-cited passage from the initial pages of *On the Plurality of Worlds*, Lewis defends his philosophical stance based on its theoretical consequences:

Why believe in a plurality of worlds?—Because the hypothesis is serviceable, and that is a reason to think that it is true. The familiar analysis of necessity as truth at all possible worlds was only the beginning. In the last two decades, philosophers have offered a great many more analyses that make reference to possible worlds, or to possible individuals that inhabit possible worlds. I find that record most impressive. I think it is clear that talk of *possibilia* has clarified questions in many parts of the philosophy of logic, of mind, of language, and of science—not to mention metaphysics itself. Even those who officially scoff often cannot resist the temptation to help themselves abashedly to this useful way of speaking. (1986: 3)

We shall return to the theoretical advantages of modal realism shortly. To begin to explain Lewis's choice, we must point out how modal realism elegantly solves the three sub-problems of possibility, which—as we may recall—are:

SPP: What does it mean to say that a certain situation is possible?
EPP: How do we come to know that which is possible?
MPP: What sort of entity is a possible entity (of any given kind—a possible individual, property, state of affairs, or …)?

To answer the semantic problem of possibility (SPP), Lewis developed *counterpart theory*, to be discussed in §4.3. Counterpart theory is a semantics for modal sentences, resting on the existence of an infinity of worlds, such that there is no individual inhabiting more than one world. Introduced in 1968—so, before modal realism—counterpart theory is the main alternative to the standard possible-worlds semantics (developed by Hintikka, Kripke, et al.), in which the very same individual may inhabit infinite worlds. As for the metaphysical problem of possibility (MPP), Lewis's solution is straightforward: a possible entity is as real as any entity of the actual world. Finally, Lewis's answer to the epistemic problem of possibility (EPP) rests on philosophical analysis: we know of the existence of other worlds and their inhabitants because conjecturing that they exist delivers the best philosophical analysis of modality, that is, a simple and elegant analysis with great explanatory power.

To position modal realism on the map of metaphysical theories of modality, it is useful to compare it to other views. Let us consider the following example:

1 There could have been more stars than there are.

The modal realist, contrary to the radical modal skeptic, believes that it is possible to grasp the meaning of (1); and, contrary to the modal expressivist, believes that (1) is not the expression of a sentiment of the person who uses it, but is about a genuinely possible scenario. According to the modal realist (and the modalist, for that matter), the analysis of (1) must begin by bringing to light the modal operator: that is, there must be a certain relationship between (1) and:

2 It is possible that there could be stars that actually do not exist.

For the modal realist (who here parts ways with the modalist), the truth of (2) is best couched in terms of possible worlds: modalities can be conceptually analyzed in terms of worlds. Finally, the modal realist project is the boldest of those that endorse possible worlds: this is because, according to Lewis, modal realism not only conceptually analyzes modalities in terms of non-modal entities (i.e. worlds), but also *metaphysically reduces the first to the second*; as we shall see in due course (§4.5.), however, whether the reduction succeeds is a point of contention.

According to the modal realist, there are many worlds, all of which are as concrete as our world; the individuals inhabiting those worlds (people, living entities, material objects, and any other entity whatsoever) exist in the same way we say the inhabitants of our world exist. Of these worlds, there is one in which there are more stars than there are in ours. Thus, (2) can be reformulated in the following manner:

3   There is a world in which there are more stars than there are in our world.

Notice that (3) is not about "possible worlds", but "worlds": this is because all worlds exist on a par, as we shall see. Therefore, for the modal realist, believing (1) simply amounts to believing (3). Generally speaking, the central tenet of modal realism—through which the PP is resolved—is the following:

MR: The sentence in natural language: "It is possible that: *s*" expresses the existence of a world in which: *s*.

The extravagance of the proposal is shocking. In order to explain the attribution of possibilities to our world, we are left with infinite *additional* concrete situations. To assess the plausibility of this view, let us now take a closer look at the main conceptual focal points of modal realism. We shall begin with the metaphysical underpinnings of modal realism, since they are the most controversial and the most central to our analysis. Afterward, we will discuss the semantic and epistemic sides of modal realism, in that order.

§4.2. Modal realism: Metaphysics

The main thesis defended in *On the Plurality of Worlds*—that there are infinite worlds, each of which exists like our own—regards modal metaphysics in particular. And yet, in order to argue for such a thesis, Lewis unfolds a much richer metaphysical picture, where modal issues are entrenched with bits of mereology (the theory of parts and wholes), as well as with a metaphysics of individuals, properties, time, and much more. Introducing modal realism, therefore, forces us to touch upon a number of additional metaphysical issues that have been at the center of contemporary debates in analytic metaphysics. Here we have made a selection of the key issues and, even so, we will not be able to discuss all of them in detail. We begin with the modal realist's conception of worlds.

§4.2.1. Worlds

Call the universe we inhabit, whose boundaries coincide with the boundaries of its spatio-temporal manifold, the *actual world*. According to the modal realist, infinite worlds exist. Some depart from the actual world in only minute details, whereas some are so different that we cannot even imagine them. For instance, there is (at least) one world differing from the actual just because, in the previous sentence, instead of "minute details" the reader finds "small ways": there is a world inhabited only by philosophers; there is a world where libraries exist and nothing else (no writers, no readers, no trees); and there is a world where only a vast amount of Hydrox-cookie ice cream exists. Play as much as you like the game of picturing worlds: as long as there is no contradiction in your picture, that world exists. But, again, do not form the impression that only the worlds we can imagine exist: there may be many more (we shall come back to this in the next section).

Each of the worlds of the modal realist possesses three key features: it is a maximal individual, it is isolated from all other worlds, and it is not metaphysically privileged, or unprivileged, with respect to any other world. One may add a fourth feature, already mentioned, which is that worlds are "concrete". Indeed, Lewis claims:

So, by and large [...] it seems that indeed I should say that worlds as I take them to be are concrete; and so are many of their parts, but perhaps not all. But it also seems that to say that is to say something very ambiguous indeed. (1986: 86)

So, yes, worlds exist in the same sense that we would say the actual world exists and, at least in this sense, they are concrete; if people in the actual world are made of flesh and blood, then other worlds contain people made of flesh and blood too. But, because of the ambiguities in the meaning of "concrete", it is best not to place too much emphasis on the claim that worlds are concrete. We will see that the key claim is, rather, that no world is metaphysically privileged, or unprivileged, with respect to the others.

The first feature, then, is that each world is a *maximal individual*. It is an *individual* because, no matter how gerrymandered a world may be, it is just a totality composed of its inhabitants; like a salad is composed of its ingredients, no matter how disparate they are, so a world is composed of its inhabitants. In fact, for Lewis a world is *nothing over and above* its inhabitants, in virtue of the (controversial) mereological principle of Composition as Identity, which he accepts, and according to which, once you have the inhabitants of a world, you have the world, and *vice versa*.

A world is a *maximal* individual because, in first approximation, it fully occupies a reticulate of external relations. At least for our world and the worlds like ours, such reticulate is a spatio-temporal relation—a specific relation for each world. The definition of maximality resorts to a maximal external relation, rather than a spatio-temporal system, because the former is a wider concept than the latter: indeed, the former, but not the latter, can be used to characterize worlds with a space-time manifold wildly different from the one we attribute to the actual world.

In more detail, the first feature delivers the following condition of maximality, which an individual must satisfy in order to count as a world:

I–MAX: w is a maximal individual if and only if all the parts of w bear a certain external and maximal relation to all the other parts of w.

This condition depends on the following two types of relations:

R–EXT: A relation R between two individuals x_1 and x_2 is external if and only if there are (at least) a part p_1 of x_1 and (at least) a part p_2 of x_2 such that: p_1 and p_2 do not overlap and R holds between p_1 and p_2.

R–MAX: A relation M is maximal with respect to a collection $x_1,..., x_n$ if and only if, for any x_i among the $x_1,..., x_n$, x_i bears the relation M to all the $x_1,..., x_n$ and there is no x_j such that: x_j is not among the $x_1,..., x_n$ and bears M to one of the $x_1,..., x_n$.

The second feature of each of Lewis's worlds is that it is *isolated*: no individual inhabits more than one world. Put together with maximality, the resulting picture has it that the inhabitants of each world are unique to it and there is one external relationship through which they are all connected. Isolatedness may seem an innocuous feature, but it is distinctive of Lewis's semantics of modal sentences and also his metaphysics of possible worlds. Because of isolatedness, Lewis's theory of identity across worlds is not based on strict identity, but rather on a specific similarity relation—counterparthood—to be discussed shortly. Furthermore, it is important to stress that isolatedness concerns individuals, not *properties* or *events*. With the exception of certain very special properties or events, for Lewis the same property is exemplified in multiple worlds, and the same event occurs in multiple worlds.

To determine whether individuals inhabiting different worlds are similar is to compare the properties that those individuals share; and causation is defined by tracking the same (sequence of) event(s) across multiple worlds, where that (sequence of) event(s) is embedded in relevantly similar sequences of events. (For a discussion of isolatedness in the context of modal realism, good starting points are Bricker (2006a), (2006b), and (2007).)

Finally, no world is metaphysically privileged with respect to the others. This feature is typically cashed out in the thesis that actuality is indexical. That is, from the point of view of each world, *that* world is *the actual* world. Expressions such as "here", "now", or "I" are indexical: without the specification of a context (an *index*) with respect to which they are employed, those expressions convey no specific meaning. Thus, the sentence:

4 Foffo is eating fish with potatoes now,

when uttered at 8:15 a.m. on Friday February 21, 2014, means:

5 Foffo eats fish with potatoes at 8:15 a.m. on Friday February 21, 2014.

But, when (4) is uttered on Saturday February 22, 2014, it means:

6 Foffo eats fish and potatoes at 8:15 a.m. on Saturday February 22, 2014.

Analogously, for Lewis, the sentence:

7 In the actual world: Foffo eats fish with potatoes,

when read by us, inhabitants of a certain world—call it W_1—means:

8 At W_1: Foffo eats fish with potatoes.

Yet, when (7) is uttered by an inhabitant of a world other than ours—call it W_2—it means:

9 At W_2: Foffo eats fish with potatoes.

Typically, we regard the actual world as privileged with respect to other worlds (see, for example, van Inwagen (1986) for a defense of this idea). Such a privilege has, among others, an epistemic foundation: we have privileged access to what happens in the actual world, and not what happens in most other worlds, because we are acquainted with only the actual world. Analogously, we tend to privilege the present, or the past, with respect to the future: for instance, as we saw in Chapter 1 when discussing the problem of Future Contingents, we regard the present and the past as fixed, whereas the future we regard as open. To Lewis, however, there is no such privilege.

§4.2.2. Plenitude and recombination

Like many other philosophers, Lewis endorses the so-called principle of *plenitude of possibility*. An intuitive, but sketchy and rather uninformative, way to express the principle is that *there is all that there could be*. To begin refining this intuitive formulation, a modal realist could say that, for any way a world could be, there is a world that is that way. This formulation nonetheless falls short of addressing the key philosophical question at stake, namely: Which scenarios are possible?

In order to answer the latter question, and thus specify which worlds exist, Lewis resorts to the so-called *principle of "Humean recombination"*, named after David Hume, chief opponent of necessary connections in metaphysics. The principle rests on the modal intuition according to which *anything can coexist, or fail to coexist, with anything else*, as long as the coexisting individuals can fit the maximal external relation of a world; for the modal realist, the intuition amounts to the belief that "patching together parts of different possible worlds yields another possible world" (Lewis 1986: 87–8). There are all the worlds that there could be by recombining whatever collection of individuals with whatever other collection of individuals. The individuals to be recombined need not belong to the same world; and neither the individuals' size nor their mereological complexity (i.e. how many parts and how they are arranged) make a difference. We can thus offer a preliminary formulation of the principle of recombination:

> PR: Any collection of individuals x_1, ..., x_n could coexist, or fail to coexist, with any collection of individuals y_1, ..., y_n, as long as they fit the maximal external relation of a world.

PR, however, is unsuitable for a modal realist. This is because the modal realist denies that any individual can inhabit more than one world, thus she cannot endorse a principle according to which anything can coexist with anything else. The modal realist must therefore translate PR into the language of counterpart theory.

Before we can arrive at a modal realist formulation of PR, we must consider parts of Lewis's semantics for modal sentences. Counterpart relations are relations of qualitative similarity among individuals; the range of properties upon which the similarity rests varies based on the sentence under consideration and the specific context in which it is used; thus, at a minimum the similarity will rest on one property and, at a maximum, it will rest on all the properties of the individuals under comparison. The flexibility of counterpart relations is a theoretical virtue when it comes to explaining the meaning of sentences embedding modal expressions; however, when the goal is to offer a formulation of the principle of recombination, such flexibility poses a problem: we are not just recombining an initial cluster of individuals (say, those of the actual world); rather, we have to devise worlds made out of counterparts of the individuals in the initial cluster, and such operation is more articulated because counterpart relation differs significantly from identity.

Lewis solves the problem of offering a modal realist formulation of PR by resorting to *intrinsic properties* and, through them, to the notion of an *intrinsic duplicate*. In contemporary metaphysics, the debate regarding intrinsic properties is complex and still open-ended (for a start, see Weatherson and Marshall (2012)). Simplifying a bit, intrinsic duplicates are those individuals that share all of their "perfectly natural" properties. Those properties have two features: first, each of them serves to explain fundamental causal relationships or to ground the similarity of natural kinds; second, each of them is *independent of accompaniment*: each belongs to an individual independently of whether that individual is, or is not, accompanied by any other collection of individuals. Perfectly natural properties comprise the core class of intrinsic properties: any other property that is intrinsic is defined as such based on its relationship to the perfectly natural properties. More precisely, the intrinsic properties of an individual are the properties that it shares with all and only its intrinsic duplicates. Intrinsic properties are thus independent of accompaniment; but, except for perfectly natural properties, intrinsic properties cannot play a major role in the natural sciences (because they do not carve nature at its joints as much as the perfectly natural properties).

Because intrinsic properties are independent of accompaniment, they will serve well the purpose of offering a modal realist formulation of the principle of recombination, which may be stated as follows (for a more in-depth discussion of the formulation, see Darby and Watson (2010)):

> PR* For any collection of individuals $x_1, ..., x_n$ that stand in a maximal external relation, there is a collection of individuals $y_1, ..., y_n$ such that: (i) each of the $y_1, ..., y_n$ is numerically distinct from each of the $x_1, ..., x_n$; (ii) y_1 is an intrinsic duplicate of $x_1, ..., y_n$ is an intrinsic duplicate of x_n; (iii) the $y_1, ..., y_n$ compose a world.

PR* expresses the thesis of the plenitude of possibility, according to the modal realist.

Before ending this section, we should recall that the principle of recombination—in its Humean or non-Humean variants—has been endorsed by other philosophers. Most notoriously, the so-called *combinatorialist theory of possibility* rests entirely on a certain understanding of the principle of recombination. We will discuss this theory in Chapter 5, especially in connection with the work of Brian Skirms and David Armstrong.

§4.3. Counterparts

In 1968, Lewis published a now-classic article on the semantics of sentences containing modal expressions: "Counterpart Theory and Quantified Modal Logic". The article presented a novel modal semantics, which paved the road for modal realism. Before examining this semantics in more detail, and to place Lewis's proposal in the context of this volume, it is important to stress three characteristics of counterpart theory. First of all, the theory moves within the framework of possible-worlds semantics, thus analyzing the meaning of modal sentences in terms of sentences making reference to possible worlds; by now, it should be clear that Lewis's semantics, as well as his metaphysics and epistemology, belong to the large group of theories that analyze modal expressions in terms of possible worlds. Second—and we have stressed that this is the element of novelty within Lewis's semantics—counterpart theory assumes that there is no overlap between the domains of each world. (It is worthwhile to note, on a side, that the contention that no world is metaphysically privileged with respect to another was not yet in place in Lewis's 1968 article on counterpart theory. Additionally, only later, when Lewis fully developed his modal realism, was this second assumption refined to the claim that worlds are isolated maximal individuals.) Third, the meaning of modal sentences, for Lewis, is analyzed in terms of the relationship of counterparthood.

Counterpart relationships, as we have already anticipated, are much more flexible with respect to relationships of strict identity (see Lewis (1968), Merricks (1999), and Borghini (2005)). To understand why, it is best to first define counterparthood:

> COUNTERPARTHOOD: An individual x_1, inhabiting a world W_1, is *a counterpart in W_1* of an individual x_2 inhabiting the world W_2 when, with respect to a given selection of properties $P_1, ..., P_n$, there is no individual in W_1 that resembles x_2 more than x_1.

Four salient characteristics of counterparthood tell it apart from identity (for a broader understanding of counterparthood, see: Forbes (1982); Mondadari (1983); Heller (2002, 2005); Dorr (2005); Fara and Williamson (2005); and Torza (2011)).

(i)   Unlike strict identity, counterparthood is compatible with qualitative dissimilarity and, thus, with an individual having more than one counterpart in a given world. For instance, Foffo, the cat, may have two cats as counterparts in another world, one having a second tail that is grey and the other having a second tail that is black; both cats are otherwise exactly like Foffo and more than anything else in their world resemble Foffo.

(ii) Like strict identity, counterparthood is *reflexive:* any individual is a counterpart of itself in its own world; it is *not* transitive: if x_1 is a counterpart of x_2 in W_1, and if x_2 is a counterpart of x_3 in W_2, it is not necessarily the case that x_1 is a counterpart of x_3 in W_1.

(iii) Unlike strict identity, counterparthood is *not* symmetric: if x_1 is a counterpart of x_2 in W_1, it is not necessarily the case that x_2 is a counterpart of x_1 in W_2; there might be some x_3 in W_2 that resembles x_1 more than x_2 resembles x_1.

(iv) Finally, unlike strict identity, counterparthood is *contextually defined* on the basis of a varying list of properties, broadly understood.

An examination of counterpart theory shows why properties play a key role in Lewis's metaphysics. It is by means of properties that the identity of individuals across worlds can be fixed. Worlds are inhabited by non-overlapping collections of individuals; on the other hand, properties are defined as sets of individuals: each of those sets includes members that span across multiple, possibly infinite, worlds. Thus, once we have the individuals and the properties, we also have a picture of the relationships of qualitative similarity between individuals inhabiting different worlds. Modal sentences express some of those similarities. It was on the basis of this metaphysical apparatus that Lewis provided a brilliant analysis of counterfactual statements in his *Counterfactuals* (1973).

To recap, for Lewis the sentence:

10 Foffo could have had milk and cookies

is not really about Foffo itself. Rather, it is about certain counterparts of Foffo, because the counterpart theorist's translation of (10) is:

11 There is a world, other than the actual, and relevantly similar to the actual, where a counterpart of Foffo has milk and cookies.

In other words, when the modal realist explains Foffo's possible meal through the existence of a world in which Foffo has a different meal, she is not speaking literally. If we take things literally, Foffo could have had a different meal seeing as there is a world in which an individual relevantly similar to the one whom in our world we call "Foffo" has such a meal. This aspect of the theory has been criticized time and again, generating the so-called *Humphrey objection*, to be discussed below (see Kripke (1980), Merricks (2003), and Sider (2006)).

We will end this section with a remark concerning the interplay of counterpart theory and Lewis's theory of individuals. For Lewis, there may be individuals that, so to speak, are not world-bound. For instance, consider the scattered whole composed of Foffo and of one of its counterparts in another world; this whole is an individual that has parts in two distinct worlds. Modal sentences from ordinary language, however, are never about such individuals. (Of course, we can generate modal sentences about counterparts, possible worlds, and so on, but those sentences belong to the language of the theory, not to natural language. More on this later, when we discuss so-called *advanced modalizing*.) Modal sentences are always about worlds or their parts. (On this point, see especially Varzi (2001).)

§4.4. Modal realism and the philosophical analysis of modality

Let us take stock. We have seen some fundamental metaphysical and semantic tenets of modal realism, according to which:

(i)   There are infinite worlds, as many as can be recombined by means of PR*.

(ii)   No individual inhabits more than one world.

(iii)   Sentences of natural language containing modal expressions are disguised qualitative comparisons of individuals (typically spread across multiple worlds), according to the relation of counterparthood.

Based on (i)–(iii), we can now more precisely reformulate the solution to the PP proposed by the modal realist:

MR*: The sentence of natural language: "It is possible that: *s*" expresses the existence of some worlds $W_1, ..., W_n$ in which "*s**"

where "*s**" is a sentence obtained from *s* by substituting all of the individuals in *s* with their counterparts in $W_1, ..., W_n$, based on the translation schemas provided by counterpart theory. (In the last section of this chapter, we shall see that the translation schema must be flexible enough to accommodate so-called advanced modalizing, that is, modal sentences that do not belong to natural language, but rather to the language of some theory—most typically, modal realism itself.)

Suppose, for the sake of the argument, that Lewis's metaphysical and semantic accounts of modality are fine and sound. A host of important episte-mological questions would remain to be addressed. How can one prove, or disprove, that Lewis's picture is correct? How are we to know what is going on in other worlds? After all, how do we even know that those worlds exist?

Lewis himself addressed these questions (cf. 1986: §2.4.). Certainly, it is *not through direct experience* that we know of other worlds. We cannot travel to them. Neither is it through *imagination*. Some philosophers have argued that the worlds that exist are all and only those which we can imagine (see the collection of essays in Gendler and O'Leary-Hawthorne (2002)). But a modal realist is not committed to this view, and may have reason to reject it. Perhaps there exist worlds that we cannot imagine. Or perhaps we can imagine having a more developed imaginative capacity than the one we have; if this is so, then there is also a world in which we have a more developed imaginative capacity; but, then, if our world counts just as much as the other in which inhabitants have more of an imagination than we do, why not believe that there are worlds that we cannot imagine, but that our possible counter-parts *can*? Furthermore, it is not necessarily true that all we can imagine exists. Lewis himself offers the following admittedly controversial example: we can imagine a square circle, but this does not mean that there is a world with a square circle. See Lewis (1986: 113–15).

We will make some progress if we start by pointing out that Lewis's answer to the question "How many worlds are there?" rests on a modal intuition, namely the intuition that anything can coexist with anything. Is it then by means of a modal intuition that we are supposed to *prove* that modal realism is true? Not quite, but that is the beginning. The rest of the argument would depend on the plausibility of the philosophical analysis of modality suggested by modal realism, and in particular the underlying conception of *philosophical analysis* itself.

The idea that Lewis's modal views should be understood in the light of, and ultimately evaluated on the strength of, his conception of philosophical analysis has been defended to a good extent by John Divers (see especially (2013, 2014c)). To illustrate Lewis's view of philosophical analysis, it is useful to start with an often quoted passage from *Counterfactuals*:

One comes to philosophy already endowed with a stock of opinions. It is not the business of philosophy either to undermine or to justify these preexisting opinions, to any great extent, but only to try to discover ways of expanding them into an orderly system. A metaphysician's analysis of mind is an attempt at systematizing our opinions about mind. It succeeds to the extent that (1) it is systematic, and (2) it respects those of our pre-philosophical opinions to which we are firmly attached. Insofar as it does both better than any alternative we have thought of, we give it credence. There is some give-and-take, but not too much [...] So it is throughout metaphysics; and so it is with my doctrine of realism about possible worlds. Among my common opinions that philosophy must respect (if it is to deserve credence) are not only my naïve belief in tables and chairs, but also my naïve belief that these tables and chairs might have been otherwise arranged. Realism about possible worlds is an attempt, the only successful attempt I know of, to systematize these preexisting modal opinions. (1973: 88)

We can derive two important lessons. The first is that we should not think of philosophical analysis as a philosophical process that solves *once and for all* the questions we ask regarding a certain topic. Thus, our analysis of modal expressions is not to be regarded as successful just in case it leaves us with no more questions regarding the meaning of such expressions. Lewis confirms this lesson just a few lines after the quoted passage:

But why should I think that I ought to be able to make up my mind on every question about possible worlds, when it seems clear that I may have no way whatever of finding out the answers to other questions about noncontingent matters—for instance, about the infinite cardinals?

The second lesson regards the philosophical method suggested by Lewis's analysis. We can divide it into three parts: Opinion, Analytic Hypothesis, and Metaphysical Basis. The Opinion is the set of naïve beliefs with which we come to philosophize about a subject matter. As we have seen, a crucial naïve belief guiding our philosophical theorizing about possibility and necessity is the naïve formulation of the principle of recombination (i.e. that anything can coexist with anything). The Analytic Hypothesis is the core contribution of a theory, defining the new terms introduced by the theory and thus specifying how they should be understood (and employed). (Typically, the Analytic Hypothesis is expressed in terms of so-called Ramsey sentences, where the empirical content of the newly introduced theoretical term is made explicit. We will not get into the details of this here, though.) Finally, the Metaphysical Basis makes explicit the ontological commitments of the theory, that is, what must exist—if anything—in order for the theory to be true.

Equipped with an outline of Lewis's method of philosophical analysis, we can now summarize his analyses of modal plenitude and of possibility and necessity. Let us begin with the analysis of plenitude:

(Opinion) There is all that there could be. Anything can coexist with
anything else.

(Analytic Hypothesis) PR*: For any collection of individuals $x_1, ..., x_n$ that
stand in a maximal external relation, there is a collection of individuals
$y_1, ..., y_n$ such that: (i) each of the $y_1, ..., y_n$ is numerically distinct from
each of the $x_1, ..., x_n$; (ii) y_1 is an intrinsic duplicate of $x_1, ..., y_n$ is an
intrinsic duplicate of x_n; (iii) the $y_1, ..., y_n$ compose a world.

(Metaphysical Basis) An infinite stock of individuals (including infinite
maximal individuals), properties, and relations (including infinite
external relations) exists.

Notice that the Metaphysical Basis countenances the possibility that worlds
contain properties completely different from those exemplified by individuals
in our world—so different that these properties are *alien* to our world (the
expression is employed by Lewis himself). So, as far as we know, the actual
world may not suffice in providing the metaphysical basis for the theory.
As we shall see, Lewis regarded this point as a virtue of his theory, shared
by none of the other major rival theories of modality employing possible
worlds (with the exception, perhaps, of fictionalism, as we will see in
Chapter 6). We shall come back to alien properties in Chapter 5, when
discussing Combinatorialism.

Let us now turn to the philosophical analysis of possibility and necessity.

(Opinion) Most situations we experience are contingent. For instance,
Pierluigi might have been with me right now; and I could have avoided
writing this sentence.

(Analytic Hypothesis) For any sentence P, P is possible if and only if
P's translation in the language of counterpart theory—call it P*—,
understood in accordance with the metaphysical tenets of modal
realism, is true.

(Metaphysical Basis) An infinite stock of individuals (including infinite
maximal individuals), properties, and relations (including infinite
external relations) exists.

The Metaphysical Basis of the analysis of possibility and necessity is the
same as the Metaphysical Basis of the analysis of modal plenitude. The
Analytic Hypotheses, however, reveal that two different bits of philosophical
theorizing are employed to analyze different sets of naïve opinions.

The analyses just provided suggest the direction taken by Lewis in
addressing the EPP: we know of the existence of other worlds, and we know
what those worlds are like, because the best philosophical theory we have
at hand says that they exist. It is not a matter of acquaintance. It is not a

matter of imagination. It is, rather, a matter of philosophical understanding. Such understanding is not an all-or-nothing affair, but rather expresses itself in a complex system of tenets, some of which may be uncontroversial, while about others we may argue back and forth; furthermore, philosophical understanding does not answer all our questions regarding the subject matter that our theories systematize. Lewis in effect proposes a rationalistic model of the epistemic justification of a theory of modality that is more modest and more open to revision than rival models. For example, recall Lowe's justification of essentialism offered in Chapter 3: there, the analysis of modality was justified by appealing to allegedly uncontroversial intuitions regarding real definitions of individuals. The analysis left little room for revisions and for dialogue between theorizing and naïve opinions. To date, the distinctive nature of Lewis's contribution to modal epistemology has been recognized, but it is yet to be studied and appreciated in more detail.

§4.5. The theoretical advantages of modal realism

Let us go back to the passage cited at the beginning of this chapter, where Lewis explains that we should believe in a plurality of worlds because of the ensuing theoretical benefits of such a choice. It is now time to discuss those benefits in more detail. We will outline five of them, drawn, by and large, from Chapter 1 of Lewis (1986).

The first theoretical benefit of modal realism is that, unlike any other theory of possibility, it aims to *reduce* modal entities to non-modal entities. That which is possible is that which exists at a certain world (the characteristics of the relevant world depend on the specific sentence expressing the possibility). That which is necessary is that which exists at all worlds. (Or, most often, at all worlds *of a certain kind*, as a tacit implicit restriction is typically embedded in a sentence expressing a necessary truth.) Modal realism thus provides an analysis of possibility and necessity in terms of existence. (Incidentally, we may notice that it is for this reason that Lewis's theory was almost immediately regarded as suspiciously *Meinongian*: Lewis seems to endorse the existence of certain things—namely, things involved in merely possible scenarios—that—it seems fair to say—do *not* exist, since they do *not* actually exist. We shall come back to Meinongianism in Chapter 8.) Although the reduction of modality to simple existence seems at first glance to be an unremarkable result, it should be noted that none of the other theorists discussed in this volume even considered this achievement within reach. To a modal realist, speaking of capacity and probability, making hypotheses, speaking of the future, *and so on*, amount to speaking of that which exists. In fact, from the modal realist's theoretical perspective, unicorns exist as much as mountain gorillas: for, surely there is a world where there are unicorns, because there seems to be no contradiction in the idea of a unicorn; and surely mountain gorillas are still around on Earth, even if only a few hundred are left. Some, like the expressionist and the skeptic, believe that possibility is merely a projection of—respectively—human sentiments or something confusing and unfathomable; others—namely the modalist and other theorists we have yet to consider—believe that what is possible exists in its own way. The modal realist is the only one who can say that that which is possible is simply no different from that which is actual, and who can interpret what we say about that which is possible in the same way as what we say about that which is actual.

The second theoretical benefit of modal realism is that it yields a particularly simple analysis of so-called counterfactuals, sentences that express a hypothetical scenario that is contrary to an actual scenario, for example:

12   If I hadn't been here writing this book, I would have gone surfing.

Counterfactuals pose an obvious problem for those who do not accept the existence of non-actual entities, as it seems that that which makes a counterfactual sentence true cannot be rooted in actuality (though this was recently called into question by Williamson (2007a, 2007b, 2010). Sentence (12) expresses a mere possibility: a scenario which is not (and was not and will not be) realized in the actual world; so, the antecedent of (12) is false in the actual world. In classical logic, a sentence whose antecedent is false is always true. But this is not the case with all counterfactuals. For instance, while I may be inclined to think that (12) is true, I may be inclined to regard the following sentence as false:

13   If I hadn't been here writing this book, I would have gone to rob a bank.

Despite the fact that (12) and (13) have the same antecedent ("If I hadn't been here writing this book"), and that this antecedent is false in both (12) and (13), my inclination is to endorse (12) and reject (13). But how to go about arguing for my intuitions? The modal realist offers an elegant philosophical analysis of counterfactuals that answers this question. According to Lewis, (12) and (13) should be analyzed as follows:

14   There is a world, and a counterpart of mine in that world, where that counterpart decided to go surfing instead of writing for the day; and that world, compared to all the other worlds in which my counterparts decide not to write today, is the most similar to the actual world.

15   There is a world, and a counterpart of mine in that world, where that counterpart decided to go rob a bank instead of writing for the day; and that world, compared to all the other worlds in which my counterparts decide not to write today, is the most similar to the actual world.

While the concept of resemblance, embedded in counterpart relations, is vague and maybe a bit elusive, the Lewisian solution offers a straightforward explanation of the contents of (12) and (13), clarifying why I may be inclined to believe (12), but to disbelieve (13): were everything to stay the same except that I would not have been writing, it seems highly implausible to me that I would have gone to rob a bank today, while it seems highly plausible that I would have gone surfing.

The third theoretical benefit of modal realism rests in the metaphysical robustness of the theory. According to modal realism, there are many more possibilities than the ones we can express in our language. We have the actual world; we have all worlds we can imagine, as long as they are not contradictory; we have all worlds that our languages can represent, as long as there is no contradiction in such representations; *and* we have any additional world that there could be. Modal realism, in other words, is compatible with a sort of metaphysical humility, according to which the actual world does not contain all the kinds of things that there could be: there may be many more kinds of things than there are in this world and that we can express or imagine. No other theory can defend such a claim, according to Lewis (see especially (1986: Chapter 3)); for this reason, modal realism is the metaphysically most robust theory on the market.

The fourth theoretical benefit is that modal realism calls for an ontology that is, in a certain sense, minimal. All there is are worlds (and their parts) and sets of worlds or their parts. The modal realist might even be able to do without these sets (see Lewis (1991)), but I will not get into the details of this proposal here. Through the worlds, their parts, and the sets of worlds and parts, we are able to define any other ontological category. A property is a set of parts of worlds; for example, redness is the set of all of the things that are red in all of the worlds. A proposition (the content of a sentence) is a set of worlds, namely, those where it is true (with the exception of so-called *de se* propositions—see Lewis (1979)). The so-called "natural kinds" (roughly speaking: the properties that play a key role in scientific laws) would be certain properties, that is, certain sets. And so on, and so forth.

The fifth and last theoretical benefit of modal realism is that it offers a simple and elegant model to explain the behavior of agents. Before acting, each one of us contemplates various propositions and then, usually, chooses to actualize one of these propositions. Each proposition corresponds to a set of worlds, as mentioned. Choosing a proposition on which to act amounts to undertaking that our world is the one in which that proposition will be realized. If I desire something that cannot be realized, it is most likely because I am contemplating a proposition that contradicts another proposition that is already true of my world. This type of model allows us to form intuitive representations—some highly complex—of the behavior of an agent. See Lewis (1986), Stalnaker (1984), and Stalnaker (2003).

The Lewisian picture of modality remains one of the most powerful and elegant philosophical theories of modality put forward: it rests on an innovative and flexible semantic theory; it is supported by a robust and elegant metaphysical view; and it is backed by a plausible epistemological story relying on philosophical analysis. And yet, readers have doubted that it really possesses the five theoretical benefits suggested by Lewis, at times harshly criticizing his arguments aimed at demonstrating such benefits, so much so that today there are a considerable number of apparently good reasons to distance ourselves from the Lewisian perspective. A selection of these will be considered in the next section.

§4.6. Modal realism and the definition of modal concepts

The criticisms made of modal realism are numerous, and most of them have generated considerable debate, making it difficult to provide a thorough overview. Lewis (1986: Chapter 2) addresses eight lines of objection, and over the years a few more have been added. The reader will find additional references to related literature in the *Further Reading* section. In this section, we shall concentrate on a particularly central criticism of Lewis's theory, according to which modal realism is *unable* to define—and therefore eliminate—modal concepts; since the reduction of modal concepts is regarded as the major theoretical prize for endorsing the bizarre idea that there are infinite worlds on a par with ours, the criticism threatens to cast serious doubt on the plausibility of the philosophical analysis proposed by Lewis.

There are different ways to rehearse the criticism. One that seems particularly straightforward begins with the principle of recombination. We shall start by recalling the final version of the principle we provided earlier:

PR* For any collection of individuals $x_1, \ldots, x_n$ that stand in a maximal external relation, there is a collection of individuals $y_1, \ldots, y_n$ such that:
(i) each of the $y_1, \ldots, y_n$ is numerically distinct from each of the $x_1, \ldots,$

x_n; (ii) y_1 is an intrinsic duplicate of x_1, ..., y_n is an intrinsic duplicate of x_n; (iii) the y_1, ..., y_n compose a world.

Principle PR* employs modal concepts in two ways. To see why this is the case, let us again unfold the reasoning at the basis of the principle of recombination. The goal of PR* is to spell out the modal intuition that *anything can coexist, or fail to coexist, with anything* in terms of a non-modal metaphysical principle. We can break down the achievement of this goal into four steps. The first step is to replace the "anything" in the modal intuition with collections of individuals. The second step is to exploit the modal realist's thesis that there are infinite worlds, thereby reducing the "can coexist" to the non-modal coexistence of counterparts in some world. The third step is to qualify those counterparts as intrinsic duplicates. The fourth and final step is to ensure that the intrinsic duplicates *can fit* a certain reticulate of external relations.

Modalities surface at the third and fourth step. Let us begin with the latter. According to the criticism under consideration, the appeal to the possibility that the intrinsic duplicates fit the reticulate of external relations introduces a metaphysical modality into PR*. It is a metaphysical modality because it countenances the possible *coexistence* of the intrinsic duplicates *and* of a certain system of external relations. So, here is the problem. The modal realist is supposed to analyze the possible ways that individuals could be in terms of the existence of counterparts of those individuals; PR* is the principle that should clarify which individuals exist, unrestrictedly, so that we generate enough counterparts to support the theory; PR* appeals to the possible coexistence of some individuals and certain reticulates of external relations among them; this appeal should be explained in terms of counterparts; thus, the very principle that is supposed to tell us what are the individuals in the theory that support the appeal to counterpart relations appeals to such relations; PR* fails to provide an adequate metaphysical basis for the theory because it cannot provide an adequate stock of individuals.

The modal realist may reply that the appeal to the possible coexistence is a case of *advanced modalizing* and, thus, does not require the existence of counterparts to have been postulated. Advanced modalizing is an important part of modal realism. Consider the sentence:

16 There could have been more worlds than there are.

Sentence (16) cannot be analyzed in terms of counterpart relations, because this would imply that there are more worlds than in fact there are, which is impossible. (Incidentally: it is on the heels of sentences such as (16) that the debate on impossible worlds ensued, starting especially with Yagisawa (1988), on the heels of Lewis (1986, §3.2); we shall return to these issues in Chapter 8, where we will discuss dialetheism.) Instead, the modal realist argues that sentences such as (16) are part of so-called advanced modalizing: modal talk that concerns *theoretical* entities and that therefore does not really involve natural language, but the language of the theory we have put forward to deal with modalities in natural language. The aim of modal realism is to provide a reductive analysis of modal talk in natural language; if the analysis cannot apply to theoretical language, that is fine: for theoretical language we can introduce a *sui generis* analysis that makes no appeal to counterpart relations. For example, the modal realist would insist that (16) be read as:

17 There are more worlds than there are,

which is patently contradictory and accords with our intuition that (16) affirms the existence of impossible worlds. On analogy with the suggested reading of (16), the modal realist could insist that the modality in the fourth step of PR* is an instance of advanced modalizing and thus involves no counterpart relation. In PR*, the appeal to an "appropriate" maximal external relation should be understood as meaning something like "matching"—where the match in question suggests instructions for how the worlds should be theoretically analyzed—and not as introducing a genuine metaphysical modality.

We shall now consider the second count on which modal realism may be accused of failing at reducing modalities. As we indicated above, this objection rests on the appeal to intrinsic duplicates in PR*. Intrinsic duplicates, we shall recall, are defined by Lewis in terms of natural properties, that is, those properties that supposedly ground fundamental scientific claims and that are independent of accompaniment (the individual possesses that property regardless of whether any other individual exists). The appeal to independence of accompaniment, however, involves yet again a modality. A good way to explain this is to point out, as have Cameron (2008) and Denby (2008), that the definition of intrinsic duplication implicitly presupposes a principle of recombination; in fact, independence of accompaniment means that a given individual is combined with other individuals *in every possible way*. Thus, PR* is spelled out in terms of intrinsic duplicates; and the latter are spelled out in terms of PR*. What we are left with is plain circularity, which can be illustrated in the following schema:

Modality
⇓
Existence of infinite worlds
⇓
Principle of Recombination
⇓

Intrinsic Duplication

⇓

Principle of Recombination

Certainly, a more modest formulation of the principle of recombination that appeals to generic counterparts, and not intrinsic duplicates, would avoid the circularity:

> PRC: For any collection of individuals $x_1, ..., x_n$ that stand in an appropriate maximal external relation, there is a collection of individuals $y_1, ..., y_n$ such that: (i) each of the $y_1, ..., y_n$ is numerically distinct from each of the $x_1, ..., x_n$; (ii) y_1 is a counterpart of $x_1, ..., y_n$ is a counterpart of x_n; (iii) the $y_1, ..., y_n$ compose a world.

But PRC has too high of a price, given the aims of the modal realist. In fact, PRC greatly limits the number of possibilities that the theory can represent, given that counterpart relations often take into account the environmental circumstances of an individual and, thus, are not independent of accompaniment. Modal realism, then, would no longer boast a greater number of possibilities than its rival theoretical proposals.

Is Lewis's modal realism a theoretical paradise for scholars of modality? As we suggested, Lewis's proposal offers simple and elegant solutions to the PP, MPP, and EPP. Probably, from this perspective, it offers the best integrated and most solid theory on the market. And yet, modal realism has important drawbacks, and not only because it compels us to accept a bizarre account of worlds. As we have seen in the current section, modal realism has some important theoretical limitations. And we have just scratched the surface. For lack of space we have not addressed other potential sources of theoretical concern: for instance, the tenability of the Lewisian definition of actuality as indexical, of cases of recombination in connection with the possibility of so-called gunk (i.e. a whole with infinite mereological complexity), and of the number of worlds. In Chapter 8, we shall return to some of these topics. Now, we shall turn to the main rival of modal realism, *ersatzism*.

Study Questions

- What is the modal realist's reply to the MPP?
- What is the principle of recombination?
- What is the modal realist's version of the principle of recombination?

- What is a natural property, according to Lewis?
- What is an intrinsic duplicate, according to Lewis?
- What is the modal realist's solution to the SPP?
- What is a counterpart relation?
- What is the modal realist's solution to the EPP?
- For Lewis, philosophical analysis involves three steps: what are they?
- What are the five main theoretical virtues of modal realism?
- Why might the principle of recombination conceal some modalities?
- What is advanced modalizing?

FURTHER READING

For an **overview** of modal realism, we recommend starting from Lewis's writings, most especially Lewis (1973: 84–91, 1986: Chapter 1). For a shorter but still detailed introduction, see especially Divers (2002: Part II) and also Melia (2003: Chapter 5). The latter two texts also illustrate, or contain bibliographical references on, specific aspects of modal realism and counterpart theory. Among the overviews of modal realism, the reader may also consult Chihara (1998: Chapter 3).

Particularly useful for framing modal realism within the broader context of Lewis's philosophical work are the following **volumes on the philosophy of Lewis**: the collection of essays edited by Preyer and Siebelt (2001), especially the first part, and also those edited by Jackson and Priest (2004), in particular Chapters 3, 12, and 20; Daniel Nolan's introduction (2005); the companion devoted to the philosophy of Lewis, edited by Schaffer and Loewer (2015); and the special issue of *Humana.Mente* edited by Carrara, Ciuni, and Lando (2011).

The original presentation of **counterpart theory** is Lewis (1968), which should be read along with its postscript, published in Lewis (1983), and integrated with the consultation of Forbes (1982; also 1985: Chapter 3) and Mondadori (1983). Counterpart theory has been criticized on various counts—to start see: Merricks (1999, 2003); Heller (2002, 2005); Dorr, Fara, and Williamson, respectively (all 2005); Borghini (2005); and Sider (2006). Additional criticisms are addressed by Lewis in his work of 1986 (see Chapter 2).

Unusually vast is the literature that critically assesses one or another aspect of **Lewis's metaphysics**. John Divers has made an important contribution for understanding the modal status of modal realism, as well as Lewis's method of philosophical analysis; see especially Divers (2012, 2013, 2014a, 2014b, 2014c). As early as 1979, William Lycan claimed that the idea of a (possible) world is in itself modal (cf. 1979). Shalkowski (1994) reiterated the doubt about whether modal realism is effective in reducing modalities to the existence of individuals at worlds. The doubts are rehearsed in Divers (2002: Part II), Melia (2003: Chapter 5). For a broader discussion of the metaphysical aspects of modal realism, see also work by ▶

Philip Bricker (in particular, (2006a, 2006b, 2007)), and by Kris McDaniel (2006). For a recent discussion of the principle of recombination, see Denby (2008), Cameron (2008), and Darby and Watson (2010). Finally, Peter van Inwagen has offered some insightful contributions to the debate on modal realism (especially 1980, 1986).

5

Ersatzism

E rsatzism counts the largest number of subscribers among the theories of modality. For this reason, it is difficult to provide a taxonomy of the ersatzist positions. All ersatzist positions share the conviction that possible worlds are a *surrogate* (in German: *ersatz*) of the actual world. The positions differ with respect to the metaphysical status of the surrogates. After a brief historical and general presentation of ersatzism (§5.1.), four positions are considered, and critically assessed: linguistic ersatzism (§5.2.), combinatorialism (§5.3.), pictorial ersatzism (§5.4.), and atomic ersatzism (§5.5.). The taxonomy, by and large, follows the one adopted by Lewis (1986), with the addition of combinatorialism.

---

* * * * *

§5.1. Introduction

L et us suppose, together with the modal realist and the modalist, that possible-worlds semantics is the best instrument available for addressing the numerous, complex conceptual nexuses related to the PP; let us also assume, together with the modal realist, that possible worlds can be philosophically analyzed, thus delivering a philosophically savvy interpretation of the diamond and box (the symbols expressing, respectively, possibility and necessity in the language of quantified modal logic (QML)). Must we, therefore, endorse the theory, advocated by the modal realist, that there are infinite worlds like ours? No. In fact, the majority of those who would explain the meaning of modal sentences in the terms of a philosophical theory of possible worlds believe that those worlds are surrogates for certain elements of the actual world. This is why their position takes the name ersatzism, from the German *ersatz*: "surrogate" or "substitute". Normally included among the supporters of this theory is Leibniz, the figure who introduced the concept of a possible world in modern philosophy (see Chapter 1).

Of the theories of possibility presented in this book, ersatzism is perhaps the one that boasts the longest tradition. It underlies the positions of a wide array of twentieth-century and contemporary authors, including Ludwig Wittgenstein, Rudolf Carnap, Alvin Plantinga, Robert Stalnaker, and David Armstrong, to cite just a few influential names. For this very reason, providing a comprehensive overview of ersatzism that takes into account the positions of its proponents with regard to the three sub-problems of possibility (SPP, MPP, and EPP), and with regard to the nature of language, truth, knowledge, existence, properties, and individuals, is an arduous task. In what follows, we will take an in-depth look at the two positions that, throughout the years, have become most prominent, namely linguistic ersatzism (§5.2.) and combinatorialism (§5.3.). We will then consider two other relevant positions, which are also illustrated in Lewis (1986: Chapter 3): pictorial ersatzism (§5.4.) and atomic ersatzism (§5.5.).

The traits differentiating the four positions under review are mainly metaphysical and epistemic; at the semantic level, they all typically endorse some version of QML, with identity of individuals across worlds (thus, they reject counterpart theory). Linguistic ersatzism contends that possible worlds are linguistic entities: each world is a maximally consistent (and possibly infinite) set of sentences; combinatorialism, by contrast, maintains that possible worlds are abstract recombinations of elements of the actual world, where a recombination is not a linguistic entity, but an abstract entity defined on the basis of the individuals, properties, and natural laws of the actual world; pictorial ersatzism replies that possible worlds are, rather, non-linguistic representations of the way the world could be (e.g. propositions or states of affairs that represent the way our world could be), so that the number of possible scenarios is not tied to the expressive powers of language; finally, atomic ersatzism proposes that possible worlds are abstract entities devoid of structure, and thus simple, atomic. Though the four positions are characterized by their metaphysical take on possible worlds, it is important to stress that such metaphysical divergences often go along with epistemic ones.

Ersatzists have been the most fierce opponents of modal realism. The key points of rupture between the two positions are semantic and metaphysical. At the semantic level, ersatzists object to counterpart theory, especially the idea that there is no overlap between the domains of individuals of any two worlds, endorsing instead the initial formulation of possible-worlds semantics, in which the same individual inhabits multiple (possibly infinite) worlds. At the metaphysical level, ersatzism affirms the priority of the actual world over all other worlds, which are indeed regarded as surrogates of actuality.

Perhaps the most natural way to think of possibility is, in fact, to believe that there is only one world: the actual world, in which we live. If, however, we believe that the ultimate explanation of the meaning of sentences containing modalities requires a theory of possible worlds, then we are faced with the problem of having to explain where these worlds can be found in the actual world. Hence the ersatzist solution to the MPP:

ME: Only one world exists, the actual world, of which possible worlds are surrogates.

Surrogates, hence, stand in as replacements for the purposes of someone's speaking or thinking intelligibly of some possibility. Consider, for example, the following sentence:

1 Foffo the cat could have had milk and cookies.

Even the ersatzist would assert that there is a strict relationship between (1) and the following:

2 It is possible that: Foffo the cat has milk and cookies.

And (2), just as for the modal realist, is in turn explained in terms of the truth of the following sentence:

3 There is a world where Foffo the cat has milk and cookies.

Yet, when it comes to clarifying the metaphysical commitments of (3), ersatzism and modal realism diverge. According to the latter, as we have seen, (3) commits us to the existence of a world that is on a par with our own and where a counterpart of Foffo (not Foffo, the cat, itself, but an individual that most resembles Foffo in that world) has milk and cookies; the ersatzist, on the other hand, would argue that (3) commits us to the existence of *surrogates* of entities of our world, including a surrogate of Foffo, the cat, and a surrogate of the milk and cookies of our world. But what exactly is a surrogate?

The various ersatzist roads diverge exactly at this point. Building upon the taxonomies adopted by Lewis (1986), Divers (2002), and Melia (2003), we will follow four main ersatzist avenues. In doing so, we will encounter four interpretations of the ontological allegiances of (3) and four sets of solutions to the MPP and EPP.

§5.2. Linguistic ersatzism

The first approach considers a possible world to be a surrogate of a set of sentences in a certain language. This position is known as *linguistic ersatzism* and is a longstanding tradition in modal theorizing. Versions of linguistic ersatzism can be attributed to some of the founders of possible-worlds semantics, including Rudolf Carnap and Jaakko Hintikka.

The key idea of linguistic ersatzism is that, in the same way that the sentence:

4   Pinocchio was carved by Geppetto

is true according to (or, in brief: at) a certain story, namely the book *Pinocchio*, so the sentence:

5   Foffo could have had milk and cookies

is true according to (or, in brief: at) a certain world. Like a book, a world is a very long—possibly infinitely long—and complex list of sentences; in fact, a world *is* the set of those sentences.

More precisely, the linguistic ersatzist will define a world thus:

WLE: A possible world is a complete and consistent description, given in a certain language, of a state of things.

A world in which Foffo has milk and cookies is nothing but a description of a state of things—given in English, for example—in which Foffo enjoys milk and cookies. As such, WLE also indicates linguistic ersatzism's answer to the MPP: in short, possible, non-actual entities are sets of sentences.

As descriptions, possible worlds are fundamentally differentiated from our world by the fact that they are not concrete, in the way that we would say our world is: our world is not a mere description; it is made of things, not words. Thus, unlike modal realism, linguistic ersatzism denies that "actual" is an indexical and that the actual world is metaphysically no more or less privileged than any non-actual world; on the contrary, there is a major difference, as possible worlds consist simply in sentences. It is at this point important to point out the danger of confusing linguistic ersatzism and modal fictionalism, a theory we will discuss in Chapter 6. One could in fact think that, if possible worlds are sets of sentences, just like books, then in a sense they are linguistic fictions. This is fine, but it is far from implying that linguistic ersatzism and modal fictionalism are one and the same theory. As we shall see, modal fictionalism treats as fictions certain *theories of modality*, such as modal realism: thus, the distinctive suggestion of modal fictionalism is—say—that we should endorse modal realism, yet treat it as a useful fiction. This is not what linguistic ersatzism advocates. So, even if linguistic ersatzism and modal fictionalism ultimately share the claim that possible worlds are linguistic entities, they differ in how such linguistic entities are generated: for the modal fictionalist, possible worlds arise out of the fiction a theory of modality. Let us now turn to the details of how possible worlds are generated for the linguistic ersatzist.

We must first specify the requirements a set of sentences must fulfill in order to count as a possible world. Afterward, we can see how such sets can be generated. Two requirements are especially relevant: completeness and consistency. First of all, the set should be detailed enough to include all that there is to describe in a world. More precisely, a set of sentences describing a world is *maximal* (or: complete) when, for every describable scenario of that world, the set includes either a description of that scenario or a description of its negation. Second, the set should be *consistent*. That is, it should not contain two descriptions of scenarios such that one is the negation of the other. According to some authors, the requirement of consistency may be given up without compromising the spirit of linguistic ersatzism; for a discussion of impossible worlds, including sets of sentences that are not consistent, see Chapter 8.

By characterizing a possible world as a maximal and consistent set of sentences, the linguistic ersatzist utilizes certain modal concepts—completeness and consistency—in order to explain another modal concept—possible worlds. Maximality is a modal concept because it appeals to *describable* scenarios; consistency is a modal concept because it appeals to the idea of incompatibility, which we expressed by the requirement that the set of sentences *could* not contain two descriptions such that one is the negation of the other. To the linguistic ersatzist, the modal circularity is not a major reason for concern, though. It is not part of the general project of ersatzism to reduce modal talk to non-modal talk, or to explain—as the modal realist attempts to do—possible and necessary entities in terms of the existence of certain non-modal entities. Linguistic ersatzism will succeed if it can provide an adequate analysis of modal sentences in terms of sets of sentences; insofar as the view provides answers to the MPP and EPP that dissipate the doubts that lead us to formulate them, it does not matter that those sets of sentences are themselves modal entities. So, the issue is: does linguistic ersatzism provide satisfactory answers to the MPP and EPP?

When it comes to the MPP, linguistic ersatzism may have an advantage over modal realism. For, unlike the latter, the former may more easily explain what a (possible) world is. For instance, it may suffice to show that a language exists independently of it being used, thereby showing also that (possible) worlds exist independently of us talking about them. The point of contention, however, is whether linguistic ersatzism is able to supply a sufficient amount of worlds to satisfy our pre-theoretical intuitions about possibility. Lewis and other authors have questioned linguistic ersatzism on precisely this point.

How does a linguistic ersatzist generate possible worlds? One way, of course, would be to describe them in a natural language. But more systematic strategies can be found. A well-known one builds upon a so-called Lagadonian language (from the language experiment of the Academy of Science at Lagado, described in Jonathan Swift's *Gulliver's Travels*). Suppose that every individual *a* in a world names itself—*a*'s name being "*a*"—and that each property *P* and relation *R* also is its own predicate—respectively, "*P*" and "*R*". At this point, a sentence that describes a world will be an *n*-tuple containing *n*–1 names of individuals and a property or a relation; for example, the triple <*R, a, b*> will be the sentence expressing the fact that the relation *R* holds between individuals *a* and *b*. So, at a world *w* it is true that *R* holds between individuals *a* and *b* if and only if <*R, a, b*> is included in the set of sentences that characterizes *w*.

If we believe that our assertions about possibility are endowed with meaning, then we would presumably also believe that the totality of the scenarios they may describe is infinite. Two apples could exist, or three, or ... It seems not contradictory for there to be infinitely many apples. Furthermore, there could be apples, but also pears, oranges, apricots ... It seems not contradictory for there to be an infinite number of other fruits, infinitely many of which did not, do not, and will not exist in our world. In order for the description of a world to be complete, it must contain *all* describable states of things. But here we encounter the difficulty of producing a number of sentences that is equal to the number of possibilities. We encounter, that is, the problem of generating worlds that are suitable to represent the scenarios that intuitively we regard as possible.

In fact, as observed by Lewis (1986: §3.2.), there could be many more worlds than those we are able to express through a language. Let us suppose that space is continuous: that is to say, between any two points in space another point can always be found. We might wish to express the possibility that each of these points can be occupied or not occupied. But a language is arguably unable to provide a description of a cardinality of states of things equal to that of the states of the things that constitute a continuous space; this is a straightforward result of our failure to prove the *continuum hypothesis*, according to which—roughly—any set of real numbers can be put into correspondence with a set of natural numbers. So, through language, we have no way of expressing the existence of a world made of points that occupy a continuous space.

The scenarios that are suggested by our modal intuitions can be even more complex: besides space, time could be continuous; or we could have infinite properties for each point. And this is all without taking into account that space and time can be extended to infinity. A natural language is far from being able to express the existence of possible worlds in which space and time are continuous and extend to infinity, and in which each spatio-temporal point is occupied by infinitely many properties. For the modal realist, this means that there is an infinity of worlds that apparently exist, but whose existence cannot be admitted by the linguistic ersatzist. This is a serious theoretical limitation.

There are only two ways out for the linguistic ersatzist. The first denies that the possibilities that cannot be described by means of a set of sentences are genuine, no matter how intuitive they may seem. According to this response, it would simply be impossible that space is continuous, because no set of sentences can describe such a scenario. This position, however, seems ultimately *ad hoc* and therefore unsatisfactory. The second option is more promising, though probably still unsatisfactory. According to it, the requisites of completeness and consistency should be understood against the background of some ideal agent who possesses a language much more powerful than the ones we in fact possess; for such an ideal agent, a possible world where space is continuous would be describable by means of a set of sentences. Thus, unfortunately we human beings do not have the ability to express in our languages all of the possible scenarios that we have reason to believe exist; but some ideal agent would be able to do so. (For more on this point, see Divers (2002) and Divers and Melia (2002, 2003)).

While the linguistic ersatzist's solution to the MPP is unimpressive, she will be able to provide a more persuasive treatment of the EPP. This is because linguistic ersatzism delivers a surprising result. Normally, knowing that a sentence is true is importantly distinct from knowing its truth conditions. (Knowing its truth conditions is just what it is to know its meaning, which in turn is part of what it is to know the relevant language.) Yet, it is part and parcel of linguistic ersatzism that understanding a sentence about a possibility is enough for understanding that that sentence is true. So, just in knowing a language—and therefore knowing the truth conditions of its sentences—one knows the truth of its sentences about what is possible. Hence, all it takes to show that we know of the existence of complete and consistent sets of sentences is, indeed, a theory of what it is to know a language (including a formal language). Coming to know the fact that Foffo could have milk and cookies—sentence (5)—amounts to understanding the conditions through which (5), when expressed in a certain language, is true. These truth conditions do not require knowledge of the details of an entire world. That is, in order to know that (5) is true, it is not necessary to know the details of the complete and consistent sentence that expresses the existence of one of the worlds in which (5) is true (presumably, (5) is true in many worlds). It would suffice to understand the meaning of the terms in (5), together with the WLE theory, according to which the truth of (5) is not possible on its own, but rather through a description of a complete and consistent set of scenarios.

Before moving on to combinatorialism, let us distill the solution to the PP proposed by the linguistic ersatzist:

LE: The sentence in natural language: "It is possible that: *s*" expresses a maximal and consistent description, given in a certain language, according to which: *s*.

§5.3. Combinatorialism

According to the second ersatzist approach we will consider, possible worlds are not linguistic entities, but are made of the components of our very world. The approach goes under the label of "combinatorialism", and is often associated with the name of David Armstrong, the philosopher who most prominently and exhaustively developed it in his work of 1989, 1997, and 2004. Combinatorialism owes its name to the fact that possible worlds are construed as recombinations of pieces of the actual world: they are thus worlds much like our own. The recombination schema, as we shall see, in part follows the principle of recombination offered by modal realism and discussed in Chapter 4, while also containing some important differences. Because worlds are ways in which elements of the actual world could be recombined, we can claim that for combinatorialism worlds are surrogates of the actual world and, thus, that combinatorialism is an ersatzist theory.

In our analysis of combinatorialism, we shall especially concentrate on how the theory purports to reply to the MPP. This is because, at the semantic level, combinatorialism can be squared with most versions of QML, with the identity of individuals across worlds. In this sense, no particular discussion of the combinatorialist's approach to the semantics of modal sentences is required. Nonetheless, there is a semantic aspect that will turn out to be relevant during our consideration of the combinatorialist metaphysics: this is the combinatorialist's understanding of the relationship of "truth in a world," which relates a sentence and a world. We shall come back to this in due course, towards the end of our presentation of the position.

Combinatorialism explains possibility in terms of actual entities *plus* the principle of recombination. The latter is regarded as a metaphysical principle, much like modal realism. Thus, the combinatorialist's answer to the EPP will depend on how we come to secure knowledge of both actual entities and, most distinctly, the principle of recombination. With respect to the latter, the most plausible strategy open to the combinatorialist follows the one suggested by Lewis and discussed in Chapter 4: the principle of recombination is known through the philosophical analysis of the key notions involved in the principle. It is indeed to such analysis that we shall now turn, while addressing the combinatorialist answer to the MPP.

§5.3.1. *States of affairs*

At the metaphysical level, combinatorialism crucially relies on *states of affairs*. While "states of affairs" has a generic connotation in English, and may be regarded as synonymous with the generic "scenario" we have employed so far, in this context the expression connotes a specific type of entity. To introduce this type of entity, let us consider the following sentence:

6   Foffo has milk and cookies and Fufi eats fish and potatoes.

According to the combinatorialist, (6) expresses the existence of a certain state of affairs. This is a complex whole made of various constituents: Foffo, Fufi, milk, cookies, fish, and potatoes. The constituents are arranged in a specific order and, for this reason, we can claim that the state of affairs described by (6) is a *structured* whole. Not all states of affairs need to be structured wholes; consider, for instance, the state of affairs expressed by the sentence:

7   It rains.

Aside from the special case of sentences such as (7), all states of affairs have some structure, that is, they will have at least two constituents, related in a specific order and fulfilling specific roles.

For Armstrong, constituents divide into two fundamental categories: individuals (or "particulars", but we will stick with "individuals", as has been our practice so far in this volume) and universals. Foffo and Fufi are individuals. *Being a cat* is a universal. There are different ways of drawing the distinction between individuals and universals. According to one that is often employed, the key difference between individuals and universals is that a universal can exist in its entirety in more than one spatio-temporal region, while an individual cannot; thus, *Being a cat* is, in its entirety, simultaneously where Foffo is *and* where Fufi is, but neither Foffo nor Fufi can be in two places at the same time. Another difference is that only universals can be *instantiated* (or: exemplified); thus, individuals *instantiate* universals, while universals cannot instantiate individuals; nor can individuals instantiate individuals. For example, Foffo instantiates *Being a cat*, so does Fufi, but Foffo and Fufi are not instantiated. Needless to say, many find the distinction between individuals and universals problematic; many, moreover, find the very idea of universals problematic; ruling out one or the other notion implies rejecting combinatorialism, as proposed by Armstrong. For the sake of the argument, we shall set aside any such objections, granting Armstrong suffi-cient metaphysical ground to display his metaphysical theory of possibility (and, hence, his answer to the MPP).

According to Armstrong, once we are equipped with a stock of individuals and universals, we can provide a full-fledged metaphysical analysis of worlds. The actual world is a vast array of individuals that instantiate a large number of universals. Combinatorialism is the view that the individuals and universals of the actual world can be rearranged. Let us offer an example. It seems possible that, instead of (6), the following scenario could have occurred:

8   Foffo eats fish and potatoes and Fufi has milk and cookies.

For the combinatorialist, (8) is possible insofar as it is a legitimate recombi-nation of constituents of the actual state of affairs described in (6). Thus, from the fact that (8) is possible we can infer that the following sentence is true:

9   It is possible that: Foffo eats fish and potatoes and Fufi has milk and cookies.

The truth conditions for (9) are explained by the combinatorialist in terms of the truth conditions for (6). We shall come back to this remark in a moment. For now, we shall sum up the combinatorialist solution to the MPP as follows:

C: A state of affairs is possible if and only if it is obtained by means of a legitimate recombination of constituents of at least one actual state of affairs.

In order to further understand the combinatorialist stance, C must be debated from different angles. We will study three of them: the notion, invoked by C, of a constituent; the principle of recombination that sustains C; and the extent to which non-actual worlds may depart from the actual one.

§5.3.2. Constituents

A recombination is defined based on the *constituents* of some state of affairs. As we have seen, according to the combinatorialist, (almost) every state of affairs possesses a metaphysical structure; this is typically established by appeal to the logical structure of the sentence that expresses the state of affairs. The logical analysis of the structure of a sentence can be made in at least two ways: through the identification of logically relevant roles, or through the identification of logically relevant constituents.

The first modality of analysis involves identifying the key roles of the sentence that expresses the state of affairs: for example, subject, predicate, and adverb. Nevertheless, in some cases, this type of analysis does not dig deep enough into the structure of the sentence: the role of the subject could be fulfilled by several different individuals; the predicate or adverb could be compound. From a combinatorialist point of view, this fact is problematic in that it does not allow us to identify the metaphysical structure of the sentence, and thus the ultimate elements subject to possible recombination: for example, it does not allow us to identify the various elements that form a subject, but rather it forces us to recombine the entire subject.

For this reason, the combinatorialists support a logical analysis based on the concept of a logical constituent of a sentence. A logical constituent of a sentence is, intuitively, a term that denotes an object or an action (including states, such as a frame of mind), or a modification of the object, action, or state of affairs. Now, an important distinction is the one between *atomic* and non-atomic constituents. An atomic individual is such that it has no proper parts, while an atomic universal is such that it is not a conjunction, a disjunction, or a structure made out of other universals. For example, in (6) we may suppose that the atomic constituents are: the predicate "to eat"; the terms "Foffo", "Fufi", "milk", "cookies", "fish", and "potatoes". On the other hand, in the state of affairs expressed by (6) there are also non-atomic constituents: "Foffo eats fish and potatoes" and "Fufi has milk and cookies". These constituents are not atomic insofar as they are obtained based on other constituents.

In the simplest model proposed by Armstrong, which shares important elements with the metaphysical picture provided by Wittgenstein, all the constituents are atomic. (See Wittgenstein (1921), Skyrms (1981), and Armstrong (1997).) Now, imagine having a stock of atomic individuals and a stock of universals such that: (i) each individual in the stock instantiates some universal and, furthermore, (ii) each universal in the stock is instantiated by some individuals. Imagine that the world fulfilling these conditions is the actual world, so that any recombination of constituents of the actual world delivers a world made of atomic constituents and the totality of recombinations associated with the actual world recombines the totality of individuals and universals we have in stock. If this is the case, then the actual world is what Armstrong calls a "*Wittgenstein world*".

As long as combinatorialism assumes that the actual world is a Wittgenstein world, the combinatorial machinery for combinatorialism is relatively straightforward. Unfortunately, this assumption is implausible. For all we know, some important constituents of the actual world (e.g. physical, chemical, or biological kinds) may not be atomic, but rather exhibit a variety of characteristic structures. How are we then to recombine structured constituents? For instance, should their parts be recombined as well? Consider how we might recombine a molecule of water: should its atoms of hydrogen and oxygen be recombined as well, or does only the whole molecule figure in the recombination? Sider (2005) raises a number of questions along these lines, which still await proper discussion. Armstrong (2004) argues that combinatorialism may indeed sit best with atomic worlds, but it is far from an established (scientific or philosophical) fact that our world is atomic. To see further into this matter, we shall now turn to the combinatorialist's formulation of the principle of recombination.

§5.3.3. Recombinations

Armstrong contends that combinatorialism is capable of providing a reductive analysis of modality on a par with modal realism. The reason is that combinatorialism explains the meaning of modal sentences in terms of the existence of non-modal, actual entities. For instance, the truth of (9) is explained in terms of the truth of (6). Constituents of the actual world are sufficient to account for all the truths that a theory of modality must explain, or so contends Armstrong.

Principle C is exempt from some of the difficulties of the concept of recombination observed during our discussion of modal realism, where counterpart theory forced Lewis to introduce the notion of an intrinsic duplicate. Because the combinatorialist admits that there is identity among individuals belonging to distinct worlds (after all, the individuals of other worlds exist as surrogates of individuals of the actual world), what she recombines are precisely individuals of the actual world. On the other hand, the combinatorialist will face some new challenges, to which we now turn.

Having clarified the notion of a constituent, we can define the concept of recombination as follows:

> R: A state of affairs S is a recombination of certain states of affairs S*
> if and only if: (i) all constituents of S belong to at least one of the
> states of affairs in S* or are obtained by interpolation or extrapolation
> from constituents of at least one of the states of affairs in S*; (ii) S is
> distinct from all the states in S*.

A state of affairs recombines other states of affairs if and only if it possesses a different order of constituents or if it relates constituents that are not related in the original state. The appeal to interpolation and extrapolation allows some departure from the actual world. A universal is obtained from interpolation of another when some of its aspects are changed: for instance, imagine that the gravitational constant had some slightly different value than in fact it has. A universal is obtained by extrapolation from another one by removing some of its aspects: for instance, imagine having an electron with no charge. Part (ii) of the definition is used to guarantee that S is not actual, but it is a mere possibility. As an illustration of principle R, consider the state of affairs S:

10 Giovanni loves Laura,

and suppose that S is a recombination of the two following states of affairs:

11 Laura loves Pietro,

12 Giovanni admires Gina.

Yet, things aren't quite that simple. In fact, not all recombinations are acceptable. For example:

13 Giovanni loves admire

is a recombination of (11) and (12), but it is not acceptable. For this very reason, C requires that recombinations be legitimate.

In order to explain which combinations are legitimate, it is necessary to reintroduce the logical analysis based on roles introduced earlier: (13) would not count as legitimate insofar as "admire" fulfills the role of a term, while it should fulfill the role of a predicate. Combinatorialism, therefore, is based essentially on a double logical analysis of sentences, which yields a double metaphysical analysis of states of affairs: that of atomic constituents and that of atomic roles.

Thus, *contra* Armstrong's contention that combinatorialism offers a reductive analysis of modality, the appeal to legitimate recombinations makes C a circular definition of the concept of possibility: possible states of affairs are those that are *possible* within the limits of the assigned metaphysical roles. Surely, this is a theoretical limitation with regard to modal realism; yet, if we consider that modal realism is the only theory that claims to be able to define the concept of possibility in a non-circular manner, the concerns raised by the limitation are minor. The combinatorialist offers us an explanation of the concept of possibility, but not a definition. And this may be considered sufficient: in order to offer adequate solutions to the PP, EPP, and MPP, it is not necessary to eliminate the concept of possibility; it need only be explained.

We can now proceed to formulate the principle of recombination for combinatorialism:

PRC: Any collection of individuals $x_1, ..., x_n$ and universals $U_1, ..., U_n$ could coexist, or fail to coexist, with any collection of individuals $y_1, ..., y_n$ and universals $V_1, ..., V_n$, as long as: (i) the individuals fit the maximal external relation of a world, and (ii) the combination delivers states of affairs.

There are two key differences between the principle of recombination, PR, seen in Chapter 4 and PRC. To begin with, PRC recombines not only individuals, but also universals; in fact, PR followed a nominalist metaphysics, where only individuals exist, while PRC rests on a so-called realist metaphysics, where universals—as well as individuals—are real. In general, PRC purports to recombine *all* constituents of states of affairs (and whether it succeeds in doing so is debated by its detractors, as we shall see). The second difference between PRC and PR is PRC's requirement that the recombination deliver a state of affairs.

PRC offers us the opportunity to consider the combinatorialist solution to the EPP. Combinatorialism seems to play upon two distinct types of knowledge. On one hand, we have the principle of recombination, which states that all legitimate recombinations are possible. It is a metaphysical principle, knowledge of which is gained (to a certain extent) independently of experience. On the other hand, we have empirical knowledge of the atomic constituents of reality: it is based on this knowledge that we can grasp the meaning of any modal sentence.

At this time an objection could be made: identifying the atomic constituents of reality is not at all banal. Can a cell be considered an atomic constituent, or is it composed of other constituents? Are colors, sounds, or tastes constituents of reality or mere figments of our imaginations? Are gaps and omissions constituents of reality?

Of course, this objection involves general philosophical problems that are not exclusive to the combinatorialist, though they do have a greater weight for her than for the modal realist, for example. The combinatorialist typically believes that it is not (only) up to philosophers to give an answer to questions of this type. Combinatorialism brings a conceptual clarity to the PP, but the fact that it cannot have the last word about what things are possible is not strange; to find out what is possible, we must also consult other disciplines.

§5.3.4. Alien possibilities

The third aspect of C that requires attention is also related to ways in which the actual world might depart from a Wittgenstein world. In particular, it concerns the possibility that the actual world may have contained either fewer or more individuals, or more universals. The simplest circumstance is the actual world containing fewer individuals; this scenario is typically referred to as a *contraction*. The combinatorialist will represent a contraction by means of a world made of a conjunction of states of affairs that jointly contain fewer individuals than the ones existing in the actual world.

More difficult is the case of an *expansion*, that is, a world that contains more individuals than the actual world. Suppose the stock of recombinable individuals from the actual world includes n individuals, and we are given the sentence:

14 There could have been $n+1$ cats.

Regardless of whether it would turn out to be true or false, (14) seems to express a state of affairs whose content is straightforward. So the combinatorialist can hardly appeal to the fact that, despite our modal intuitions, (14) expresses an impossible state of affairs. Yet how can her theory represent such a state of affairs if there are not enough individuals in the actual world to deliver it?

A solution may be to add a clause endorsing the legitimacy of recombinations obtained through the *iteration* of elements of the actual world: if in the actual world there is only one pope, a state of affairs with two popes is possible insofar as it is derived from the actual world by the iteration of a certain constituent. Thus, a world in which there are more individuals than there are in the actual world becomes a possibility by iterating some items of the actual world. Whether iteration should be regarded as a legitimate operation, from a metaphysical point of view, may nonetheless be doubted.

Despite the potential merits of her view, there is a type of possibility that the combinatorialist does not seem to be able to explain: *alien universals* (which we encountered in Chapter 4). Not only can we think that there are worlds with more individuals than there are in our own; there could also be worlds with individuals whose qualities and abilities are completely distinct from those of the individuals of our world. At one time, such possibilities were excluded by invoking the so-called *principle of plenitude* for the actual world, according to which God created (in the actual world) everything God could have created, not only with respect to number (which is debatable, but less relevant), but also, and more importantly, with respect to variety. The fact remains that this principle does not seem to have a clear empirical confirmation: there are undoubtedly many species of living organism, but why should we believe that there couldn't be, or couldn't have been, even more? Or why couldn't the periodic table, for example, have included more elements than the ones it already includes? In other words: why believe that we live in the most variegated world that could exist? A combinatorialist cannot account for the plausibility of these questions and yet it is not easy to set them aside. We are, therefore, left with a serious theoretical limitation.

A final objection to combinatorialism arises from the semantic tie "being true in", which relates a sentence and a world. For the combinatorialist, worlds *make-true* the sentences that they make true out of necessity; for instance, (9) is necessarily made true by any world containing the states of affairs depicted in (9). However, the necessity of the truthmaking relationship cannot be analyzed in modal terms. Thus, we are stuck with a primitive kind of modality, despite Armstrong's contention that combinatorialism manages to reduce modalities.

To this objection, the combinatorialist may point out that the necessity of the truthmaking relationship is expressed through a kind of advanced modalizing (see Chapter 4), which is not subject to the same sort of analysis as modal sentences in natural language. It is therefore to be expected that the theory cannot explain truthmaking in terms of recombinations of actual states of affairs.

§5.4. Pictorial ersatzism

The two ersatzist positions we have seen up to this point have taken advantage of the representative power of language and of the notion of recombination of actual states of affairs, respectively. The third position we will consider— pictorial ersatzism—is in some respects a cognate theory of combinatorialism because, ultimately, both theories employ non-linguistic and non-material structured entities. On the other hand, pictorial ersatzism and combinatorialism differ with respect to how the existence of a world is motivated: the combinatorialist relies upon a principle of recombination rooted in actual individuals, properties (universals), and laws; but, for the pictorial ersatzist the maximality and consistency of a world will typically be defined independently of the laws of the actual world.

The label *pictorial ersatzism* comes from Lewis (1986: Chapter 3). Versions of pictorial ersatzism can be attributed already to classic authors, such as Wittgenstein (1921) and Carnap (1947), and perhaps even Leibniz. After the development of QML and possible-worlds semantics, pictorial ersatzism became a predominant position and was developed in different directions by, among others, Alvin Plantinga (1974a, 2003), Robert Adams (1974), Robert Stalnaker (1984, 2003), and Peter van Inwagen (1980, 1986). Because of the large number of authors who have endorsed pictorial ersatzism, there is no uncontroversial taxonomy of its variants. Our discussion will distinguish three of the main versions: according to the first, worlds are maximally consistent sets of propositions; according to the second, worlds are complex states of affairs (but not recombinations of actual states of affairs); according to the third variant, possible worlds are images. Let us analyze the variants in this order.

§5.4.1. Worlds as sets of propositions

The first variant of pictorial ersatzism proposes one of the most intuitive views of possible worlds, according to which they are sets of propositions. Let us begin by reasserting the basic distinction between sentences and propositions. Consider the following two sentences of, respectively, English and Italian:

15 It rains.

16 *Piove.*

Now, (15) and (16) are clearly not the same sentence—they even contain a different amount of words; on the other hand, they convey the same content—that it rains. We call the content of a sentence the *proposition* expressed by the sentence.

Insofar as we have reason to believe that our sentences and our thoughts do convey some content, we have reason to believe that they express propositions. Or, so claim the authors who endorse the existence of propositions. Since we seem to have good reasons to believe that propositions exist— reasons that are independent of our theorizing about modality—the proposal to analyze modal sentences in terms of propositions is far less controversial, from a metaphysical point of view, than most other competing proposals on the market, including modal realism. Because of this, some authors (e.g. Divers (2002) and Melia (2003)) included this variant of pictorial ersatzism among the so-called *quiet moderate realist* positions, in contrast to the extreme realism of David Lewis.

The defender of the first variant of pictorial ersatzism takes the theory of propositions one step further. She contends that the content of our modal sentences can be explained by fine-tuning our theory of propositions. This operation requires several adjustments and different authors have suggested alternative ones (see Adams (1974) and Stalnaker (1984) for some examples). In our view, it takes at least four adjustments to a basic theory of propositions in order to produce a suitable pictorial ersatzist account of possible worlds. (i) We must make sure that the propositions out of which worlds are constructed are neither incomplete nor contradictory (as would be the content expressed by sentences such as, respectively, "Socrates thinks about" and "Socrates is and is not Athenian"). Some deny that propositions of this sort exist *tout court*, but we need not be so demanding, as it suffices to require that no such proposition is part of a world. (ii) We must require that propositions exist independently of the existence of actual entities and that they exist independently of a language expressing them. This adjustment allows us to claim that a proposition about non-actual entities (e.g. unicorns) is true or false even if there actually are no such entities. This adjustment allows modal sentences that express mere possibilities, including alien possibilities, to be meaningful. Moreover, it grants the pictorial ersatzist with a basis for maintaining that there may be some scenarios that are so alien to us that we cannot express them in our language. (iii) We shall define a world as a *set* of propositions, since one of them will typically not be enough to fully capture all that there is to a world. Such a set should be *maximal* and *consistent*, as also required by the linguistic ersatzist (and a similar requirement will hold for the other two variants of pictorial ersatzism). And, it is important to remark that these requirements render the analysis of modality circular. (iv) We shall define a relationship of *"truth at"* as holding between sentences and (maximal and consistent) sets of (complete and non-contradictory) propositions. To illustrate, the sentence:

17   It is possible that: Foffo plays with Fufi

is true if and only if there is a maximal and consistent set of propositions such that, at such a set, (17) is true; and (17) is true at that set when (17) is included in the set.

The key tenet of the first variant of pictorial ersatzism can be summed up as follows:

PEP: The sentence in natural language: "It is possible that: *s"* expresses a proposition *p*, and is true if and only if there is a maximal and consistent set of (complete and non-contradictory) propositions at which *p* is true.

The view is pictorial because possible scenarios are specific entities (i.e. specific sets of propositions) that *depict* how the actual world could have been. The theory employs three metaphysical primitives: propositions, sets, and the relation "true at". In a way, these primitives are common to many solutions of the MPP, regardless of the details of any theory of modality providing such solutions. On the other hand, pictorial ersatzism is far from innocent, for two chief reasons. First of all, it compels us to buy into a theory of propositions as entities that exist independently of actual entities. Second, if the theory is to have some plausibility, it must endorse a view of propositions as structured entities of some sort, so that the truth of a proposition is explained by recurring to its structure. (For example (17), if true, is true in virtue of the structure of the proposition it expresses—a structure made up of Foffo, Fufi, and the relation between them.) To many philosophers, these two features alone are reason enough to look elsewhere for a solution to the PP and its sub-problems.

§5.4.2. Worlds as sets of states of affairs

The second variant of pictorial ersatzism resembles the first, but its key metaphysical primitive is not the proposition. A theory resting on propositions, as we have seen, starts off as intuitive, by insisting on the tie between sentences and propositions; but it ends up introducing unlikely constraints on our view of propositions, which depict them as abstruse and perhaps even obscure entities. Plantinga (1974a) and subsequent authors opt for an ersatzist position where the role of worlds is played by states of affairs.

We encountered states of affairs during our discussion of combinatorialism. While the latter was developed after, and under the influence of, the pictorial ersatzist variant under consideration, the views are distinct. The two chief differences between them regard the relationship between actual entities and the constituents of states of affairs, and the nature of the constituents themselves. Let us discuss them in order.

While combinatorialism crucially relied upon a principle of recombination that operated upon actual individuals and universals, no such appeal is required in the variant of pictorial ersatzism under consideration. That is, combinatorialism delivers only non-actual states of affairs whose constituents are (obtained by iteration, interpolation or extrapolation from) constituents of actual states of affairs; the variant under consideration, instead, allows for constituents that are non-actual. Thus, the variant cannot regard states of affairs as endowed with causal powers or at least as part and parcel of the causal structure of reality; on the other hand, it can accommodate the existence of alien possibilities more readily than combinatorialism.

Second, the variant under consideration explains the existence of non-actual constituents by postulating that constituents of states of affairs are *necessary existents*, endowed with *individual essences*. Suppose that Fufi, the cat, could have had a twin sibling, Fefe. Fefe is an unactualized cat. According to the variant under consideration, it is necessary that there is a state of affairs of which Fefe is a constituent and, in this sense, Fefe exists out of necessity. Moreover, Fefe has an individual essence, that is, there are certain properties of Fefe that define what sort of entity it is (among other things, a cat and a sibling of Fufi): Fefe retains those properties in any state of affairs and it is identified by means of them (for a discussion of essentialism, see Chapter 3).

Equipped with the theory of states of affairs just outlined, we can define worlds as maximal and consistent sets of states of affairs. More explicitly:

PES: The sentence in natural language: "It is possible that: *s*" expresses a state of affairs *S*, and is true if and only if there is a maximal and consistent set of states of affairs at which *S* is true.

The analysis of modalities provided by PES is even more circular than the one proposed by PEP: it relies not only on maximality and consistency, but also on individual essences and necessary existent individuals. We shall come back to necessary existents in Chapter 8, both in conjunction with Meinongianism (the view that *there are* certain things that *do not exist*) and when considering the theory of necessary existents suggested by Timothy Williamson.

§5.4.3. Worlds as images

The third pictorial ersatzist proposal envisions worlds as images, as opposed to representations that possess a logical or linguistic structure. Images, here, do not stand for figures embodied in some material object or drawn by some agent, but for figures that exist independently of such material inscriptions. After all, it is still possible that a prism with 30,827 sides could exist, even if—say—no material object has the form of such prism and no one has ever drawn it. Why, then, should we not believe that there is an image for every possible world and that possible worlds are nothing but those images, no matter whether the images represent some actual material inscription?

The chief advantage of pictorial ersatzism over the other ersatzist positions we have seen lies in the fact that pictures have a greater expressive power than descriptions or recombinations. By embracing pictorial ersatzism we can assert that there are worlds with a cardinality of individuals similar to that of the continuum, just as we are able to represent worlds with a variety of individuals that are not attainable through the recombination of actual varieties.

That said, pictorial ersatzism must admit that it provides, not a definition of possibility, but, more modestly, an explanation of it. The figures that represent possible worlds are those whose interpretation is consistent and complete. A figure, in and of itself, does not constitute a representation; the representation is obtained only once the figure has been interpreted. (Similarly, a figure, in and of itself, is not a map; we have a map only once the criteria for interpretation of the figure have been provided.) But consistency and completeness (as seen in the foregoing discussion of linguistic ersatzism) are modal concepts: that is, they are concepts that presuppose an understanding of possibility.

The notion of interpretation raises a second problem. From what has been said, it emerges that a possible world cannot consist simply of a figure, but of an *interpreted figure*. Thus, pictorial ersatzism's solution to the PP would be the following:

PEI: The sentence in natural language: "It is possible that: *s*" expresses an interpreted figure such that: the figure represents *s*; and, according to the interpretation, the figure constitutes a maximal and consistent representation.

The problem is that PEI itself lacks a clear interpretation. What are interpreted figures? In what sense can we consider them to be surrogates for entities of the actual world? Moreover, doubts could be raised with regard to how the figures to which PEI refers are known. Certainly, these questions will have to be adequately answered if this version of ersatzism is to attract broader consensus.

§5.5. Atomic ersatzism

The final ersatzist position that merits a closer look is atomic ersatzism. This can seem to be a strange position at first, because it rests on a very simplistic metaphysical proposal, according to which possible worlds are atomic, simple entities. That is, according to atomic ersatzism, the answer to the MPP is straightforward and can be summed up as follows:

MAE: A scenario is possible if and only if there is an atomic entity that is abstract and maximal and that represents that scenario.

According to the atomic ersatzist, worlds have no structure at all; they seem to represent possible scenarios by magic: hence the label that Lewis reserved for this position: *magical ersatzism*.

Up until this point in our discussion of the ersatzist positions, we have spoken of worlds as entities that have certain constituents: elements of a language, abstract correlates of concrete constituents of the actual world, propositions, states of affairs, or images. But we might imagine that a world is a single entity, without real parts. Of course, we can imagine an object being divided into parts, but this does not mean that the object is dividable: for example, we can think of a quark being divided into parts, but this does not mean that it can be done. In other words: metaphysical atoms do not necessarily coincide with topological or conceptual atoms.

For the atomic ersatzist, as in the case of any other ersatzist position, actuality is metaphysically privileged. There are many worlds. Each of them is a maximal entity in the sense we defined (for the other ersatzist positions). Only one of them is actual. All of the others are abstract. But they are not obtained through a recombination of parts of the actual world, parts of figures, or parts of a language. They exist; period. And they represent the way in which our world could have been because they are distinct from our world. Their being distinct is explained in terms of their representational powers, which vary from world to world, but which cannot be analyzed in terms of constituents.

The appeal to representational power raises some perplexities. Given that worlds are metaphysical atoms, we cannot say much about them. We know that they are atomic: that is, they do not have parts. We know that they are maximal: that is, it is not possible to add any part to any world. We know that they are abstract. But, what are they abstractions of? It appears that, as we saw with pictorial ersatzism, atomic ersatzism also requires that its preferred metaphysical material be interpreted in order to deliver possibilities. MAE must, therefore, be reformulated as follows:

> MAE*: A scenario S is possible if and only if there is an atomic entity $S*$ that is abstract and maximal, and of which there is at least one interpretation according to which $S*$ counts as a representation of S.

MAE* contains a double appeal to modal concepts: the maximality and the validity of representation. Furthermore, given that $S*$ is atomic, there is no *reason* that it should count as a representation of S: it represents it because it represents it. By virtue of this distinctive feature of the theory, the representational powers of each world seem magical.

The solution to the PP proposed by atomic ersatzism can now be stated:

> AE: The sentence in natural language: "It is possible that: s" expresses an atomic entity $S*$ that is abstract and maximal, and of which there is at least one interpretation according to which $S*$ counts as a representation of the scenario expressed by the sentence "s".

Some words are needed in order to explain the plausibility of atomic ersatzism. In this chapter, we have examined five ersatzist conceptions of possible worlds, in addition to atomic ersatzism. Each of them suggested complex analyses of the elements of which a world is allegedly composed. And yet, we have seen that thinking of such elements as linguistic entities, images, structured propositions, or structured states of affairs leads to complications regarding the kinds of entities worlds are or regarding the extent of the possibilities that worlds are able to represent (including especially alien possibilities). The atomic ersatzist takes a different route. She maintains that worlds are simple entities. Thus, the issue of alien possibilities is solved: we can have as many simple entities as we need in order to represent all the possibilities that the theory should. Explaining the representational powers of a world is, of course, the most delicate aspect of atomic ersatzism. But, just as a single symbol, such as an ideogram, can stand for many words and, as such, for some complex scenarios, so a single abstract entity can stand for the complex scenario that is a possible world.

While the other ersatzists have tried to explain the complex scenario that is a world by complicating the metaphysical structure of worlds themselves, the atomic ersatzist discharges that responsibility by complicating the relation of representation between a world and a scenario. Yet such representation happens by magic and cannot be explained in metaphysical terms, as we have seen; and for this reason atomic ersatzism may be regarded as implausible. On the other hand, atomic ersatzism can describe the representation by means of semantics: the representation consists in all the sentences that a certain world makes true. Furthermore, it may by now be clear that the metaphysics of modality forces any account to adopt some-or-other unwelcome (at times incredible) tenet; atomic ersatzism is, thus, in good company in making a seemingly bizarre metaphysical choice, and we should at least concede that atomic ersatzism cleverly exploits a theoretical possibility that had not yet been seen among the theories in this volume.

Study Questions

- What is the meaning of the term "ersatz"? And why is it appropriate for characterizing ersatzism?
- What is the main characteristic of ersatzism at the metaphysical level?
- What is the main contention of linguistic ersatzism?
- How does linguistic ersatzism generate possible worlds?
- What are the chief drawbacks of linguistic ersatzism?
- What, according to a combinatorialist, is a state of affairs?
- What, according to a combinatorialist, is a constituent?
- What is a Wittgenstein world?
- What is the principle of recombination in combinatorialism?
- What are the principal difficulties for combinatorialism?
- What is a proposition?
- What are the main difficulties for using propositions in conjunction with pictorial ersatzism?

▶

- What is the distinctive trait of states of affairs, for the pictorial ersatzist variant that employs them?
- What is the advantage of supposing that worlds are images?
- What are the drawbacks of supposing that worlds are images?
- How does atomic ersatzism explain the meaning of a modal sentence?
- What motivates the supposition that worlds are atomic?

FURTHER READING

Along with modal realism, ersatzism is the most debated position in the philosophy of modality. There is a crucial difference between the two theories, though: while modal realism has been openly endorsed by only a handful of philosophers, plenty are those who have professed allegiance to ersatzism or advanced a theory that seems ersatzist. It is for this reason not uncontroversial to systematize the spectrum of ersatzist positions, and the reader is invited to explore the debate along several paths. For an **introductory survey** of the various ersatzist positions, see Lewis (1986: Chapter 3), Divers (2002: Part Three), and Melia (2003: Chapters 6 and 7). Also useful to consult are Sider (2002) and Stalnaker (2012). Some classic readings include: Carnap (1947), Cresswell (1972), Plantinga (1974a, 2003), the collections of essays in Linsky (1974), and Loux (1979), Kripke (1980), and Skyrms (1981).

For a discussion of **trans-world identity**, see: the texts collected in Loux (1979), Kripke (1980), van Inwagen (1985), and Lewis (1986: Chapter 4).

For a formulation of **linguistic ersatzism**, see Roy (1995) and Stalnaker (1984, 2004). For a critical discussion, see McMichael (1983), Lewis (1986, §3.2.), and Heller (1996, 1998).

For a systematic formulation of **combinatorialism,** see Armstrong (1986, 1989). Important follow-ups are Armstrong (1997, 2004). For a critical assessment of the position, see Kim (1986), Bradley (1989), Lewis (1992), Thomas (1996), Sider (2005), Efird and Stoneham (2006), and Wang (2013).

For a formulation of the various **pictorial ersatzist** positions, see Adams (1974), the essays contained in Loux (1979), Stalnaker (1984, 2003), van Inwagen (1980, 1986), and Plantinga (1974a, 2003). For a critical discussion, see especially Lewis (1986, §3.3.). Also useful is Brogaard (2006).

For a critical presentation of **atomic ersatzism**, see Lewis (1986, §3.4.). For a defense of the position, see Denby (2006). Also in connection with atomic ersatzism, it is useful to consult Brogaard (2006).

6

Modal fictionalism and modal agnosticism

Fictionalist strategies in metaphysics have been endorsed with respect to a wide variety of subjects, ranging from meta-ethics to truth and the ontology of mathematical entities; the first half of this chapter considers how fictionalism has been applied to modalities. First, modal fictionalism is illustrated and three different formulations of it are given (§6.1.); then, five problems for modal fictionalism are discussed (§6.2.). In the second half of the chapter, a more recent modal theory is taken up—modal agnosticism—which proposes to delimit the range of modal sentences expressing true or false propositions. After a distinction between strong and moderate variants of modal agnosticism (§6.3.), two objections to this view are examined (§6.4.).

* * * * *

In this chapter we will consider the final two theories of possibility that are based on possible-worlds semantics: modal fictionalism and modal agnosticism. Both develop what seems to be the most immediate advantage of possible worlds: references to them do not have to be taken literally and, thus, we need not make special room for worlds in our conception of reality. This feature of possible worlds evidently runs counter to the theoretical core of both modal realism and ersatzism, which aimed—each in its own way—to provide a suitable metaphysical and epistemological story to pair up with the semantic benefits of possible-worlds semantics. Furthermore, both modal fictionalism and modal agnosticism were formulated after modal realism and ersatzism: the first article to defend a fictionalist theory of modality is typically considered to be Rosen (1990) (Rosen's view being further developed in 1993 and 1995), though Armstrong (1989) also discusses the hypothesis of a fictionalist theory which, as we will see, differs from Rosen's theory in several ways. Agnosticism had not received adequate consideration before Divers (2004).

Let us now take a closer look at the two positions. The first half of this chapter discusses how fictionalism has been applied to modalities (§6.1.) and why that's problematic (§6.2.). In the second half of the chapter, we will take up modal agnosticism (§6.3.) and point out some difficulties for it (§6.4.).

§6.1. Fictional worlds

In recent years fictionalist approaches to metaphysical questions have received considerable attention in the analytic philosophical community, and have been developed in diverse philosophical areas: from the philosophy of science to the philosophy of mathematics, and from the commonsense ontology of objects to modality and ethics. (For a general overview, see Kalderon (2005) and Eklund (2007).) The distinguishing feature of modal fictionalism is that it considers what is arguably the most useful discourse we have for explaining modality—possible-worlds semantics—to be a useful fiction. (For a comparison between modal fictionalism and modal ersatzism, see Brogaard (2006).)

Before examining the details of the theory itself, we must make a clarification. It is rather ambiguous to say that a certain discourse must be treated as a useful fiction, because it is unclear which aspects of the discourse should be regarded as fictional. It could be hypothesized, that all fictions are nothing but discourses introduced for the purpose of explaining other discourses. When we say that Pinocchio is a piece of literary fiction, we do not believe that the things *The Adventures of Pinocchio* tries to shed light on—certain traits of human nature, let's say—are also fictional. Thus, Pinocchio is a fiction in the sense that the sentences contained in the book are not literally true or false; but certain other sentences, closely connected to those contained in the text, seem to be true.

Understanding this point is crucial for understanding the modal fictionalist's theory and its difficulties. The modal fictionalist does not claim that modal sentences are fictional in and of themselves; we are not feigning when we say that Foffo could have had milk and cookies; we are feigning when we try to explain that scenario through a language that makes reference to (possible) worlds. Therefore, the modal fictionalist typically does not deny the truth of what theories considered to be fictional try to explain, but simply the truth of those theories.

With this clarification under our belt, we can now move on to the formulation of the fundamental theory of modal fictionalism, which sets out to resolve the PP as follows:

F: The sentence in natural language: "It is possible that: *s*" is true if and only if its orthodox possible-worlds analysis is true.

For instance,

1   Foffo the cat could have had milk and cookies

is true only if, in the fiction of a theory of possible worlds,

2   There is a world in which Foffo the cat has milk and cookies

is true.

In other words, modal fictionalism tries to join together two observations, both of which appear to be valid, but which are in tension with one another: (i) modal sentences need a theory in order to be explained and the best one on the market seems to be the theory that makes reference to possible worlds; (ii) theories that take the existence of possible worlds seriously encounter significant problems when trying to explain the nature of the entities to which they refer. The modal fictionalist sets out to use a theory that makes reference to possible worlds in order to explain the meaning of modal sentences, while at the same time denying that the theory should be taken seriously. Is this feasible?

Before taking into consideration some of the numerous objections that have been raised against modal fictionalism, we must make certain clarifications and elucidations regarding F. Let us begin with the following expression: "in the fiction of a theory of possible worlds". The lack of reference to a specific theory should be noted. In fact, among the theories of possible worlds illustrated in the previous two chapters, the fictionalist can afford to choose whichever she prefers. They are all fictions. But how is she to choose?

After weighing the pros and cons, it seems it would be a good idea to choose modal realism, as Gideon Rosen did when he first formulated modal fictionalism, in 1990. In fact, as we have seen, there are few doubts regarding the greater conceptual potential of modal realism compared to the various ersatzist proposals: modal realism is able to account for a greater number of possibilities (see Chapter 4 and the cardinality objection in §5.2). Therefore, if we were to choose a theory independently of what the theory suggests exists, modal realism would come out on top—hence, Rosen's decision. It is, nonetheless, important to clarify that the fictionalist is akin to a spectator on the debate between theories of possible worlds, and may at any point change sides. Typically, fictionalists choose whichever theory proves most conceptually potent.

Another element of F that must be clarified is the reference to an undetermined fiction of possible worlds and, therefore, the translation of s into s^*. Rosen suggests that the theory may be determined using a simple prefix—"according to the story ..."—to be placed in front of an exposition of the relevant theory—such as, for him, the modal realism of Lewis (1986). The result is the following principle, in which s stands for a sentence in ordinary language and s^* stands for the orthodox possible-worlds analysis of s:

> RF: The sentence in natural language: "It is possible that: s" is true if and only if, according to the story told in Lewis (1986), "s^*" is true.

Rosen's strategy is clever and points to an anti-realist solution of the PP that had been overlooked until 1990. Possible-worlds semantics allows the most sophisticated logical and semantic treatment of sentences embedding modalities; however—as modal skeptics, modal expressivists, and modalists have pointed out—possible-worlds semantics raises a host of metaphysical and epistemic problems that are difficult to solve. An ideal compromise is to retain the depth of analysis proper to possible-worlds semantics, while avoiding the metaphysical commitment. That is the aim of modal fictionalism. The solution is hence found in endorsing the best comprehensive theory of (possible) worlds—that is the theory that provides the most persuasive answers to SPP, MPP, and EPP—while regarding that theory as a useful fiction.

But this is not the only way we can interpret the fictional framework. We could assume, following a suggestion of Armstrong (1989), that there is more than one framework: not only is the whole of modal realism a story; it is a story made of infinite stories: one for every possible world. The exact formulation of the F principle would, therefore, be the following:

> AF: The sentence in natural language: "It is possible that: s" is true if and only if, according to the story told in Lewis (1986), there is a collection of stories such that, according to at least one of them, s's equivalent "s^*" is true.

If, on the other hand, s is a sentence that expresses the necessity of a situation, then s is true if and only if according to all the stories within the collection (i.e. all of the worlds) s^* is true. The idea, then, is that the fiction of the modal fictionalist has two layers: the first being Lewis (1986), the second being each world countenanced by modal realism. Two remarks about AF are in order. First, it is important to remark that "collection" does not refer to an entity in and of itself, but should be understood simply as a list of stories. Second, as we shall see later on, adding a second layer is not free from important theoretical consequences. On one hand, it provides a clear-cut fictionalist interpretation of each world within the modal realist framework; on the other hand, it risks weakening modal fictionalism enough to make it less attractive than RF. Ultimately, then, the choice between RF and AF is not free of theoretical consequences and may resolve in favor of the former.

A general point about modal fictionalism that should be highlighted is the fact that F (and its variants RF and AF) maintains that the truth of a sentence in a fictional discourse has the role of establishing the truth of a modal sentence in ordinary language. At first sight, this comes off as a controversial affirmation: after all, a fiction is not true; nor is it necessarily false; it is simply a fiction. Therefore, the notion that the truth of our modal sentences is set by a fiction certainly comes off as suspicious. We could make a criticism such as this: possible-worlds semantics unquestionably assigns certain truth values to modal sentences; yet, for fictionalists, possible-world semantics is nothing but a fiction; if fiction tells us that a certain sentence is true or false, why should we believe that it in fact is?

Upon more careful reflection, the affirmation contained in F may appear more plausible. In a certain sense, it depends on our basis of comparison. Admittedly, we may be unwilling to concede that—absent an adequate inter-pretation—that which is written in the story of Pinocchio could be directly translated into truths concerning human nature: after all, the noses of liars do not grow, and we don't just happen to bump into the cat, the fox, or the fairy with turquoise hair. However, our perspective may be different if we consider fictions that are put to different uses. For instance, take the case of an interior decorator, who speaks of sofas, chairs, tables, empty spaces, etc. while furnishing a house; the decorator is also employing a fiction, which is useful to furnishing a house. However, the decorator's case seems to be different from Pinocchio's: even while referring to fictional entities, the decorator establishes what we must or mustn't do in our house. Why, then, should we not assume that the case of the modal realist is more similar to that of the decorator than to that of Pinocchio? By simply using a fiction, the modal realist, like the decorator, determines the truth regarding a certain discourse—modal discourse.

In conclusion, the distinctive answers to the SPP, MPP, and EPP provided by the modal fictionalist consist in borrowing the answers of another theory—typically, modal realism—and treating those as fictions that are useful for the philosophical purpose of solving the PP. Although such a move may seem innocuous at first, we shall see that it is not. To establish itself as a plausible theory of modality, modal fictionalism needs to supply many more details, in particular with respect to the metaphysics and epistemology of the fictions that allegedly found modal discourse. Whether RF or AF or WF is the principle of choice will make a big difference already; the detailed interpretation of each principle will then decide the plausibility of the modal fictionalist proposal.

§6.2. Five problems for modal fictionalism

The modal fictionalist program has been criticized in many respects. We will highlight five of them here. The list of objections we will consider is not exhaustive and we will privilege some underrepresented ones. In fact, a number of objections were considered already by Rosen (1993) and Brock (1993) themselves; most notably, this includes the so-called Brock-Rosen objection, which in brief goes as follows. According to the modal fictionalist, at all worlds it is true that there are many possible worlds. But then—by the definition of necessity as truth in all possible worlds—, according to the modal fictionalist, it is necessary that there are many possible worlds. This is precisely what the modal fictionalist denies, however. It is still debated whether fictionalism can solve this objection (cfr. Nolan 2011 for an overview) and the subtleties of the dispute cannot be dealt with here.

The first criticism we will consider claims that the very formulation of modal fictionalism makes use of modal concepts. The particular part of F that has been in the limelight is, "in the fiction of a theory of possible worlds". Some have found in it an implicit reference to a counterfactual; in fact, the best way to interpret the passage would be the following: "if the fiction of a possible-worlds theory were to be realized". (This criticism is already considered in Rosen (1990), but see also Divers (1995, 1999).) In other words, according to the criticism, F would be better interpreted as follows:

> F*: The sentence in natural language: "It is possible that: *s*" is true if and only if is true if and only if, were the orthodox possible-worlds analysis to be true, then the sentence would also be true.

In light of what we have previously said, we are able to clarify why the modal fictionalist would not be willing to accept F*. According to the modal fictionalist, the critic who proposes F* does not fully appreciate the strength of F. Modal fictionalists do not believe that the truth of sentences in ordinary language is determined by the sentences of possible-worlds semantics, provided said theory were true; rather, the truth of sentences in ordinary language is determined by what is stated in fiction, without any suppositions. Therefore, F does not call upon any modalities. It should also be noted that the interpretation F* could be accepted by a proponent of a bland version of modal fictionalism—such as Divers (1999). In fact, for these supporters, modal fictionalism does not claim to determine the truth of modal sentences in ordinary language, but simply to explain them; and F* could be an explanation.

A variant of the first criticism is raised by Bob Hale (1995a, 1995b), and concerns the modal status of the F principle. Though this criticism is also related to F*, it is often presented independently of the criticism we have just considered. Hale (1995b) states that the following question presents a dilemma for the modal fictionalist: is the fiction referred to in the F principle contingently or necessarily false? If it is necessarily false, then F* is not a plausible interpretation of F, insofar as the antecedent of the counterfactual ("if that theory were to be realized") would be false in any case—and, therefore, by definition, the consequent would be true. If it is contingently false, then the sentence "Possibly, the possible worlds fiction is true" is true. If we apply to such sentence the fictionalist's analysis suggested in F*, then we obtain the following: "If the possible worlds fiction is true, then there is a world where the possible worlds fiction is true." Now, the latter is trivial, but the claim that the possible worlds fiction is possibly true is not trivial! Thus, when we suppose (per the second horn) that the possible worlds fiction is contingently false, F* gives us the wrong analysis of "Possibly, the possible worlds fiction is true".

However, Hale's question does not seem to pose a true dilemma for the modal fictionalist. As previously clarified, the modal fictionalist would deny F*: in and of itself, fiction determines the truth of modal sentences in ordinary language. Whether fiction is contingently or necessarily false is not a question that affects F in any way, insofar as it does not affect the role that fiction would have in establishing the truth of modal sentences in ordinary language.

The second criticism, proposed in Peacocke (1999: 154), concerns the choice of fiction. Of all imaginable fictions, F must choose some theories that make use of possible-worlds semantics (one of the theories illustrated in the previous two chapters): but why make that choice in particular? Is there perhaps an implicit *obligation* in F to do so?

This criticism naturally suggests a delicate point which has not been sufficiently stressed in the extant literature. By way of explaining her choice, the modal fictionalist could appeal to the greater conceptual capacities of possible-worlds semantics. In and of itself, however, this is insufficient reason to land on modal realism in particular, as many modal fictionalists do. It seems that their choice implies an appeal to plausibility, which it is fair to make explicit:

F**: If we wish to judge in the most apparently philosophically plausible way the truth of the sentence in natural language: "It is possible that: *s*" then

we *must* assert that said sentence is true if and only if its equivalent "s *",
in the fiction of a possible-worlds theory, is true.

But F** contains a modal term, "must"; therefore, the fictionalist is implicitly relying upon modality when formulating his principal theory: how are we to interpret this implicit modality?

Alas, there is no compelling answer to this question to date. The modal fictionalist could bite the bullet and accept that there is a modal assumption in his theory that cannot in turn be analyzed as a fiction; after all, as we have seen, some primitive modalities have to be accepted not only by modalists and ersatzists, but also by modal realists; the modal fictionalist would simply be joining the bandwagon. Still, if the point highlighted by F** is correct, then the most appealing trait of modal fictionalism—deferring the analysis of *all* modal talk to the best theory of modality on the market—is undermined, and we are left with little clue as to how the modal fictionalist's core principle is supposed to be interpreted.

The third criticism relates to the relevance of the fiction invoked in F and has so far gone unnoticed in the literature. How are we to believe—one might object—that a fiction can have such a relevant role in our lives that it can determine—say—whether Elena should be punished for drunk-driving because, *according to a fiction*, the fictional character representing her does harm someone? More important to us is what Elena does in our world, not what happens in some fiction, no matter how useful such a fiction may be claimed to be. Ultimately, modal fictionalism commits the same fallacy committed by the counterpart theorist (encountered in Chapter 4, when discussing modal realism): explaining possibility in terms of entities that are not the ones for whose behavior we sought an explanation. We want to know how to judge the entities of our world, and we are instructed to consider other entities—other-worldly ones in the case of counterpart theory, and fictitious ones in the case of modal fictionalism.

The modal fictionalist, like the modal realist, holds the cards in terms of devising a response to this criticism. Ultimately, F is an explanation of the meaning of our modal sentences; it would seem legitimate for an explanation to involve entities we had not foreseen when we raised the question. If we go to the doctor with a simple stomachache and she, in response, brings up entities we have never heard of before (certain types of bacteria and enzymes), which we were unaware had anything to do with stomachaches, it would not come as a surprise to us. Many accept principles that explain who we are and how we must act in this world in terms of what we have done in previous lives, or of what a deity mandates; yet, before learning of these explanations, we never thought of those previous lives or of the deity and its teachings.

We should not be misled by one of the critical features of the dispute over possibility: the fact that possibility must, inevitably, find solutions that go far beyond what we can establish by empirical observation, if it is to take a cognitivist stance (a point we illustrated in Chapter 2, when discussing radical modal skepticism). If the explanations of the modal realist and modal fictionalist do not prove to be convincing insofar as they involve entities that are not causally related to those of our world, this has more to do with the nature of the philosophical problem than with the specificity of the theories that stand accused. Not every theory of possibility can speak of causal explanations, as the doctor or the theologian does; therefore, from this point of view, modal realism and modal fictionalism are neither more nor less prone to criticism than their rival theories. And the fact that they involve entities that are distinct from those invoked when the problem is raised is not a unique feature of these theories: doctors and theologians, among others, do the same.

The fourth criticism, raised in Nolan (1997: 264–6) and more recently in Kim (2005), concerns the ontological status of the fiction invoked in F. We might be wondering whether it is a fiction in the sense that Pinocchio is fictional or in the sense applicable to a non-Euclidean geometry. In other words: according to the modal fictionalist, is the modal realist's fiction an artifact (such as a character invented by an author), or is it an abstract and eternal entity, whose existence is independent of our conceiving it, which the modal realist finds himself describing?

There appear to be reasons to accept both of the options. On one hand, if fictions were abstract and eternal entities, whose existence is independent of our conceiving of them, then how they are fictions would not be clear: the same would go for numbers, geometric shapes, and laws of logic. On the other hand, the possible worlds of which the modal realists and ersatzists speak must have specific characteristics, such as maximality and consistency. Even if they were artifacts, their authors would be constrained in their creativity by the need for these characteristics.

Let us, at this point, clarify that the answer to the question about the ontological status of the fiction depends partly on the specific version of F we are considering. According to RF, for example, the fiction is not possible worlds *tout court*, but possible worlds as described by Lewis (1986); given that, for Lewis, there may be worlds that cannot be known by us, worlds would have more in common with numbers or geometric shapes than with invented characters such as Pinocchio. If, on the other hand, we endorse AF, then each world is treated as a fiction of its own. At this point, Pinocchio turns out to be a more useful point of comparison; but, we also lose—at least *prima facie*—the option of claiming that there may be worlds that cannot be known by us. That option is, nonetheless, regained, if we make reference to possibly existing and yet unknowable fictions—a move that would appear to be countenanced by Lewis's modal realism. Modal realism would then be a fiction, according to which there are infinitely many fictions, some of which we cannot know.

It would certainly be possible to argue that all works of literary fiction obey certain rules of construction: for example, if we wanted to write a sonnet, we would have to adhere to a certain metric schema. Of course, some genres, such as the novel, are more liberal, but we could not write a one-page text and legitimately call it a novel. The case of theories of possible worlds, then, is not peculiar: if we accept that sonnets and novels are fictions, despite the constraints on their creation, then we can also accept that a theory of possible worlds is a fiction, despite *its* constraints.

Some theorists, such as Nolan (1997) and Kim (2005), have insisted that the analogy between a possible-worlds theory and a novel seems to dissolve if we consider the distinguishing trait of an artifact: the need for an author. A novel has an author, but the fact that Foffo could have had milk and cookies does not; the latter could even have happened without anyone having conceived of it. The connection between fiction and reality is not analogous to that between possibility and reality.

It would seem, however, that this variant of the fourth objection reflects an incomplete understanding of modal fictionalism. The theory does not deny that our modal sentences are true or false; therefore, for a modal fictionalist, the fact that Foffo could have had milk and cookies does not depend on the existence of someone who conceives of it. At the same time, the modal fictionalist would claim that the *explanation* of that fact in accordance with the fiction of a possible-worlds theory depends on the existence of an author. A person does not have the power to do or undo modal facts, but she does have the power to explain or not explain them. The fiction of which the modal fictionalist speaks is the explanation itself, without which we cannot learn what is or is not possible.

The metaphysical aspects of a fiction raise a fifth and final problem, regarding the incompleteness of the descriptions we can give of a world. In fact, the modal realist or the ersatzist can be exempt from the obligation to provide a consistent and complete description of possible worlds, even if they believe they exist; they can be so exempt insofar as they are able to argue that worlds exist independently of those who speak of them. The modal fictionalist, on the other hand, does not have this possibility: possible worlds are fictions, just as a novel is; if a fiction is not described to the fullest, then it is incomplete.

This is a delicate point for modal fictionalism. It is a tall order to provide a consistent and complete description of all worlds; even more so if the fiction is that of modal realism, according to which there could be worlds we will never be able to imagine (see especially Woodward (2012) on this point). Also relevant here is the interpretation of F under discussion—whether RF or AF. In effect, it seems RF must admit that the modal realist's fiction is incomplete because it does not fully describe all the worlds of the theory. A key point of modal realism is that it countenances more worlds than we can represent (see Chapter 4), thus the fiction proposed by Lewis is such that it cannot possibly describe all the worlds it suggests exist. Therefore, the truth conditions of the sentences in our language can only be given in an approximate manner, with the proviso that a consistent and complete story of some worlds can be provided only (and at best) on a case-by-case basis.

AF, by contrast, seems to have a more compelling solution. In fact, according to this interpretation of F, worlds are fictions within the fiction of a general theory of worlds: the latter fiction—the principal fiction—is not incomplete; what are incomplete are the fictions that it unfolds. Therefore, AF can maintain that there is no incompleteness in the fiction that defines the modal fictionalist theory, and that the incompleteness of the fictions of individual worlds does not nullify the evaluation of the truth of a sentence because, in accordance with what the modal realist or the ersatzist claim, such incompleteness is irrelevant for the purposes of the evaluation.

§6.3. Modal agnosticism

One last theory of possibility that uses possible-worlds semantics remains to be considered: modal agnosticism. As in the case of modal fictionalism, agnosticism was developed in different philosophical realms: for example, in the philosophy of science (see Van Fraassen (1980)) and in the philosophy of mathematics (for a similar, but not strictly agnostic, approach, see Field (1980, 1989)). Articulate defenses of an agnostic theory of modality are recent, and derive primarily from an essay by John Divers (2004); see also Humberstone (2007).

Like modal fictionalism, modal agnosticism itself operates in relation to a theory of possible worlds. As indicated by the term itself, modal agnosticism gives no definitive answer regarding the truth of the theory it uses. Thus, it shares with modal fictionalism a certain anti-realist strategy that aims to exploit the theoretical strength of possible-worlds semantics—and possibly of a full-blown theory of worlds such as modal realism—without committing to the existence of worlds, and so without having to tell a *sui generis* story about how we come to know modal truths. Indeed, Divers (2004) begins with two observations regarding modal realism: that its analysis of modal concepts is deeper than that of its rival theories; and that it commits us to the existence of an infinite number of strange entities, that is, worlds just like ours which, by definition, we cannot experience. The solution proposed, as in the case of modal fictionalism, sets out to take advantage of the conceptual analysis while, at the same time, avoiding a commitment to the existence of worlds.

But this time, the idea is to deny assent to—to remain agnostic toward—the sentences whose translation into modal realism (or another chosen possible-worlds theory) commits us to the existence of worlds that are not our own. This can be done in two ways, which give rise to two types of agnosticism: strong and moderate.

Strong agnosticism denies assent to all sentences whose translation into modal realism (or another possible-worlds theory) commits us to the existence of worlds that are not our own. The moderate agnostic, on the other hand, denies assent to only the sentences that commit us to the existence of worlds whose existence we have reason to doubt (because we do not have empirical proof of them, for example).

An analogy with the case of non-observable entities in physics can be useful for clarifying this point. Let us suppose that a theory in physics commits us to the existence of entities that are not directly observable, but that behave in a way that is entirely similar to the behavior of molecules of water; the strong agnostic would deny her assent to the theory in question, while the moderate would offer it. The moderate agnostic, however, would deny her assent to a theory that postulates the existence of non-observable entities whose behavior is dissimilar to that of entities we are able to observe: for example, he would deny assent to a theory according to which causal laws between non-observable entities are not subject to any fundamental laws of physics (e.g. conservation laws), but follow other *sui generis* laws instead.

The most attractive modal agnostic position—at least in terms of a theory of modality—seems to be the moderate position. In fact, the strong modal agnostic would deny assent to interpretations in modal realism (or another possible-worlds theory) of almost any modal sentence; the only exclusion would be the sentences that concern our world alone. The moderate modal agnostic, on the other hand, would accept all sentences whose translation into modal realism (or another possible-worlds theory) concerns situations that are similar to those of our world. For example:

3   Foffo the cat could have eaten lava

is true if and only if:

4   There is a world in which Foffo the cat eats lava

is true. Since the cat, Foffo, and the lava mentioned in (4) are very much like the cats and the lava found on our world, and since it does not seem contradictory to believe (although it is unheard of) that Foffo, the cat, eats lava, the moderate agnostic—unlike the strong agnostic—could accept (4) as true. But if the sentence under evaluation were:

5 Donkeys can fly,

whose translation into modal realism is:

6 There is a world in which donkeys fly,

the moderate agnostic would suspend assent with regard to (6).

Although modal agnosticism superficially resembles the modal skepticism introduced in Chapter 2, the difference between them should be clear: the former accepts the plausibility of a theory of possibility—in particular, of modal realism—but it denies assent regarding the truth of the modal assertions in ordinary language whose translation into modal realism requires the existence of situations that occur in worlds that are not our own and that are entirely dissimilar to situations that occur in our world. It should be noted that this position follows in the footsteps of the position defended in Mondadori and Morton (1976), which tries to found the meaning of modal sentences on what occurs and exists in the world in which we live; in the case of sentences that do not have such a foundation, we are better off remaining uncommitted. (We must point out, however, that Divers (2004) makes no mention of Mondadori and Morton (1976).)

In light of what has been said, we can now introduce the concept of an *admissible sentence*: for a modal agnostic, a sentence s is admissible if and only if it is possible to express assent or dissent toward s. Hence the following agnostic solution to the PP:

AGN: The sentence in natural language: "It is possible that: s" is true if and only if: (i) its equivalent "$s*$" in modal realism (or another chosen possible-worlds theory) is true; and (ii) "$s*$" is admissible.

It should be emphasized once again that AGN does not commit us to accepting modal realism, but rather leaves open the question regarding which possible-worlds theory is to be used. Ultimately, the agnostic simply accepts what is proposed by a possible-worlds theory, within the limits of admissible cases. The specific replies to the SPP, MPP, and EPP endorsed by the modal agnostic will thus depend on which theory of possible worlds the modal agnostic endorses, with a special proviso of admissibility for the EPP: we cannot know of a modal fact unless the sentences describing it are regarded as admissible by the specific version of modal agnosticism (moderate or strong) that we have endorsed. But what counts as admissible? Is admissibility an epistemic or metaphysical notion? We shall see in the next section that, as innocent as it may appear at first, the proviso of admissibility, which limits the range of sentences the modal agnostic is willing to regard as either true or false, has important philosophical consequences for the modal agnostic.

§6.4. Modal agnosticism and possible worlds

We will examine two criticisms of modal agnosticism: the first is found in Divers (2004); the second will be proposed here for the first time.

The plausibility of the modal agnostic proposal depends largely upon that of point (ii) in AGN: only if there is a sufficiently large number of admissible modal sentences will modal agnosticism be able to differentiate itself from modal skepticism, reconcile the conceptual benefits of modal realism (or another possible-worlds theory) with the refusal of its metaphysical costs, and avoid having to rely on controversial entities such as fictions. But can the agnostic supply a sufficient number of admissible sentences?

Let us take the following case as an example. Let us imagine a situation in which a doctor has just developed a new pill, which we shall call p; the pill is anticipated to defeat the HIV virus, but it has not yet been tested. It would seem plausible to assert that, nonetheless, the following sentence is either true or false:

7   The pill p can defeat the HIV virus.

The reason for which (7) is either true or false even before the test is performed is that the test is not needed to instill certain capacities in the pill, but rather to reveal the capacities the pill already has.

Nevertheless—it could be noted—the agnostic does not appear to have the resources to assent or dissent to (7), and thus to say that it is either true or false. That is, she could still express assent or denial to (7), but those expressions would offer a thin bridge with truth and falsity. Thus, since there are no situations in our world that are comparable to the one described in (7), the sentence would not be admissible. Consequently, it would be neither true nor false that the pill has certain capacities. (For a more complex but analogous example, see Divers (2004: 681).)

The moderate modal agnostic has a reply to this criticism. In fact, the problem raised does not appear to concern the metaphysics of possibility, but rather its epistemology. And—the modal agnostic could insist—admissibility is a metaphysical concept. The moderate modal agnostic, that is, could point out that it is not true that there are no situations in our world that can be compared to the one described in (7); there are, but, at the time of the test they have not yet been realized and, therefore, the doctor in the example provided is not yet aware of them. Hence, the problem is epistemological, not metaphysical: if the admissibility of a sentence depends on that which occurs and exists *in the actual world*—in its spatial and temporal totality—then in the actual world there is a test and, therefore, there is a way to judge the truth of (7). However, in the example given, the test has not yet been performed and, therefore, the doctor would not know if (7) is true or false. But, this is simply an epistemic problem.

Let us suppose we were to change our example slightly by adding the condition that the pill *p* was created with materials that do not exist in our world and that cannot be obtained from materials of our world through any process of manipulation whatsoever. At this point, (7) would arguably become non-admissible, insofar as the test we are speaking of cannot be carried out in our world. It should be noted, however, that the modified example has a much lower argumentative appeal than the previous one: in the end, we have good reason to doubt that the proposition expressed by a sentence that we cannot test is either true or false.

For the strong modal agnostic, of course, the range of scenarios that would be non-admissible is larger than for the moderate modal agnostic. It includes all situations that do not obtain in our world, including, for instance, the case of a pill that is created in our world but never tested: we cannot truthfully attribute any causal power to such a pill, according to the strong modal agnostic. Here, the modal intuition seems to be that the pill has causal powers, even if they are never tested; thus, the strong modal agnostic pays a higher price than does the moderate.

Let us now consider the second critical observation, which looks into the specific relationship between modal agnosticism and modal realism. The modal agnostic claims that it is possible to accept modal realism, even without believing that there are worlds other than our own: the evaluation of the truth of modal sentences is carried out by taking into consideration the only world that we have reason to believe there is: ours.

Since we are moving within the context of modal realism, the modal agnostic strategy must make use of counterpart theory; in particular, for evaluating admissible sentences, the modal agnostic will find the relevant counterpart in our very world (see Divers (2004)). For example, Foffo, the cat, could have had milk and cookies because, in the actual world, there is an individual who is similar to Foffo—let's say, Fufi, the cat—who has milk and cookies. In other words, according to modal agnosticism, a sentence is admissible only if, given its translation in counterpart theory, in our world there is at least one counterpart for each individual the sentence speaks of.

At this point, we might be asking ourselves whatever happened to the worlds. It would appear that the modal agnostic proposes the following interpretation of (possible) "worlds" in the language of her theory: all of the worlds that, in the theory, are obtained through the simple recombination of elements in the actual world, denote our world; all other worlds do not denote it.

There are two problems with this interpretation. The first is that it exacerbates the objection that when we speak of what Foffo could have done, we do not mean to speak of what Fufi is doing. The agnostic simply replaces the individuals (of our world) of which modal sentences seem to speak with other individuals (of the same world): yet, if we had wanted to speak of certain individuals rather than of others, we would have. We did not mean to speak of Fufi, but of Foffo.

The second problem is that modal agnosticism does not benefit from the two principal conceptual advantages of modal realism. First, since all admissible sentences concern worlds that are obtained through the simple recombination of elements of the actual world, the modal agnostic could never admit the existence of alien possibilities, as the modal realist does. Secondly, since AGN makes reference to the modal concept of admissibility, AGN does not *reduce* modalities, as modal realism aspires to do; more simply, AGN explains them.

§6.5. Conclusions

The objective shared by modal fictionalism and modal agnosticism is to borrow the philosophical strengths of modal realism (or of any other possible-worlds theory that proves more philosophically palatable than others) while avoiding its metaphysical costs. If achieved, the objective would deliver an anti-realist paradise for modal theorists. Yet what emerges from our analysis is that, for different reasons, both projects encounter numerous difficulties in realizing their objective.

Modal realism, ersatzism, modal fictionalism, and modal agnosticism exhaust the range of theories relying upon the existence of (possible) worlds in order to solve the MPP and the EPP. We shall now turn to one last theoretical option, which makes use of a new set of modal primitives in order to deal with the truth or falsity of the propositions expressed by our modal sentences: the so-called new actualism.

Study Questions

- What are the modal fictionalist's solutions to the SPP, MPP, and EPP?
- What does it mean to be a fiction, according to the modal fictionalist?
- What types of things count as fictions, according to the modal fictionalist?
- What are the main objections that can be raised against modal fictionalism?
- What is the distinguishing feature of modal agnosticism?
- What is the difference between strong and moderate modal agnosticism?
- What are the main objections that can be raised against modal agnosticism?
- What are the common denominators of modal fictionalism and modal agnosticism?

FURTHER READING

Modal fictionalism was first introduced by Rosen (1990). Some important objections to the theory, and some possible modifications of it, were presented shortly thereafter by Menzies and Pettit (1994) and Rosen himself (1995). For an **introductory discussion** of modal fictionalism, see Nolan (2007); to situate the fictionalist perspective within the broader context of fictionalism in philosophy, see Kalderon (2005) and also Eklund (2007). The debate about fictionalism has been lively and bears on several important details of the theory; among the many **discussion articles**, see: Brock (1993); Rosen (1993, 1995); Noonan (1995); Hale (1995a, 1995b); Divers (1995, 1999); Nolan and O'Leary Hawthorne (1996); Nolan (1997); Baldwin (1998); Yablo (2001); Kim (2002, 2005); Dever (2003); Brogaard (2006); Divers and Hagen (2006); Liggins (2008); Woodward (2008, 2011, 2012); Sauchelli (2013); and Armour-Garb (2015).

Modal agnosticism is introduced by Divers (2004). A discussion of the specific modal logic and modal semantics that best pair with modal agnosticism is found in Humberstone (2007). An important paper discussing some ideas that are later developed in modal agnosticism is Mondadori and Morton (1976).

7

The new modal actualism

The last place we will explore on our map of theories of modal metaphysics is the so-called "new modal actualism". Its proponents deny that our approach to modality should start from necessity and possibility: they suggest that we start instead from alternative notions—such as dispositions, essences, or other modal properties—which we already have reason to include in our inventory of reality. After an overview of the new modal actualism (§7.1.), two broad versions of the view are discussed. The first is a version resting upon essences, which in turn divides into individual essentialism and property essentialism (§7.2.). The second version rests upon dispositions, and gives rise, in particular, to the so-called dispositional theory of possibility (§7.3.).

* * * * *

§7.1. The new modal actualism

The last type of theory of possibility we will analyze covers some relatively recent proposals that are not usually regarded as part of one and the same theoretical perspective; following Vetter (2011a), we shall label this type of theory *new modal actualism*. Vetter introduces new actualism as follows:

> These new actualists, as I shall call them, do not feel the onus of providing an actualist account of possible worlds. Possible worlds, they say, may be a useful formal device in modal logic (as well as in other formal contexts),

> but they have little to do with the metaphysics of modality. Instead of accounting for possible worlds, then, these theorists seek to provide an account of modality directly; their shared aim is to identify, within the actual world, the grounds, source or truthmaker of modal truths.
>
> —Vetter (2011a: 742)

All the proposals falling under the label of new modal actualism share two important tenets. First, these theories deny that possible worlds provide a viable analysis of modal sentences. For this reason, Contessa (2010) suggests a different label for these proposals: *hardcore modal actualism*. The idea is that the soft-core modal actualists contend that the actual world is ontologically privileged with respect to all other worlds, while making use of possible worlds to make sense of modal sentences; the hard-core modal actualists, on the other hand, aim to provide an analysis of modal sentences that does away with possible worlds. The new modal actualism thus shares with the views discussed in Chapter 2 and Chapter 3 the rejection of possible worlds. It is the second tenet that distinguishes the new modal actualism from the views discussed in those early chapters. New modal actualists aim to substitute talk of possible worlds with talk of modalities that are possessed by individuals, such as essences, dispositions, or other modal properties. In so doing, and unlike the theories we discussed in the forementioned chapters, the new modal actualists offer a cognitivist analysis of modality.

By now, our reader will have noticed that different theories of possibility approach their task by privileging one or two of the three sub-problems of the problem of possibility (PP). Those, let us recall, are the semantic problem of possibility (SPP), the metaphysical problem of possibility (MPP), and the epistemic problem of possibility (EPP):

> PP: What does it take for a certain situation to be possible?
> SPP: What does it mean to say that a certain situation is possible?
> EPP: How do we come to know that which is possible?
> MPP: What sort of entity is a possible entity (of any given kind—a possible individual, property, state of affairs, or ...)?

As Vetter remarks in the passage cited earlier, the new modal actualism seems to pay special attention to the MPP. In particular, the new modal actualism calls into question the way that the MPP has been discussed for the past fifty years. It has been standard in quantified modal logic (QML) to privilege the two modalities of necessity and possibility—represented, as we have seen, by the box and the diamond symbols. Theories of possibility have been driven to solve the MPP by postulating the existence of possible worlds just insofar as they have conformed with this semantic decision.

Possible worlds suit the two modalities of necessity and possibility and are in accordance with the semantics suggested to complement both QML and counterpart theory; although, as we have seen (Chapters 4 to 6), it is very difficult to provide a sound theory of possibility in terms of possible worlds. Thus, for the past fifty years, discussion of the MPP has been largely dominated by the view that, if modal sentences do express content, they are about possible worlds—whatever these turn out to be.

The new modal actualist denies that our approach to the PP should start from necessity and possibility: instead, she suggests that we start from alternative notions—such as dispositions, essences, or other modal properties—which we already have reason to include into our inventory of reality. Thus, instead of talking about possible worlds, the new modal actualist will carry forward a theoretical analysis of possibility founded on one (or more) of these alternative notions; necessity and possibility will have to be explained in terms of those notions. While the new actualism stakes its claim to a place on the map of theories of possibility on a metaphysical point, it is nonetheless important to stress that arguments for versions of that approach can depend on broader reasons, having to do with achieving a suitable philosophical explanation of modal sentences or with semantic considerations. We shall see an example of an appeal to semantic considerations in the new essentialist's insistence on the foundational explanatory role of essences,

What is the alleged theoretical advantage of doing away with necessity and possibility as the core concepts by means of which to analyze modal sentences? Different new modal actualist views will provide different answers to this question. In general, we can point to two advantages. First, modal notions such as dispositions or essences are *specific to individuals*, thus they allow for some finer explanatory distinctions. A notable example was provided by Kit Fine: by invoking a modal theory that uses the notion of essence, we can easily explain why Socrates is intuitively *more fundamental* than the singleton (a set with exactly one element) that contains Socrates as its sole element; according to Fine, this is because it is part of the essence of Socrates's singleton to have as its sole element Socrates, while it is not part of the essence of Socrates that there is a singleton of Socrates. No such account is open to the theories based on possible worlds discussed in Chapters 4 to 6, because allegedly Socrates and its singleton exist in exactly the same worlds. Of course, supporters of theories based on possible worlds can try to devise some explanation, based for instance on impossible worlds; nonetheless, their view will pay a theoretical price to accommodate cases that Fine's theory does not have to pay, because it makes use of essences.

The second theoretical advantage of new modal actualism is to simplify the philosophical explanation of modal sentences by having it draw from the philosophical explanation of other philosophical issues that involve modalities.

For instance, dispositionalism starts from the observation that we already need dispositions in order to account for the ascription of certain properties and powers to actual entities; if this is the case, then why not try to employ dispositions to explain modal sentences involving other types of scenarios as well? Similarly, Fine's view starts by pointing out the need for essences in explaining important metaphysical differences, such as that between Socrates and its singleton; once this is acknowledged, we may then try to employ essences to shed light on other types of scenarios as well.

Our discussion of new modal actualism will concentrate on two types of theories: the new actualist essentialism (§7.2.) and dispositionalism (§7.3.). The new actualist essentialism encompasses at least two different views: one—championed by Fine and labeled *individual essentialism*—that is more attentive to the essences of necessary existents, such as Socrates and its singleton; and another—championed by Michael Jubien and Brian Ellis and labeled *property essentialism*—that views essences as types of properties. The two views share some common ground, and may perhaps be developed into a unified view in the years to come; also for this reason, we shall treat them together. Dispositionalism, for its part, moves from the widespread underlying intuition that the world is imbued with powers, capacities, and dispositions; the view was partially anticipated by Mondadori and Morton (1976) and Martin and Heil (1999); it has been more recently developed by Pruss (2002), Borghini (2003), Borghini and Williams (2008), and Contessa (2010).

Before moving on, however, we should recall another theory that some readers may associate with new modal actualism: the proposal put forward by Timothy Williamson in a series of recent writings—including those of 2005, 2007b, and 2010—according to which the concept of what is possible is subject to the concept of the counterfactual situation; in other words, the response to the PP proposed by Williamson plays upon the ability of human beings to imagine counterfactual situations: possibility is simply a concept derived from the expansion and systematization of this ability. Because of Williamson's insistence on the idea that all individuals are necessary existents, we shall discuss this view in the next and final chapter—Chapter 8.

§7.2. Individual essentialism and property essentialism

We have encountered essentialism twice already: the first time was in Chapter 4, while discussing a metaphysical variant of modalism inspired by the work of Jonathan Lowe; the second time was in Chapter 6, when considering Alvin Plantinga's *ersatzist* view, according to which worlds are states of affairs constituted by individual essences and their properties (including essential properties). These positions differ from one another both in their understanding of essences and in the roles that essences play in the explanation of modal sentences. According to Lowe, an essence is the real definition of an individual; Foffo, the cat, *is* identical to its essence. For this reason, Lowe's proposal can provide an adequate foundation for modalism. According to the modalist, truths in QML must be accepted without recurring to possible worlds, and positing the existence of essences (as real definitions) helps us found modal truths of QML on what is actually the case. On the other hand, Plantinga's essences are part and parcel of possible worlds, conceived as states of affairs. Plantinga's position seems compatible with the view that essences are real definitions of individuals and are identical to them; however, for Plantinga there are some essences that are not actual, and yet exist as constituents of possible worlds. In his view, then, essences found the truth of sentences of possible-worlds semantics, which the modalist refuses to accept as true.

We shall discuss two versions of the new actualist essentialism: individual essentialism and property essentialism. These share two commitments. For one, essences—and not necessity and possibility—are the starting point in explaining matters concerning modalities; second, essences provide a suitable metaphysical terrain to propose a novel semantics and epistemology of modality. That said, the two views differ significantly with respect to the theory of essence they support. Thus, while it is reasonable to think that a unified new actualist essentialist view may be proposed, such a view would require adjusting some important details of its ingredient theories. Let us discuss each view, in order.

Individual essentialism shares a great deal with Lowe's understanding of essences; indeed, Lowe explicitly cites Fine as a source of inspiration for his work. As we suggested in Chapter 4, Lowe's project can be regarded as part and parcel of modalism, only to the extent that essences are invoked to provide the metaphysical foundation of the language of QML. However, if essences act as the foundation for a more updated semantic theory of modal sentences that proposes itself as an alternative and *sui generis* view of modality, then what we have is no longer a modalist view. Because Fine's proposal aims to explain modality in terms of the essences of actual individuals, it fits the new actualist essentialist tag.

Fine defended individual essentialism in a number of papers, including those published in 1994 and 1995. His argument moved from a polemic against the view that essence is a modal notion:

It is my aim [...] to show that the contemporary assimilation of essence to modality is fundamentally misguided and that, as a consequence, the corresponding conception of metaphysics should be given up. It is not my view that the modal account fails to capture anything which might reasonably be called a concept of essence. My point, rather, is that the notion of essence, which is of central importance to the metaphysics of identity is not to be understood in modal terms or even to be regarded as extensionally equivalent to a modal notion.

—Fine (1994: 3)

For Fine, explaining metaphysical necessity requires, not possible worlds, but rather identity. (For an argument showing that the notion of essence cannot be captured in terms of possible—or the combination of possible *and* impossible—worlds, see Torza (2015).) The proper understanding of identity delivers a theory of essences, according to which an essence defines an entity; such a definition can then act as the explanatory foundation for metaphysically necessary truths. We have described the workings of a similar doctrine in Chapter 4, and the reader can refer back to that discussion for more detail on the underlying conception of essence. Fine's doctrine licenses the following answer to the PP:

IE: The sentence in natural language: "It is possible that: *s*" expresses the existence of an individual whose essence grounds the truth of that sentence.

It is important to clarify an aspect of Fine's view that will be discussed again in Chapter 8: according to Fine, there are different varieties of necessity depending on the domain of discourse.

[E]ach class of objects, be they concepts or individuals or entities of some other kind, will give rise to its own domain of necessary truths, the truths which flow from the nature of the objects in question. The metaphysically necessary truths can then be identified with the propositions which are true in virtue of the nature of all objects[1] whatever.

—Fine (1994: 9)

Essences found metaphysical truths; logical truths, instead, are founded upon logical necessity, which does not rely on a doctrine of essences; scientific truths rely on nomic necessity, which again has *sui generis* foundation. Thus, individual essentialism and the theory of essences that accompanies it do not provide a full-fledged account of all modal talk; more modestly, they provide an answer to the MPP for those modal claims that do indeed concern

---

[1]What Fine calls "objects" here is what we refer to in this book as "individuals", and for the sake of consistency, we stick to the terminology previously adopted in the volume.

metaphysical truths. It is in this sense that individual essentialism differs from the version of modalism that is inspired by Lowe's doctrine of essences: the latter aimed to provide a general theory of modality grounded on essences, while individual essentialism suggests a piecemeal approach.

The second version of the new actualist essentialism is *property essentialism*. According to this theory, the solution to the MPP is rooted in the essences of the properties of actual entities. The details of the theory have been articulated in two ways, which we will label, respectively, *intrinsic essentialism* and *scientific essentialism*. Most notably defended by Jubien (2007, 2009), intrinsic essentialism argues that the essences of properties depend upon the intrinsic character of properties; thus, if Foffo is a cat, Foffo is essentially an animal because it is the intrinsic character of the property *Being a cat* to entail the property *Being an animal*; this notion of intrinsic character, moreover, founds the possibility that Foffo is black. Thus, Foffo's property of *Being a cat*, in virtue of its essence, founds many (possibly infinite) metaphysical truths about Foffo.

Scientific essentialism, on the other hand, sees the roots of metaphysical necessity in the fundamental properties discovered by the natural sciences. It is necessary that salt dissolves in water because the property *Being a molecule of salt* and the property *Being a molecule of water*, in virtue of their essences, bear a certain necessary relationship to each other; such necessary relations found the laws of nature concerning water and salt. Analogously, all metaphysical truths are founded upon the relationship that properties bear to each other in virtue of the essential character of fundamental properties. Brian Ellis (2001) and Alexander Bird (2007), who develop ideas found in Shoemaker (1980), are among the most notable supporters of this view, which has received considerable attention in contemporary metaphysics of science.

Finally, we can condense the two articulations of property essentialism as follows:

PE: The sentence in natural language: "It is possible that: *s*" expresses the existence of a property whose essence grounds the truth of that sentence.

Individual essentialism and property essentialism rest on two quite different readings of the doctrine of essences. Indeed, Fine has openly criticized scientific essentialism (e.g. 2002) and he would probably not endorse intrinsic essentialism either. Still, the two versions of the new actualist essentialism do share an important aspect: they both reverse the order of metaphysical explanation, contending that, at the metaphysical level, necessity and possibility are explained in terms of what holds true of essences (whatever these turn out to be). The two versions are relatively new to the literature on the metaphysics of possibility and we may one day see a theory that conjoins individual and property essentialism, properly revised—a core new actualist essentialist view.

Our discussion of the new actual essentialism illustrates a characteristic trait of the new modal actualism *tout court*. Over the past fifty years, theories of possibility have attempted to provide a *unified* philosophical analysis of all modal sentences that is cohesive and systematic; such analyses have ultimately rested on a cohesive semantic picture, be it specified in terms of the more familiar possible-worlds semantics, counterpart theory, or a simplified modalist account. The new modal actualism proposes a different methodology, rooted in a piecemeal explanation of modal sentences. As attractive as it may seem at the semantic level, the cohesive picture also required bizarre solutions to the MPP and the EPP. The new modal actualism proposes local but more palatable solutions to the three sub-problems of possibility, with particular attention to the MPP.

§7.3. Dispositionalism

Let us now turn to dispositionalism. We are all accustomed to attributing certain abilities to people, animals, things, and events: Giovanni can ride 8m waves; Foffo, the cat, can climb up to the top of the cherry tree in a total of 5 seconds; the magnificent Etruscan statue that we saw at the museum of Tarquinia is very fragile (and thus *able* to break); the sea storm is so strong that it could swallow up the largest ship of the fleet. And we have a name for these abilities: *dispositions* (or, as we will also call them, *dispositional properties*); in attributing abilities to people, animals, things, or events, we are attributing dispositions to them. The tendency in ordinary language is to consider dispositions to be properties of the entities they are attributed to: just as we say that Giovanni lives in Volterra and measures 1.8m in height, so, too, we say that he can ride 8m waves. *To live in Volterra*, *to have a height of 1.8m*, and *to be able to ride 8m waves* are all properties of Giovanni. Dispositionalism adopts this tendency as its own, and sets out to include among the properties of the actual world certain dispositional properties; the dispositionalist theory, then, explains the meaning of modal sentences of ordinary language in terms of the dispositions of the entities of the actual world.

The idea is simple to put into words, but a bit more complex to develop. The exposition of the theory will be divided into two parts here: the first will show that, in order to explain the attribution of certain abilities to Giovanni, we must postulate the existence of dispositional properties; the second will show that dispositional properties are enough to explain the meaning of modal sentences.

§7.3.1. Dispositions

What are dispositions? First and foremost, they are properties that are attributed to the entities of the world. They are properties with a particular characteristic: they do not manifest themselves constantly, but only occasionally—and, in some cases never. It is entirely natural to say that the Etruscan statue is very fragile: and yet, the statue has never manifested its fragility—and we hope it never will. We are the ones who have attributed that property to the statue, based on our observation of other individuals composed of the same material. For this reason, dispositional properties are distinguished from *categorical* properties: the latter properties are always active, so to speak, provided they are possessed by an individual. For a more in-depth discussion, see Mumford (1998: 64–92).

This particular trait of dispositions is responsible for their aura of philosophical diffidence in empiricist circles, which is deeply rooted in the work of Hume and Ryle (1949). In simple terms, empiricists do not believe in the existence of that which does not manifest itself through a sensory experience; and dispositions are, by definition, entities that can be hidden from our senses. An empiricist would not admit that the Etruscan statue has the property of being fragile: of course, we say that it is fragile based on our observation of other individuals composed of similar material; but this is only a projection of our minds, just like when we begin a role game by declaring that the salt shaker is the wife and the sugar bowl is the jealous husband.

A more detailed description of the empiricist strategy is as follows: every sentence that contains one or more dispositional terms (terms that seem to refer to an ability or dispositional property) must be interpreted as a sentence in a conditional form (such as: "If ..., then ...") in which the dispositional terms are eliminated. The truth of the conditional sentence is then evaluated based on the relevant evidence that we have accumulated in the past.

Let us take an example. Let us once again consider the Etruscan statue in the museum in Tarquinia; we can say that:

1 The Etruscan statue at the entrance of the Etruscan museum in Tarquinia is very fragile.

An empiricist would interpret (1) in the following manner:

2 If the Etruscan statue at the entrance of the Etruscan museum in Tarquinia were subjected to even a feeble blow, then it would be shattered.

Whether what is stated in (2) is true will be established based on certain observations made regarding the behavior of individuals comparable to the Etruscan statue, both in structure and in material. Accordingly, there is no need to postulate the existence of the dispositional properties of the statue; we are the ones who project upon it certain conditions.

Nonetheless, there is an entire philosophical tradition that has made use of dispositions, beginning with Aristotle. And it is in light of this tradition that, starting with the works of Harré (1970), Mellor (1974), and Mondadori and Morton (1976), dispositions have been rehabilitated within the realm of analytic philosophy. Today, there are numerous theories that postulate the existence of dispositions, namely Martin (1994), Ellis (2001, 2002), Molnar (2003), and Heil (2003). Philosophers such as Karl Popper have made use of them as well (1990).

The chief motive behind this blossoming interest is the vast spectrum of philosophical questions that dispositions can help to answer; in fact, they have been used in the philosophy of mind, for example, to explain certain mental attitudes (such as belief or desire); in the philosophy of science, they have been used to explain what a law of nature is; in economics and rational choice theory, they have been used to explain the behavior of agents.

Yet, insofar as it denies the existence of entities that can only be partially experienced, such as dispositions, the empiricist theory has the merit of simplifying metaphysics. What, then, are the reasons to admit the existence of dispositions?

There are ultimately two reasons, and they have been brought to light in the recent debate mainly by—among others—Martin (1994), Mumford (1998), Molnar (2003), Schrenk (2009), Mumford and Anjum (2011), and Contessa (2013). The first has to do with the interpretive strategy: attempting to explain a dispositional term based on certain conditions is often a hollow exercise. Sentence (2), for instance, is not a correct interpretation of (1): it is not enough to mention a blow, feeble as it may be, in order to specify the conditions under which the statue would break. The blow's impact is a necessary condition, but it is not sufficient. If the statue were to be encased in solid cellophane, it would not shatter, even if it were flung to the ground; if certain laws that govern the interaction among the particles that compose the statue were to change while it were flung to the ground, it would not shatter.

The empiricist would respond that it would suffice to add a clause in which it is assumed that the environmental conditions (physical, chemical, atmospheric, and so on) remain the same (these are the so-called *ceteris paribus* clauses):

3 Provided that the environmental conditions remain the same, if the Etruscan statue at the entrance of the Etruscan museum in Tarquinia were subjected to an even feeble blow, then it would be shattered.

The theorist of dispositions would not be satisfied with this solution, however. Asserting that the actual conditions must remain the same does not explain which necessary conditions cause the statue to be fragile; consequently, it does not explain what fragility consists in. As noted by Carnap (1936), the sufficient conditions that allow an individual to manifest a disposition can be manifold. We might consider, for example, the conditions that cause a vineyard to be able to produce a good wine: certain temperature values, atmospheric conditions, the presence or absence of organisms in the environment ... Who could list them all? It would seem more reasonable to assert that the vineyard has the ability—that is, a certain disposition—to produce good wine.

Furthermore, there is at least one additional problem for the conditional analysis: what type of relationship subsists between the antecedent and the consequent of the conditional statement expressed in (2) and (3)? We are certainly not dealing with a simple conditional statement such as "If ... then", as (2) and (3) suggest; in fact, if this were so, it would be enough for the antecedent to not be satisfied to make the conditional statement true. A more accurate analysis must therefore be produced; in order to do so, we must use a modal notion—for example, we could affirm that: in the case in which the conditions remain the same, if the antecedent were to be true, then the consequent would follow *necessarily*. In order to explain the modal notion that has been introduced, the empiricist must turn to one of the theories previously illustrated; and, if she aspires to find a satisfying interpretation, she will no longer have to rely solely upon past observations, but also on certain merely possible situations.

Let us now turn to the second difficulty encountered by an empiricist approach to dispositions—and second reason to admit their existence. It is based on a simple observation: it would seem reasonable to assert that some dispositions, though they exist, do not manifest themselves. Let us once again consider the statue. Fortunately, it has never been broken. But let us suppose that the museum curator has secretly been tempted on multiple occasions to melt it in the old furnace nearby (with all due respect to the curator!) One night, falling prey to an unusually strong temptation, the curator starts the furnace and tosses the statue among the flames, and it slowly melts without breaking. The statue has never been broken and never will break. Nevertheless, it seems plausible to remain of the opinion that the statue was fragile: how can an empiricist justify this opinion?

There are, fundamentally, two solutions, both of which are problematic. The first, attempted by Quine (1974), is based, in simple terms, on the fact that the statue is an individual of the same type, in structure and materials, as individuals that have broken in the past; it is, therefore, legitimate to attribute fragility to the statue. However, the relevance of resemblance cannot be taken as a primitive fact: why do we assume that a resemblance in structure and materials will be accompanied by a resemblance in behavior? In order to provide an adequate answer, we must refer to a modal notion—that of natural law, for example. And so we find ourselves once again dealing with a modality.

The second, perhaps more persuasive, but certainly more bizarre, solution was proposed by David Lewis. For the modal realist, it is sufficient for a world to exist in which a statue that is particularly similar to the one at the entrance of the Etruscan museum in Tarquinia breaks in order to verify that the statue in our world could have broken.

This solution is not satisfying, however. As demonstrated first by Martin (1994) and Bird (1998), it cannot be applied to cases in which the intrinsic properties of individuals change. Let us suppose that, after years of research, a factory successfully produces a material that, when it is not subjected to the kind of blow that would be fatal for a statue like the one in the museum, is fragile; if, however, the material is subjected to such an impact, it goes from being fragile to indestructible; as soon as the force ceases, it becomes fragile once again. Suppose we make a new statue from this material. How could we appeal to possible worlds to justify our belief that the statue is fragile? In the end, given that the disposition to go from fragile to indestructible is intrinsic to the statue, no possible world exists in which it does not possess this property. It should be noted that denying that it is possible to make a statue like the one described amounts to forgoing one of the virtues of modal realism: its practically unlimited ability to represent possible scenarios. The modal realist, therefore, is able to explain the dispositions that do not manifest themselves, but not those that change.

In sum, the empiricist analysis of sentences that contain dispositional terms proves insufficient, both because it is unable to provide an adequate translation of sentences in terms of conditional sentences, and because it is unable to account for the possibility that the dispositions of an individual change through time. For these reasons, many have deemed it necessary to include dispositions among the entities of the world.

§7.3.2. The dispositional theory of possibility

The idea at the heart of dispositionalism ensues from what has just been concluded: if we have reasons that are not *ad hoc* to postulate that there are properties with a modal character, then why not attempt to explain metaphysical modality in general using these properties?

The first thing to note about the dispositionalist proposal is its methodological approach. Again, the order of metaphysical explanation is reversed with
respect to the theories we examined in Chapters 4 to 6: the metaphysical
possibility and necessity of certain situations is explained in terms of the
dispositions possessed by actual entities. While the possible-worlds theories
are prompted by a theory of the meaning of modal sentences (e.g. possible-
worlds semantics), dispositionalism is inspired by certain metaphysical
considerations: the theoretical opportunity to include dispositions among the
entities of our world. Dispositionalism therefore takes its cue from its solution
to the MPP, that is, its explanation of what a possible entity is. According to
the dispositionalist, the entities whose possibility or necessity we express are
situations; what we are left with is the following principle (see also Borghini
and Williams (2008) for a more thorough discussion of P):

P: A situation *s* is possible if and only if there is at least a disposition
    whose manifestation includes *s*.

It should be noted that P does not require dispositions to be manifested:
all that is needed is their existence. Of course, if they were to manifest
themselves, all the better. But, as we explained previously, one of the
reasons to include dispositions among the entities of the world is precisely
the fact that they could exist without manifesting themselves; therefore, we
cannot eliminate them in favor of their manifestations. The statue can break
precisely because it has the disposition to break under certain circumstances;
it does not need to manifest its disposition in order for that disposition to be
attributed to it; and we must postulate the existence of the disposition since
we do not have a better alternative for explaining that the statue can break.

Another distinctive feature of the theory is that a single disposition
can be used to account for various possibilities. For example, the fragility
of the statue would also account for the possibility of a scandal occurring at
the museum, or of the collection of contemporary Etruscan works losing one
of its most cherished pieces.

Finally, the dispositionalist draws upon the metaphysical theory P in order
to respond to the more general PP in the following manner:

D: The sentence in natural language: "It is possible that: *s*" expresses
    the existence of one or more dispositions whose manifestation
    includes the situation expressed by "*s*".

It should also be pointed out that, for the dispositionalist, the EPP remains in
the background, as is the case for many of the theories we have considered.
Typically, a division of roles is invoked. How to come to know of the existence

of the dispositions that make a given modal sentence true is a task that applies not only to the dispositionalist philosopher, but—as a matter of principle—to all other members of society as well.

§7.3.3. Two problems for dispositionalism

Although dispositionalism was formulated only recently, as we have noted, it is rooted in a long tradition of philosophical work that makes use of dispositions. For this reason alone, the view is vulnerable to certain established objections. We will focus on two here. Other critical remarks and objections have been raised recently by Vance (2014), Wang (2015), Yates (2015), and Austin (2015).

The first objection concerns the number of possibilities dispositionalism is able to account for. Among the motivations that drive the dispositionalist to begin with the MPP when considering modality is eliminating the ontological commitment to the existence of an infinity of possible worlds. The dispositionalist maintains that there is only one world, our world, in which there is an infinity of dispositions. However, this could come off as a theoretical limitation. Are dispositions enough to account for the immense variety of possibilities there appear to be in our world?

This is certainly a delicate point of the theory. Fortunately, the dispositionalist is able to account for a greater number of possibilities than there might initially appear to be. In fact, it should be noted that, if manifested, each disposition brings into being the existence of other dispositions. In other words: with the passage of time, the entities of the world manifest some of their dispositions, from which more and more dispositions arise. For example, Giovanni can ride 8m waves with great skill; if manifested, this disposition gives rise to Giovanni's additional disposition of being among the athletes who have been summoned for the next world surfing championship; if manifested, this disposition gives rise to Giovanni's additional disposition of advancing to the next round of the world surfing championship; and so on and so forth.

In light of this observation, we are able to distinguish various types of dispositions. We give the name *first-degree dispositions* to those dispositions that an entity (or a collectivity of entities) is able to manifest simply if the right environmental conditions present themselves (that is: without the entity, in turn, having to change). We give the name *second-degree dispositions* to those dispositions that an entity is able to manifest if and only if a first-degree disposition manifests itself; we give the name *n +1 degree dispositions* to those dispositions which an entity is able to manifest if and only if an *n* degree disposition manifests itself.

The dispositionalist would argue that her theory includes all dispositions of all degrees. Consequently, there would also be dispositions that are far from manifesting themselves, as they describe scenarios which could have been realized if a whole other series of occurrences had been realized, though it never was. For example, Foffo could have eaten oysters in Oristano on December 13, 2013, since there is an n degree disposition to do so that could have manifested itself if a whole series of other dispositions had manifested itself. This is how the dispositionalist is able to account for remote possibilities such as: that dinosaurs had never been extinct, that life had never developed in the universe, or that Rino Gaetano had given a concert in Bulgaria in 2003.

Yet, this result may not be enough to answer the criticism. The modal realist, in particular, would point her finger at alien possibilities: certainly the dispositionalist would be able to account for all of the possibilities that have to do with the way in which our world could have been. But why not also imagine that there are genuine possibilities that are not ways in which our world could have been?

At best, the dispositionalist could reply that our world—itself—could have developed in different ways from the start, giving rise to worlds that are a far cry from the one in which we live. Yet, she must admit that there is no way to include the existence of possibilities that our world has not been, is not, and will never be, to any degree, inclined to manifest.

The second objection to dispositionalism concerns the very nature of dispositions. (For more on this point, see Borghini (2009).) A disposition is always defined in terms of a certain situation whose manifestation it can contribute to. It would almost appear that a situation contains the seeds of something that does not exist, something that it intends to bring to completion, if certain conditions were to present themselves. Some have identified in this scenario two related problems: first, it would appear that dispositions have an intentional character, similar to our thoughts; second, it would appear that this character compels us to admit the existence of the situations that dispositions intend to bring to completion. Nevertheless, it would seem absurd to attribute intentions to the Etruscan statue; and, if the dispositionalist were to admit that situations have intentions, then she would also have to admit the existence of possible worlds.

There is at least one way to respond to this criticism. In fact, the two problems that it raises originate from a single, erroneous temptation: to define dispositions. The dispositionalist would insist that the concept of disposition is primitive: if we could define it in terms of certain situations, we would. In reality, speaking of intentional situations and characters gives us nothing more than a partial and metaphorical explanation of what a disposition is. It is metaphorical because the concept of intention would not be applied to dispositions in the same way we apply it to a mind: it is not associated with natural language, and much less with the idea of free will. It is partial because many dispositions cannot be fully understood through the description of certain situations.

At the beginning of the book, we alluded to the theory that that which is, is what it is in virtue of that which it could be. In other words: actual and possible existence are strictly and indivisibly connected. To some extent, dispositionalism is founded on this theory. It is able to naturally account for the way we seem to conceive of that which surrounds us. A chair is such as it is because it has the disposition to carry out a certain function for human beings; a gene is such as it is because it has the disposition to carry out a certain function in the development of an organism; a piece of material is gold because it has the disposition to melt at a certain temperature, or to become worn with time much more slowly compared to other materials; Giovanni was elected as chief executive not only in virtue of what he did, but also in virtue of what he can do. Certainly, things can also be seen differently. But the interpretation offered by dispositionalism is compelling. We need only admit that, among the entities of our world, there are also certain properties that, as a matter of principle, are not always observable. Considering the complex and obscure theoretical commitment of possible worlds, this does not seem to be an absurd price to pay.

Study Questions

- What are the two distinctive aspects of the new modal actualism?
- What is individual essentialism?
- What is intrinsic essentialism?
- What is scientific essentialism?
- Why do individual essentialism and property essentialism seem incompatible?
- What is a disposition?
- What characterizes an empiricist approach to dispositions?
- What is the relationship between dispositions and conditionals?
- How is possibility explained, according to the dispositionalist?
- What is the degree of a disposition and why is it relevant for the dispositionalist?

FURTHER READING

The new actualism is a recent development of the debate on modality and it is not systematically treated in introductory texts on the topic. Useful first readings are Vetter (2011a and, especially 2015).

A good starting point to appreciate the theory of essence underlying **individual essentialism** is Lowe (2012). The classic texts that outline the position are by Fine (1994, 1995); for a broader perspective, see also the papers collected in Fine (2005). Fine's view has been widely discussed in recent years and expanded into the so-called "theory of metaphysical grounding", which will be discussed in Chapter 8; for an overview of this latter theory, see Bliss and Trogdon (2014).

Intrinsic essentialism is defended in Jubien (2007, 2009). **Scientific essentialism** has a connection with the views on metaphysical necessity proposed by Putnam and Kripke in the 1970s; for a classic exposition of the theory, see Ellis and Lierse (1994) and Ellis (2001, 2002); an important contribution was given by the more recent Bird (2005, 2007); for some background texts, see especially Shoemaker (1980) and Swoyer (1982). For some early criticisms of the theory, see Bealer (1987); for a more updated discussion, see Kistler (2002), Anderson (2005), and Corry (2011).

For an introduction to the theory of **dispositions**, see the classic by Mumford (1998). Among the works that defended a form of realism regarding dispositions, see Harré (1970), Mellor (1974), Popper (1990), Martin (1994), Ellis (2001, 2002), and Molnar (2003). For the relationship between dispositions and intentionality, see Borghini (2009). A wider and ongoing debate regards the role of conditionals in defining dispositions; for some recent contributions, see: Kment (2006); Manley and Wasserman (2008, 2011); Schrenk (2009, 2010); Vetter (2011b, 2013a, 2013b, 2014); and Nolan (2015).

Among the articles that predate **dispositionalism** and anticipate some of its ideas, see Mondadori and Morton (1976), Martin and Heil (1999), and Pruss (2002). The view was first proposed in Borghini (2003), and then in Borghini and Williams (2008), Jacobs (2010), Mumford and Anjum (2011), and Vetter (2015). A wide debate has more recently ensued, which contains important developments; see especially, Contessa (2010), Vance (2014), Austin (2015), Wang (2015), and Yates (2015).

8

Necessities, necessary existents, and their bounds

While possibility and necessity are logically and, therefore, theoretically entangled with one another, certain questions pertaining to the truth of necessary statements deserve to be discussed independently of specific theories of possibility. First of all, a more thorough analysis of the different varieties of necessity (e.g. logical, natural, metaphysical, deontic, normative) is in order (§8.1.). Then, by means of the theory of *grounding*, an array of truths is analyzed, typically concerning mathematical entities, such as geometrical figures and numbers, as well as abstract entities such as sets and moral values (§8.2.). Next on the agenda is the theory of necessary existents proposed by Timothy Williamson (§8.3.). Completing the picture is a discussion of two views that challenge the boundaries of—respectively—what seems to exist and what seems to be possible: the first view is Meinongianism (§8.4.), according to which there are things that do not exist; the second view is dialetheism, according to which some sentences are such that, at the same time, they are true, *and* their negations are true, as well (§8.5.). At the very end, an epilogue reviews the main principles discussed in the volume, and draws two general conclusions regarding the philosophical analysis of modal talk (§8.6.).

*****

So far we have been especially concerned with theories of possibility and, in particular, with their metaphysical underpinnings. Necessity has been kept in the background. It is now time to confront the relevant questions concerning necessity, in order to deliver a well-rounded picture of the metaphysics of alethic modalities.

As we explained in the Introduction, alethic modalities concern both that which is possible, and that which is necessary. Possibility and necessity are most often regarded as twin concepts: to say of a certain situation that it is necessary amounts to saying that it is not possible that it does not obtain; conversely, to say of a certain situation that it is possible amounts to saying that it is not necessary that it does not obtain. Nonetheless, when elaborating a theory of modality, it is standard to discuss possible scenarios, leaving to the side the issue of how necessity claims shall be adjudicated. An underlying presumption may be that, once matters of possibility have been settled, matters of necessity will follow suit. For instance, a theorist endorsing the existence of possible worlds may work under the presumption that what is true at all possible worlds is what is necessary: thus, for that theorist necessity is spelled out in terms of the boundaries of the possible.

Nonetheless, claims of necessity deserve separate treatment. This is because there is controversy over where to draw the boundaries of possibility and, once we start delving into this issue, *sui generis* difficulties arise. The aim of this chapter is to introduce us to these difficulties and point out the primary ways of addressing them. To begin, there seem to be different varieties of necessity. We have been focusing especially on metaphysical necessity, but this modal notion is also often employed to convey the lack of an alternative from other points of view, such as: logic (logical necessity); natural science (nomic necessity); duty (deontic necessity); laws and norms (normative necessity); or simply pragmatic considerations. A proper discussion of the varieties of necessity will therefore be in order (§8.1.). Second, this book has seen several mentions of theories of essences. In recent years, much attention has been devoted to the special relationships of dependence between entities that *essentially* depend on each other; the most important outcome of this strain of research is the so-called *theory of grounding*. Essential dependence most strikingly concerns mathematical entities, such as geometrical figures and numbers, and abstract entities, such as sets; but, to the extent that essences are attributed to concrete entities— such as chairs, trees, and people—a theory of essential dependence will help clarify claims about them as well. So we shall discuss the theory of grounding (§8.2.). Next on the agenda is the theory of necessary existents— of those entities that exist out of necessity, regardless of what scenario we are entertaining. Timothy Williamson has famously defended the view that every individual exists out of necessity; we shall discuss Williamson's view and explain how it sits with respect to the theories of possibility covered in the previous chapters (§8.3.). We shall complete our treatment of necessity by discussing two views that challenge the boundaries of—respectively— what seems to exist and what seems to be possible: the first view is Meinongianism (§8.4.), according to which there are things that do not exist;

the second view is dialetheism, according to which some sentences are such that, at the same time, they are true *and* their negations are true as well (§8.5.).

§8.1. The varieties of necessity

In the previous chapters of this book, we have studied the problem of possibility and its cognate semantic, epistemic, and metaphysical problems. It is now time to consider a parallel set of questions pertaining the other classic alethic modality: necessity.

> PN: What does it take for a certain situation to be necessary?
> SPN: What does it mean to say that a certain situation is necessary?
> EPN: How do we come to know that which is necessary?
> MPN: What sort of entity is a necessary entity (of any given kind—a possible individual, property, state of affairs, or ...)?

Clearly, the answers to the problems of possibility we have considered translate also to the problems of necessity. Typically, for instance, a linguistic ersatzist will tend to provide a linguistic ersatzist account of necessity, regarding a necessity claim as true when there is a complete and consistent description of a world according to which it is true (cf. Chapter 5); or, a modal fictionalist will regard a necessity claim as true when, once we pretend that modal realism is true, the claim comes out as true (cf. Chapter 6). Yet the problems of necessity bring to light more vividly an issue that has loomed large in our discussion of modality, but that we have not directly addressed: the classification of alethic modalities into two sole notions, possibility and necessity, falls short of fulfilling the theoretical and explanatory roles that we need. Theories of modality are employed to address issues that concern different sorts of entities, from numbers to ordinary material objects to the entities postulated by the natural sciences; it would not be surprising if, depending on the sort of entity under consideration, a different modal notion would apply. Hence, it would not be surprising if it were to turn out that our notions of mathematical necessity, metaphysical necessity, and natural necessity were distinct from one another.

Kit Fine has prominently defended the importance of recognizing a variety of independent modal notions, primarily necessities:

> The earlier literature on modality, arising from the work of Quine, was characterized by an unwarranted contempt for modal notions. The subsequent

literature, arising from the work of Kripke, has been characterized by an unwarranted enthusiasm. This enthusiasm has taken two different, though related, forms. The first, which we may call "modal mania", is a matter of seeing everything as modal; every notion which is somehow associated with modal features is itself taken to be modal. The second, which we may call "modal myopia", is a matter of seeing all modality as metaphysical; every modality is somehow to be understood as a form of metaphysical modality.

—Fine (2005: 9)

We have encountered an instance of "modal mania" in our discussion of essentialism (see Chapter 7). Fine's and Lowe's proposal to regard essence as a non-modal notion stood in contrast to the modal–maniac perspective (prompted by the work of Kripke) that defines essences in terms of possible worlds. We shall return to "modal mania" in the next section, where we will consider alternative takes on the notion of grounding, some of which are modal and some non-modal. For the time being, though, we are going to concentrate on the challenge faced by the "modal myopic": Is there really a plausible way to subsume all sorts of necessity under one sort of necessity and, likewise, all sorts of possibility under one sort of possibility? Let us call *modal monism* the view that gives a positive answer to this question. The modal monist, that is, will contend that—say—metaphysical necessity and possibility suffice as basic notions, in terms of which to account for all modalities. On the other hand, let us call *modal pluralism* the view that gives a negative answer to the question. Modal Pluralism comes in various forms: from those who hold that there are only two or three fundamental modalities to more liberal positions. We shall consider some examples. For now, we should note that under the modal pluralist umbrella falls also the view recently defended by Mumford and Anjum (2011), according to which dispositional modality is a third modal notion, not fully analyzable in terms of possibility or necessity (see also Chapter 7, where this view was recalled in connection to the dispositional theory of possibility).

It is first important to point out the intuition—and ensuing theoretical *desideratum*—motivating modal monism. Start from our most unrestricted sense of possibility: according to it, all sorts of things are possible for Foffo, the cat. Foffo could grow wings and start flying; Foffo could turn into a mango juice, but for five minutes alone; and so on. Now, take all the things that Foffo could be: this fixes the range of what is *metaphysically possible* for Foffo; by doing so, we will also be making explicit what is *metaphysically necessary* of Foffo (this may include its being a cat, or its having a certain origin, or, more modestly, its bearing a certain name). The modal monist intuition is that any other notion of alethic possibility that applies to Foffo is obtainable by appropriately *restricting* the range of scenarios capturing what Foffo could be; conversely, any other notion of alethic necessity that applies to Foffo is obtainable by appropriately *enlarging* the range of features that Foffo must possess.

For instance, it is an alleged *biological necessity* that Foffo evolved from wild cats, because (as far as we know) members of the species *Felis catus* were domesticated members of the species *Felis silvestris*; such necessity can be explained in terms of the driving intuition by simply adding the requirement of being domesticated from *Felis silvestris* to the list of necessary features that metaphysically characterize Foffo. On the other hand, while it is biologically necessary that Foffo evolved from wild cats, one could play with the idea that it is allegedly not a *physical necessity* that Foffo evolved from wild cats: the physical molecules that compose Foffo now could have been arranged as they are independently of any other previous arrangement of particles (e.g. a lab scientist could have arranged them in that way). So, among the physically necessary features of Foffo we do not find evolutionary features; but we do find physical features, such as being made of electrons: arguably, Foffo must be made of electrons, according to physics. This is how we can tell that physical necessity is a restriction of metaphysical necessity: *Being made of electrons* is a physically necessary feature of Foffo, but not a metaphysically necessary feature (Foffo could be made of some particle alien to our world, for instance); at the same time, there are no metaphysically necessary features that are not *also* physically necessary features of Foffo: thus, every scenario that is physically possible for Foffo is also metaphysically possible for Foffo. An equal line of reasoning applies to the relationship between biological modalities and metaphysical modalities. Hence, the driving intuition of modal monism leads to the theoretical *desideratum* that alethic modalities can all be understood in terms of one sort of modality, typically metaphysical modalities. Ideally, alethic modalities would even be hierarchically nested: at the top we find metaphysical modalities, followed by—in order—physical, chemical, biological, ... All modalities, in the end, would be understood as varieties of the metaphysical sort. (On the relationship between natural and metaphysical necessity, see also Sidelle (2002, 1989).)

Modal monism descends from the Kripkean idea that necessity, essence, and identity are captured in terms of truth at all possible worlds. By restricting or enlarging the number of worlds that we consider possible, we can envisage different notions of necessity, essence, and identity. Ideally, there will be one unrestricted domain of worlds, encompassing all possibilities and fixing the most fundamental truths about necessity, essence, and identity. If other domains of discourse employing modalities can be hierarchically arranged, from the most general to the most specific, we can then envisage these as nested restrictions of that initial domain.

For a Quinian modal skeptic, modal monism does not even get started: the Quinian would stop the monist right at the outset, arguing that we cannot intelligibly speak of *the* necessary features of an entity, such as Foffo (cf. Chapter 2). For this reason, the Quinian and the modal monist—as noted by Fine in the foregoing passage—stand at opposite ends of a spectrum. The position defended by Fine is intermediate: it is a form of modal pluralism.

Modal pluralism can be advocated more on the basis of general methodological considerations than by moving from specific arguments. It is indeed not easy to see how a scenario could be naturally possible—that is to say, physically, biologically, or chemically possible—and yet metaphysically impossible, though perhaps some taxonomic puzzles, such as the platypus, or some strains of bacteria may suggest nice examples (cfr. respectively Eco (1999) and Ereschefski (2010)). But, the general methodological point is that metaphysics is an autonomous domain of inquiry with respect to—say—physics, chemistry, or biology. It makes little sense to try to *understand*, much less *explain*, metaphysical necessities and possibilities in terms of natural necessities and possibilities. Arguably, there is more to metaphysics than what the natural sciences contemplate, while there may be modal truths in the natural sciences that are hard to square with some metaphysical tenets, as taxonomic puzzles indicate. We are better off thinking of the domains as autonomous, though of course we can ask from time to time, when it seems opportune, whether the domains are related or what sorts of theoretical incompatibilities they might generate.

Fine's view is a form of *sparse pluralism*, because according to him there are only three distinct and autonomous sources of necessity: metaphysical, natural, and normative. All other sorts of necessity and possibility can be accounted for in terms of one of those three. We can envisage much less parsimonious forms of pluralism—forms of *abundant pluralism*—which distinguish between dozens of varieties of modality.

We shall not venture into the details of abundant pluralism. Let us nonetheless consider the modest plurality of forms of modality introduced by the distinctive nature of mathematical and logical truths. Such truths seem indeed to enjoy a special status with respect to spatio-temporal events and facts. Consider first a material entity—say Foffo, the cat—and take the following sentence expressing an alleged necessary truth regarding Foffo:

1   Necessarily: Foffo is a cat.

One way to render the content expressed by sentence (1) is to see it as suggesting that, *whatever is the case*, Foffo is a cat. The alleged truth expressed by (1), that is, explains how Foffo is connected to all worldly phenomena: Foffo can play the cat role, and only that role, in those phenomena. By contrast, consider a sentence expressing an alleged necessary mathematical truth:

2   Necessarily: 2 + 2 = 4.

This time, it seems that the content expressed by (2) is not about the necessary role that numbers play in the workings of worldly phenomena. More than informing us that "2 + 2 = 4" is true whatever the case, (2) is telling us that "2 + 2 = 4" *no matter what is the case*. The necessity of mathematical truths, that is, seems to rest on their *independence from* what is the case, rather than on a fixed role *in* what is the case (as in Foffo being a cat). Similar considerations apply to logical truths and, perhaps, truths in certain other fields (such as music theory). The distinction between the two ways of being necessarily true—having a fixed role in worldly phenomena versus being independently true—is sometimes rendered by claiming that mathematical and logical truths are *transcendent*. Regardless of the specific terminology, it is evident that there are good reasons to consider the source of necessity for mathematical and logical truth distinct from the source of necessity for natural and, perhaps, metaphysical truths. Modal monists face the challenge of finding one unitary source for such disparate modalities.

It is opportune to recall that this volume is confined to alethic modalities. Modal monism, as described here, is the contention that all alethic modalities can be subsumed under one set of modalities. As we discussed in the Introduction, there are several additional modalities besides the alethic, including the temporal, the deontic, and the epistemic. A far more radical form of monism would therefore contend that any modality—not only the alethic ones—can be subsumed under one set of modalities. Typically, such a position is suitable only for those who believe that all there is descends from a single principle or entity. For instance, if God is ultimately the source of all that there is and all truths—including all necessary and possible existents and all necessary and possible truths—then perhaps we have reason to endorse a form of radical modal monism; or, consider the position of those who believe that we cannot escape language—that all there is is but a linguistic construction: in this case, too, there may be room to endorse a radical form of modal monism.

Before bringing this section to a close, let us note one form of necessity that is at times subsumed under alethic necessity: normative necessity. Some people contend that what is good can ultimately be explained in terms of laws of nature (that is, certain natural necessities) or in terms of certain metaphysical necessities. The positions that defend either of these claims are far too numerous and articulated to be discussed here. But it is important to recall the link between alethic modalities and normative ones.

Bringing into focus necessity, rather than possibility, has allowed us to start recognizing a complex universe of modalities—a universe about which, in principle, each of the theories discussed in the previous chapters has something to say. We shall now turn to some specific notions and problems of the debate regarding necessary entities and truths, before returning at the very end of the chapter to the intersection between theories of possibility and necessity.

§8.2. Grounding

We shall now examine the so-called notion of grounding, with a particular focus on its relationship to necessity. We will start with some examples of grounding. Consider the following sentences:

3 The singleton of the singleton of Foffo exists because the singleton of Foffo exists.

4 When Luca calls out "Foffo!", Foffo comes to Luca, because Luca always called it "Foffo".

5 Foffo is a good cat because Foffo likes to play.

These sentences illustrate three varieties of grounding. Sentence (3) exemplifies ties typical of mathematical or logical entities: the hierarchy of sets that has Foffo as an initial element (Foffo, the singleton of Foffo, the singleton of the singleton of Foffo, ...) is *grounded* in Foffo. Were Foffo not to exist, the hierarchy would not exist. And yet, because Foffo exists the hierarchy exists also, and so does any specific relationship between its elements. The key feature—at least for our purposes—of the relationship between the singleton of the singleton of Foffo and the singleton of Foffo is that the relationship cannot be captured simply in terms of possible worlds. For any world where the singleton of Foffo exists, the singleton of the singleton of Foffo also exists; and *vice versa*. And yet, the singleton of Foffo is arguably *more fundamental* than the singleton of the singleton of Foffo. Such fundamentality is captured precisely by saying that the singleton of Foffo grounds the singleton of the singleton of Foffo.

Sentence (4) exemplifies the semantic ties between words and worldly phenomena or entities. There is an element of contingency in having called Foffo, the cat, "Foffo"; and yet, Luca's consistent use of the name throughout Foffo's life is *grounded* in the fact that "Foffo" names Foffo. Such a grounding tie is not causal: by naming Foffo, the cat, "Foffo" Luca did not really cause any of his subsequent speech acts (at best we may say he somehow influenced them). Moreover, semantic grounding ties cannot be captured in terms of possible worlds: for any world in which Foffo, the cat, exists, Foffo is "Foffo". Thus, the semantic tie between Foffo and its name cannot be captured in terms of either causation or possible worlds: we introduce grounding as a special notion standing for such a tie. Notice that the element of contingency regarding the fact that Foffo, the cat, was named "Foffo" by Luca is likewise unable to be explained in terms of possible worlds: if Foffo bears its name necessarily, I cannot really depict a world were Foffo is not named "Foffo", because that would be a world where Foffo is not Foffo. Such semantic contingency is indeed best explained in terms of a semantic notion of necessity, understood as distinct from the metaphysical notion of necessity that fixes the identity of Foffo.

Sentence (5) exemplifies theoretical ties between different facts. The fact that Foffo likes to play *grounds* the fact that Foffo is a good cat. The relationship between the two facts is arguably not causal: Foffo's playfulness may tend to generate fondness in those who encounter Foffo, but it seems prudent to keep separate such a psychological reaction from a judgment regarding whether Foffo is a good cat or not. The relationship between the two facts cannot be captured in terms of metaphysical necessity—not unless we grant the controversial assumption that facts about a cat's playfulness metaphysically necessitate facts about its goodness. What might instead be operative here is some other notion of necessity, probably of a normative variety.

Sentences (3), (4), and (5) indicate the range of grounding ties. The sampling by no means shows the full spectrum of grounding ties: for instance, grounding can be employed to depict the ties between laws, institutional facts, moral facts, professional standards, just to name a few. Such an impressive spectrum explains why it is disputed whether "grounding" picks out a single notion or several distinct ones. We find here an element of analogy with the discussion of the varieties of alethic necessity: on one hand it would be desirable to subsume a number of case studies under a single notion; on the other, once we try to do that, we incur the risk of leaving key subtleties out of our analysis, so that we end up with an unsatisfactory result. The examples set by (3), (4), and (5) demonstrate the need for an account of grounding that is nuanced enough to capture the different ties conveyed in each sentence. If a single notion of grounding is to pick out ties between mathematical entities, semantic links, and theoretical claims about cats' goodness, it must possess an amazing flexibility.

It may not have escaped notice that I referred to grounding *ties*, and not to grounding relations. This is because it is important to remain neutral, at this preliminary stage, regarding the sort of entity involved in grounding. Both early logical analysis of grounding, such as Fine (2001), as well as notable, more recent developments, such as Correia (2010) and Fine (2012), treat grounding as a sentential connective, leaving somewhat open its metaphysical details. This seems a sensible move, especially if we aim to have a notion that is able to pick out a diverse range of scenarios. Thus, it may turn out that, on some occasions grounding concerns facts, on others, propositions, on others still, material objects or other individual entities; and yet, despite such metaphysical differences, the same notion is at play.

Our brief foray into grounding is meant especially to emphasize the alleged inadequacy of alethic necessity—in particular when understood as truth in all possible worlds—for capturing absolute or universal ties. Semantic ties, the nexuses between sets within a hierarchy, and the links between theoretical facts cannot be readily accommodated in possible-worlds semantics. For this reason, grounding may be regarded as a topic that reveals the shortcomings of modal monism.

That said, further inspection may reveal that the cases assembled under the label of grounding do not involve modal notions after all, or at least not alethic modalities. Scenarios displaying grounding would likely then fall into more than one non-modal category. For instance, some examples of grounding may concern identity, which may be argued to be a non-modal notion; other examples may involve normative necessity, which—as we saw in the previous section—may well be autonomous with respect to alethic necessity; other instances may involve semantic necessity, which again is arguably independent of the alethic; and so on. So, modal monism may be salvaged, if we are able to show that instances of grounding do not call upon alethic modalities.

One important lesson for our discussion of alethic modalities can be learned from considering the problem of grounding. At their most ambitious, some modal monists (including prominent ones, such as Lewis) hoped to explain even the problem of grounding itself in terms of alethic modalities; those among them who were possible-worlds theorists and modal realists hoped to reduce *all* modal talk to the non-modal existence of certain entities in certain worlds. The past few years have cast severe doubts on the aspirations of modal monists. More than fifty years have gone by since the formulation of possible-worlds semantics; the semantics has proved very useful in a number of cases; yet it seems far from providing sufficient conceptual resources to analyze even the primary cases of grounding. If we add that the reductivist efforts of modal realism also face formidable challenges, as we saw in Chapter 4, we can conclude that it is important to take a piecemeal approach to modal talk.

§8.3. Necessary existents

Next on our agenda is a discussion of so-called necessary existents. This is a longstanding issue that occupied philosophers such as Fine and Plantinga in the 1980s (see Fine's "Postscript" to Prior and Fine (1977), Plantinga (1983, 1985), and Fine (1985)). In more recent years, Linsky and Zalta (1994, 1996) and most notably Williamson revived the debate. Here we shall focus especially on Williamson's work; in the **Further Reading** section, the reader will find additional bibliographical information regarding classic texts on this topic, direct replies to Williamson, and recent contributions to the debate.

In 2013, Williamson published an influential study on the logic and metaphysics of modality titled *Modal Logic as Metaphysics*. The volume developed and refined some of the central ideas Williamson had presented in previous works, including those of 1990, 1998, 2000, 2002, and 2007b. A controversial idea emerging from Williamson's writings is that the domain of individuals inhabiting different possible worlds is fixed: any individual that inhabits a world is a *necessary existent*, that is, it exists in all worlds. Foffo, the cat, for instance, is—according to Williamson—a necessary existent: that is, Foffo cannot fail to exist, despite any modal intuition to the contrary we may have.

Williamson's argument for the theoretical need to posit necessary existents is strikingly simple and flies in the face of our most basic modal intuitions, as he himself notes:

> It seems obvious that I could have failed to exist. My parents could easily never have met, in which case I should never have been conceived and born. The like applies to everyone. More generally, it seems plausible that whatever exists in space and time could have failed to exist. Events could have taken an utterly different course. Our existence, like most other aspects of our lives, appears frighteningly contingent. It is therefore surprising that there is a proof of my necessary existence, a proof that generalizes to everything whatsoever.
>
> —Williamson (2002: 233)

The alleged "proof" comes in five sentences.

(A) Necessarily, if I do not exist then the proposition that I do not exist is true.

(B) Necessarily, if the proposition that I do not exist is true then the proposition that I do not exist exists.

(C) Necessarily, if the proposition that I do not exist exists then I exist.

(D) Hence, necessarily, if I do not exist then I exist.

(E) Necessarily, I exist.

Let us briefly assess the argument, illustrating some ways in which its controversial assumptions can be resisted (for further discussion, see the **Further Reading** section). Sentence (A) establishes a necessary link between a negative scenario (*viz.* that I do not exist) and the existence of a proposition. Notoriously, philosophers have sought to deny that negative sentences, such as "I do not exist", require the existence of negative states of affairs or facts in order to be regarded as true. If I do not exist, then I am featured in no states of affairs or facts, and there is therefore no proposition featuring me. Thus, a first way to resist the argument is to deny that my nonexistence necessitates the existence of a *proposition* regarding me because there is no proposition whatsoever where I am featured. That is, let us concede that my nonexistence necessitates the existence of a proposition; that proposition, nonetheless, is about entities other than me (one could maintain, for instance, that it is about a total fact, where I am not featured). Whether all negative sentences can be explained-away in terms of non-negative states of affairs or facts is, however, controversial. Thus, sentence (A) has at the very least some plausibility.

Sentence (B) lays out a thesis about the metaphysics of propositions: true propositions must exist. A way to resist such a thesis is to argue that not all true propositions must exist: some of them can be *metaphysically reduced* to other propositions. In the case in question, the proposition that I do not exist can be metaphysically reduced—say—to a proposition about the totality of existents, in which I do not feature. But such a move would require considerable work on the metaphysics of propositions.

Sentence (C) exemplifies the thesis that every individual featured in a true proposition must exist. Strategies to resist this claim have been endorsed in contemporary metaphysics by conventionalists, for example, who wish to maintain that propositions about things such as tables and chairs are true, while denying that there are tables and chairs (see Hirsh (1997, 2009) and Varzi (2002) for some examples).

Sentence (D) follows from sentences (A) through (C), and cannot be questioned unless we give up basic inference rules of logic. The same goes for sentence (E), even though it employs the more controversial logical principle that, from a contradiction, anything follows; dialetheists, whom we shall discuss in section §8.5., reject this principle and would therefore deny that, because sentence (D) states a contradiction, sentence (E) follows.

Williamson's argument, whether sound or not, puts in evidence a major issue in modality, especially in connection with possible-worlds semantics: our conception of propositions is deeply entrenched with the analytic results of our modal theory. This is a vivid example of the interplay between logic, semantics, and metaphysics: we end up with a metaphysical claim concerning necessary existents based on some theses concerning propositions and truth. Specifically, if we endorse the three main theses displayed in sentences (A) through (C) of Williamson's argument, then we end up with a fixed domain of entities for all possible worlds. While Williamson goes on to construct a full-fledged modal theory based on this result, other authors would regard the result as a major problem because it overrules—rather than accommodating—modal intuitions as basic as that I might not have existed. (For a comparison of Williamson's and Lewis's modal theories that is particularly relevant to the ends of this volume, see Divers (2014d).)

§8.4. Meinongianism

Are there entities that do not exist? This question, which is about the boundaries of reality, probes our ideas regarding the limits of possibility, and therefore also regarding what is *necessarily* the case. It is thus important to address this question in the context of a discussion of necessity and its boundaries. So-called Meinongians answer the question positively. They have enjoyed a poor reputation in logic and metaphysics; but, building on the works of authors such as Parsons (1979, 1980) and Routley (1980), today, they are having a comeback (see Nelson (2012) and Priest (2005) for an overview). In this section, we shall focus especially on how Meinongianism is entangled with the debates on the metaphysics of possibility and necessity.

Meinongianism—which owes its name to Alexius Meinong, an Austrian philosopher and psychologist renowned for his theory of non-existent entities (see Marek (2013))—is motivated by some simple and commonplace intuitions. Consider Foffo, the cat. Thus far, we have presumed that Foffo actually does exist; but, we must confess, Foffo does not actually exist: Foffo is a creature of our imagination. Now, in a certain sense, even though Foffo, the cat, is not of this world, it still makes sense to maintain that Foffo *does* exist; after all, we have been talking about this cat for an entire volume, illustrating complex theories of modality thanks to it. Assuming that at least some content was passed along through our illustrations involving Foffo, such illustrations must have been about *something*. Foffo is no different than the entities we encounter in novels, stories, movies, or in our imagination, and that do not actually exist: to the extent that we interact (even only at the level of imagination) with them, we may want to concede that they exist. That is what the Meinongian does: according to the Meinongian, Foffo, along with all other intentional entities, does exist.

Admitting the existence of non-actually existent entities stretches the bounds of possibility. David Lewis's modal realism seems to give in to a form of Meinongianism and was indeed accused of being Meinongian shortly after being presented (see Linsky (1991)). If to be a Meinongian means to accept the existence of non-actual entities, then Lewis certainly fits the description. For Lewis, there are infinite worlds and "actuality" is an indexical expression: there is no world such that it is true, in that world, that all existing entities are actual. Meinongianism—understood as the thesis that there are entities that are non-actual—therefore turns out to be necessarily true in modal realism. The affinity between Lewisian modal realism and Meinongianism also helps to explain why modal realism is theoretically more powerful than rival theories of possibility on the market: in a sense, Lewis's theory makes room for the existence of an infinity of non-existents, thereby expanding the bounds of possibility.

Nonetheless, contemporary Meinongians would regard Lewis's modal realism as a spooky version of Meinongianism. This is because Lewis's worlds are complete and consistent: for any property and any individual inhabiting any world, it is determinate whether that individual has that property at that world. But, our starting intuition was much simpler than that. It seemed to require a much more naïve principle, which is taken to characterize so-called naïve Meinongianism:

Naïve Principle: For any condition on entities, there is a unique entity satisfying exactly that condition.

The condition, here, stands for any assortment of properties; the requirement of uniqueness is to ensure that the same specific entity is picked out on any occasion—for example, that when we speak of Foffo we speak always of the same entity.

Naïve Meinongianism faces several problems, some of which nicely illustrate the link between Meinongianism and theories of alethic modality. Two of these problems deal precisely with completeness and consistency, the two requirements that we find in modal realism (as well as in all other theories of possibility we have surveyed so far) but that are not mentioned in the Naïve Principle. First, consider incompleteness. According to the Naïve Principle, there is exactly one entity that exemplifies the condition *Being Foffo the cat*. That entity has only one property—*Being Foffo the cat*; anything else about that entity is indeterminate: it is neither true nor false that it is white, neither true nor false that it ate fish and potatoes, and so on. Most philosophers dislike incomplete entities because they violate the so-called principle of bivalence, according to which any sentence (expressing a proposition) is either true or false. According to the view under discussion, there are infinite sentences about the entity that exemplifies the condition *Being Foffo the cat* that are neither true nor false. Is it really possible that entities violating bivalence exist?

The Naïve Principle violates not only bivalence, but also the principle of non-contradiction (contradictory sentences cannot both be true at the same time). According to the Naïve Principle, there is exactly one entity that exemplifies the condition *Being Foffo the cat and Being better than any cat*. But, if so, then this entity is better than itself (since it's better than *any* cat). Not only that, but according to the Naïve Principle there is also exactly one entity that exemplifies the condition *Being Foffo the cat and Being self-distinct.* This entity, then, *is and is not* identical to Foffo, the cat. Is it really possible that entities violating consistency exist?

The third problem (already raised by Russell in response to Meinong; see Nelson (2012)) is that, according to Naïve Meinongianism, there is no restriction on the conditions on entities. We may require as a condition that the entity exist. So, according to the Naïve Principle, there is exactly one entity that exemplifies the condition *Being Foffo the cat and existing*. We started from the intuition that there is a certain Foffo the cat that we have been talking about and that does not exist, and Naïve Meinongianism has forced us to admit its existence. This is striking and seems just plain wrong.

Meinongians have come up with different strategies to cope with the difficulties of the Naïve Principle. One such strategy, famously defended by Parsons (1980), distinguishes between *nuclear* and *extra-nuclear* properties: the nuclear properties alone fix the identity (or, as some people say, the "nature") of an entity, while the extra-nuclear do not. The alleged violations of bivalence and non-contradiction concern extra-nuclear properties and thus are not really violations of bivalence and non-contradiction, after all; as for existence, it is regarded as an extra-nuclear property, so it cannot be added to the condition regarding Foffo, the cat. A second strategy (see Zalta (1988) and (1983)) distinguishes between *exemplifying* and *encoding* a property: exemplification is the familiar relation between entities and properties, while encoding is the special relation at work in the case of conditions on intentional entities, such as Foffo, the cat. According to this strategy, the Naïve Principle specifies only encoded properties; but, we shall not worry if encoded properties violate bivalence or contradiction, or if they violate intuitions about existence: since it is not exemplification to be at stake, no real theoretical problem is posed. A third strategy (see Priest (2005) and Berto (2013a) and (2012)) goes in the direction of Lewisian Meinongianism and is known as Modal Meinongianism; the strategy consists in modifying the Naïve Principle, adding the proviso that any condition is fulfilled *at some world*:

Modal Meinongian Principle: For any condition on entities, there is a
   unique entity satisfying exactly that condition at some world.

The Modal Meinongian Principle may superficially bear some resemblance to Lewis's principle of recombination (see Chapter 4), but it differs in key respects. Unlike Lewis's principle of recombination, the Modal Meinongian Principle has no requirement for completeness or consistency of worlds: it is as liberal as a principle can be with respect to conditions on entities.

While the debate on Meinongianism is traditionally kept separate from the debate on alethic modalities, the remarks offered in this section should suffice to show how closely interconnected the two debates are.

§8.5. Impossible worlds

Since the contributions of Morgan (1973) and Hintikka (1975), on one hand, and Yagisawa (1988) and Mortensen (1989), on the other, which respectively address logical and metaphysical issues regarding the impossible, a distinctive stream of the discussion on modality has focused on impossibilities and, especially, impossible worlds. Not only do these topics have theoretical relevance *per se*; impossible worlds have been particularly handy for explaining particular phenomena, such as the behavior of agents who hold inconsistent beliefs, or the truth conditions of systems of propositions (e.g. legal systems) that contain contradictory claims (see Lewis (1986) and Berto (2013a)). In this section we shall introduce the key ideas and issues related to impossibilities and impossible worlds.

The temptation to speak of impossible scenarios and impossible worlds is pervasive; two lines of thought will help us appreciate this temptation. The first combines theories of possible worlds with the basic sense of possibility. In possible-worlds semantics, we are provided with a list of possible worlds; we typically also assume that the list contains a certain number of worlds, say N. Here, the sense of possibility pipes up: if N is the number of possible worlds, surely we can think otherwise; there seems nothing contradictory in thinking that this number could have been different. But we cannot represent this possibility by means of a possible world, because we have agreed that N is the number of possible worlds on the list and we are now considering *additional worlds* to those on the list. Hence, we need to posit some impossible worlds in order to account for the modal intuition that the number of possible worlds could have been different. This line of reasoning is especially worrisome when applied to realist theories of possible worlds and it was indeed initially entertained as a *reductio ad absurdum* of Lewis's modal realism (see Skyrms (1976) and Naylor (1976)). Soon after, however, bolder theoretical proposals were put forward which countenanced the existence of impossible worlds and exploited their theoretical potential (see especially the articles in Priest (1997)).

The second line of thought builds upon intuitions concerning impossible scenarios and does not require the idea of possible worlds. In particular, it rests on the hypothesis that some scenarios are not only counterfactuals (against what actually is the case), but counterpossibles (against what possibly is the case). If a certain contradictory claim were true, then what? For instance, if Foffo were at the same time a cat *and* a dog, could Foffo eat fish and potatoes? Counterpossibles enter the stage more frequently than it might at first appear: we find them in constitutions and other crucial pieces of legislation, we spot them in scientific papers, novels, movies, and—we must confess—philosophy books. Since they have an impossible antecedent, which turns out to be always false according to classical logic, counterpossibles risk being trivially true; additionally, they cannot be analyzed in terms of a possible-worlds semantics, because they involve scenarios that are not caught by possible worlds. Yet, it would be desirable to be able to discriminate between counterpossibles, sorting out those that rely upon intuitively sound reasoning and those that do not. Positing the existence of impossible worlds can help us do exactly that. See Brogaard and Salerno (2008) and Beall and van Fraassen (2003) for some recent treatments of counterpossibles.

If we have good, intuitive reasons to consider admitting impossible scenarios and impossible worlds to our modal theories, we also have some good, intuitive reasons not to do so. As Berto (2013a) reminds us, the empiricist tradition maintained that we cannot entertain thoughts on the impossible and that, while the practically impossible may perhaps be conceived (e.g. the thought that Foffo can fly to the moon today), the theoretically impossible is inconceivable (e.g. the thought that Foffo has round–square eyes). Lewis (1986), for instance, rejects the idea that round-squares are conceivable as well as the idea that there are impossible worlds (see also Vacek (2013)). Here is a well-known passage in which Lewis (1986) illustrates why a realist about worlds cannot accommodate the existence of impossible worlds:

> suppose travellers told of a place in this world—a marvellous [sic] mountain, far away in the bush—where contradictions are true. [...] to tell the alleged truth about the marvellously contradictory things that happen on the mountain is no different from contradicting yourself. But there is no subject matter, however marvellous, about which you can tell the truth by contradicting yourself. Therefore there is no mountain where contradictions are true. An impossible world where contradictions are true would be no better. The alleged truth about its contradictory goings-on would itself be contradictory. (7, fn. 3)

Since the end of the 1990s, a variety of strategies have been developed to fix the language in which we talk about impossible worlds and, thus, overcome objections, such as the one Lewis raises. The strategies exploit the longstanding discussion of how to deal with apparent cases of contradictions, also known as dialetheias. A *dialetheia* is a sentence such that both it and its negation are true. Some apparent dialetheias, such as those arising in connection with the so-called Liar's Paradox, have been well-known for millennia. *Dialetheism* is the view that accepts that there are dialetheias, and tries to accommodate them within logic and language (see Priest and Berto (2013) for an introductory discussion). The logic and language developed to deal with dialetheism can be employed to provide a theory of impossible worlds.

We now seem to have sufficient logical and conceptual resources to deal with impossible scenarios and impossible worlds. Impossible scenarios and worlds have the potential to considerably enrich the metaphysical apparatuses of the theories of possibility discussed in the previous chapters. Yet, how innocent are impossible worlds from a metaphysical point of view? What is the theoretical cost of accepting them into one's metaphysics? These questions remain to be fully addressed. We must ascertain, on a case-by-case basis, whether and how each view (e.g. modal realism, modal fictionalism, linguistic ersatzism, and so on) can integrate impossible worlds into its theoretical framework. For some recent contributions on this issue, see especially Yagisawa (2010) and Jago (2014).

Study Questions

- What is the modal myopia that, according to Fine, characterizes the contemporary debate about modalities?
- What is modal monism?
- What are some chief motivations for modal monism?
- What is modal pluralism?
- What are some chief motivations for modal pluralism?
- What is the distinction between worldly and transcendental necessary truths?
- Put forward at least three different and original illustrations of grounding.
- What is the relationship between grounding and alethic necessity?
- What is the relationship between grounding and non-alethic necessity?
- What is a necessary existent?
- What is Williamson's alleged proof of necessary existence?
- What reasons can be advanced to resist Williamson's proof?
- What is Meinongianism?
- What is naïve Meinongianism?
- What problems does naïve Meinongianism face?
- What strategies can be used to address the problems of naïve Meinongianism?
- What are the two lines of reasoning that invite us to postulate impossible worlds?
- What reasons do we have for not endorsing impossible worlds?
- What is a dialetheia?

FURTHER READING

Standard readings on the **varieties of necessity** are Sidelle (1989, 2002), as well as Fine (2005). An essential reading, important for appreciating the contemporary debate, is Kripke (1980); other classic readings include Farrell (1981), Hirsch (1986), Plantinga (1992), Peacocke (1997), and Shoemaker (1998). For some recent work on metaphysical necessity, see Drewery (2005), Williamson (2005), Bealer (2006), the essays in Hale and Hoffman (2010), Cameron (2010), Nolan (2011), and Correia (2012).

Bliss and Trogdon (2014) and Raven (2015) provide an exhaustive and short overview of **metaphysical grounding**, with an updated bibliography; other starting points can be Clark and Liggins (2012) and Trogdon (2013). An opinionated introductory reading on the topic is Fine (2012). In general, the essays contained in Correia and Schnieder (2012) can be a good starting point to delve deeper into the issue of metaphysical grounding.   ▶

The argument for **necessary existents** is most concisely presented in Williamson (2002). It builds upon previous work of Williamson—in particular his works of 1990, 1998, and 2000—and the works of Linsky and Zalta (1994, 1996). To appreciate the importance of the debate on necessary existents, see Prior and Fine (1977: "Postscript"), Plantinga (1983), and Fine (1985). For recent discussion of Williamson's argument, see Rumfitt (2003), Wiggins (2003), Morato (2006), Sider (2009), Stalnaker (2010), Efird (2010), Speaks (2012), Rasmussen (2013), and Pruss and Rasmussen (2015).

A concise, and yet fairly exhaustive, initial reading on **Meinongianism** is Nelson (2012). For some classic readings, the reader may want to start from Meinong's classic essay (1904) and then move to contemporary classics, including Parsons (1979, 1980), Zalta (1983, 1988), and Priest (2005). The contemporary debate on Meinongianism is lively, and often entangled with issues concerning alethic modalities. For a recent study, see Berto (2012).

The main metaphysical issues surrounding **impossible worlds** are concisely and clearly discussed in Berto (2013a) and Nolan (2013); for an introductory reading on dialetheism, see Priest and Berto (2013); for the logical issues regarding impossible worlds, see Beall and van Fraassen (2003), Priest (2005), and Goble (2006). Classic readings on impossible worlds include Hintikka (1975), Yagisawa (1988), and the essays contained in Priest (1997). For some recent and thorough studies, see Yagisawa (2010) and Jago (2014). Other recent discussion pieces include McDaniel (2004), Brogaard and Salerno (2008), Berto (2010, 2014), Jago (2013a, 2013b), and Krakauer (2013).

Epilogue: Modal talk and the analyses of modality

We have now reached the conclusion of our analysis of the eight theories of possibility that have emerged from the last fifty years of debate in analytic metaphysics, and that now characterize this branch of philosophy. Along the way, we encountered nineteen solutions to the PP, which are worth recalling; let us list them:

EXP: The sentence in natural language: "It is possible that: *s*" expresses a certain (conventionally codified) sentiment, on behalf of the person who asserts it, toward *s*.

M: The sentence in natural language: "It is possible that: *s*" expresses the existence of a modal fact of our world: the fact that it is possible that *s*.

MR*:   The sentence of natural language: "It is possible that: *s*" expresses the existence of worlds W_1, ..., W_n in which *s**.

ME: Only one world exists, the actual world, of which possible worlds are surrogates.

LE: The sentence in natural language: "It is possible that: *s*" expresses a maximal and consistent description, given in a certain language, according to which: *s*.

C: A state of affairs is possible if and only if it is obtained by means of a legitimate recombination of constituents of at least one actual state of affairs.

PEP: The sentence in natural language: "It is possible that: *s*" expresses a proposition *p*, and is true if and only if there is a maximal and consistent set of (complete and non-contradictory) propositions at which *p* is true.

PES: The sentence in natural language: "It is possible that: *s*" expresses a state of affairs *S*, and is true if and only if there is a maximal and consistent set of states of affairs at which *S* is true.

PEI: The sentence in natural language: "It is possible that: *s*" expresses an interpreted figure such that: the figure represents *s*; and, according to the interpretation, the figure constitutes a maximal and consistent representation.

AE: The sentence in natural language: "It is possible that: s" expresses an atomic entity $S*$ that is abstract and maximal, and of which there is at least one interpretation according to which $S*$ counts as a representation of the scenario expressed by the sentence "s".

F: The sentence in natural language: "It is possible that: s" is true if and only if its orthodox possible-worlds analysis is true.

RF: The sentence in natural language: "It is possible that: s" is true if and only if, according to the story told in Lewis (1986), "$s*$" is true.

AF: The sentence in natural language: "It is possible that: s" is true if and only if, according to the story told in Lewis (1986), there is a collection of stories such that, according to at least one of them, s's equivalent "$s*$" is true.

F*:   The sentence in natural language: "It is possible that: s" is true if and only if, were the orthodox possible-worlds analysis to be true, then the sentence would also be true.

F**:   If we wish to judge in the most philosophically plausible way the truth of the sentence in natural language: "It is possible that: s" then we *must* assert that said sentence is true if and only if its orthodox possible-worlds analysis is true.

AGN: The sentence in natural language: "It is possible that: s" is true if and only if: (i) its equivalent "$s*$" in modal realism (or another chosen possible-worlds theory) is true; and (ii) "$s*$" is admissible.

IE: The sentence in natural language: "It is possible that: s" expresses the existence of an individual whose essence grounds the truth of that sentence.

PE: The sentence in natural language: "It is possible that: s" expresses the existence of a property whose essence grounds the truth of that sentence.

D: The sentence in natural language: "It is possible that: s" expresses the existence of one or more dispositions whose manifestation includes the situation expressed by "s".

To this already striking list, we should add the two skeptical options seen in Chapter 2. Additionally, we should recall that, for each of the nineteen solutions, we can ask how it would be affected by the varieties of necessity and possibly enriched with Meinongianism or a theory of impossible worlds.

Two main lessons can be drawn from our lengthy discussion. The first concerns the metaphysical status of modality: even if we endorse the most powerful and radical theory—that is, modal realism—we are unable to fully reduce modal entities to non-modal ones. Regardless of any reductive aspirations, therefore, and given our best metaphysical theories, *some modal entities are nonetheless here to stay.*

The second lesson is that *a piecemeal approach to the metaphysical (and, arguably, philosophical) analysis of modality has the best payoffs.* We need not pick one view to fit all modal talk. We can choose, depending on the sort of modal scenario in need of analysis. For instance, we can endorse dispositionalism when it comes to natural necessity; a particular version of fictionalism when it comes to mathematical necessity; linguistic ersatzism when it comes to metaphysical necessity; and expressivism when it comes to normative necessity. In particular, we should not think of possible-worlds semantics as the only framework within which to discuss modality: we should use such semantics where opportune, and drop it where some other option seems to work better. This lesson is particularly in keeping with modal pluralism, according to which different varieties of possibility and necessity are autonomous.

The lessons in brief: no metaphysical theory of modality is reductive and none is exhaustive. As for which theory should be chosen, if it is true that all that which is is what it is partly in virtue of that which it could be, then we can only hope that the theoretical possibilities we have offered in this book are sufficiently many and diverse for a fruitful choice.

The pleasure of choosing, o reader, is now yours.

Bibliography

Adams, R. M. (1974), "Theories of Actuality". *Noûs* 8: 211–31.

Anderson, E. (2005), "How General is Generalized Scientific Essentialism?" *Synthese* 144: 37–39.

Armour-Garb, B. (2015), "New Problems for Modal Fictionalism". *Philosophical Studies* 172: 1201–19.

Armstrong, D. M. (2004), "Theorie Combinatoire Revue et Corrigée." In J. M. Monnoyer (ed.), *La Structure du Mond: Objets, Propriétés, États et Choses*. Paris: Vrin: 185–98.

Armstrong, D. M. (1997), *A World of States of Affairs*. Cambridge: Cambridge University Press.

Armstrong, D. M. (1989), *A Combinatorial Theory of Possibility*. Cambridge: Cambridge University Press.

Armstrong, D. M. (1986), "The Nature of Possibility". *Canadian Journal of Philosophy* 16: 575–94.

Armstrong, D. M. (1978), *Nominalism and Realism* (2 vol.). Cambridge: Cambridge University Press.

Austin, C. J. (2015), "The Truthmaking Argument Against Dispositionalism." *Ratio* 28: 271–85.

Ayer, A. (1936), *Language, Truth, and Logic*. London: Victor Gollancz Ltd.

Baldwin, T. (1998), "Modal Fictionalism and the Imagination". *Analysis* 58: 72–5.

Ballarin, R. (2010), "Modern Origins of Modal Logic". In E. N. Zalta (ed.), *The Stanford Encyclopedia of Philosophy* (Winter 2014). Available from http://plato. stanford.edu/archives/win2014/entries/logic-modal-origins/

Barrett, R. B. and R. F. Gibson (1990), *Perspectives on Quine*. Cambridge: Basil Blackwell.

Bealer, G. (2006), "A Definition of Necessity". *Philosophical Perspectives* 20: 17–39.

Bealer, G. (1987), "The Philosophical Limits of Scientific Essentialism". *Philosophical Perspectives* 1: 289–365.

Beall, J. C. and B. Van Fraassen (2003), *Possibilities and Paradox. An Introduction to Modal and Many-Valued Logic*. Oxford: Oxford University Press.

Beebee, H. and N. Sabbarton-Leary (eds) (2010), *The Semantics and Metaphysics of Natural Kinds*. New York: Routledge.

Bennett, J. (1994), "Descartes's Theory of Modality". *The Philosophical Review* 103: 639–67.

Berto, F. (2014), "On Conceiving the Inconsistent". *Proceedings of the Aristotelian Society* 114: 113–21.

Berto, F. (2013a), "Impossible Worlds". In E. N. Zalta (ed.), *The Stanford Encyclopedia of Philosophy* (Winter 2013). Available from http://plato.stanford. edu/archives/win2013/entries/impossible-worlds/

Berto, F. (2013b), "Modal Meinongianism and Actuality". *Humana.Mente* 25: 155–76.

Berto, F. (2012), *Existence as a Real Property. The Ontology of Meinongianism.* Dordrecht: Synthèse Library, Springer.

Berto, F. (2010), "Impossible Worlds and Propositions: Against the Parity Thesis". *The Philosophical Quarterly* 60: 471–86.

Berto, F. (2007), *How to Sell a Contradiction: The Logic and Metaphysics of Inconsistency.* London: College Publications.

Bird, A. (2009), "Essences and Natural Kinds". In R. Le Poidevin (ed.), *The Routledge Companion to Metaphysics.* New York: Routledge: 497–506.

Bird, A. (2007), *Nature"s Metaphysics: Laws and Properties.* Oxford: Oxford University Press.

Bird, A. (2005), "Laws and Essences." *Ratio* 18: 437–61.

Bird, A. (1998), "Dispositions and Antidotes". *Philosophical Quarterly* 48: 227–34.

Bird, A. and E. Tobin (2015), "Natural Kinds". In E. Zalta (ed.), *The Stanford Encyclopedia of Philosophy* (Spring 2015). Available from http://plato.stanford. edu/archives/spr2015/entries/natural-kinds/

Blackburn, S. (1998), *Ruling Passions.* Oxford: Clarendon Press.

Blackburn, S. (1993), *Essays in Quasi-Realism.* New York: Oxford University Press.

Blackburn, S. (1984), *Spreading the Word.* New York: Oxford University Press.

Blackburn, S. (1971), "Moral Realism". In J. Casey (ed.), *Morality and Moral Reasoning.* London: Methuen: 101–24.

Bliss, R. and K. Trogdon (2014), "Metaphysical Grounding". In E. Zalta (ed.), *The Stanford Encyclopedia of Philosophy* (Winter 2014). Available from http://plato. stanford.edu/archives/win2014/entries/grounding/

Blumenfeld, D. (1973), "Leibniz's Theory of Striving Possibles". *Studia Leibnitiana* 5: 163–77.

Bobzien, S. (2014), "Ancient Logic". In E. N. Zalta (ed.), *Stanford Encyclopedia of Philosophy* (Spring 2014). Available from http://plato.stanford.edu/archives/ spr2014/entries/logic-ancient/

Bobzien, S. (2011), "Dialectical School". In E. N. Zalta (ed.), *Stanford Encyclopedia of Philosophy* (Fall 2011). Available from http://plato.stanford.edu/archives/ fall2011/entries/dialectical-school/

Bobzien, S. (1998), *Determinism and Freedom in Stoic Philosophy.* Oxford: Clarendon Press.

Boghossian, P. A. (2009), "Content". In J. Kim and E. Sosa (eds), *A Companion to Metaphysics*, 2nd edn. Oxford: Blackwell: 188–91.

Boghossian, P. A. and C. A. B. Peacocke (eds) (2000), *New Essays on the A Priori.* Oxford: Oxford University Press.

Borghini, A. (2009), "Dispositions and Their Intentions". In G. Damschen, R. Schnepf, and K. Stueber (eds), *Debating Dispositions: Issues in Metaphysics, Epistemology, and Philosophy of Mind.* Berlin: De Gruyter: 204–19.

Borghini, A. (2005), "Counterpart Theory and Mereological Essentialism". *Dialectica* 59: 67–74.

Borghini, A. (2003), "Un mondo di possibilità. Realismo modale senza mondi possibili". *Rivista di Estetica* 26: 87–100.

Borghini, A. and N. E. Williams (2008), "A Dispositional Theory of Possibility". *Dialectica* 62: 21–41.

Bradley, R. (1989), "Possibility and Combinatorialism: Wittgenstein Versus Armstrong". *Canadian Journal of Philosophy* 19: 15–41.

Bricke, J. (2011), "Hume on Liberty and Necessity". In E. S. Radcliffe (ed.), *A Companion to Hume*, Oxford: Blackwell.

Bricker, P. (2007), "Concrete Possible Worlds". In J. O'Leary-Hawthorne, T. Sider, and D. Zimmerman (eds), *Contemporary Debates in Metaphysics*. Oxford: Blackwell: 111–34.

Bricker, P. (2006a), "Absolute Actuality and the Plurality of Worlds". *Philosophical Perspectives* 20: 41–76.

Bricker, P. (2006b), "David Lewis: On the Plurality of Worlds". In J. Shand (ed.), *Central Works of Philosophy, Vol. 5: The Twentieth Century: Quine and After*. London: Acumen Publishing: 246–67.

Brock, S. (1993), "Modal Fictionalism: A Response to Rosen". *Mind* 102: 147–50.

Brogaard, B. (2006), "Two Modal-Isms: Fictionalism and Ersatzism". *Philosophical Perspectives* 20: 77–94.

Brogaard, B. and J. Salerno (2008), "Remarks on Counterpossibles". *Synthese* 190: 639–60.

Bueno, O. and S. A. Shalkowski (2015), "Modalism and Theoretical Virtues: Toward an Epistemology of Modality". *Philosophical Studies* 172: 671–89.

Bueno, O. and S. A. Shalkowski (2013), "Logical Constants: A Modalist Approach". *Noûs* 47: 1–24.

Bueno, O. and S. A. Shalkowski (2009), "Modalism and Logical Pluralism". *Mind* 118: 295–321.

Burgess, J. P. (1997), "*Quinus ab Omni Naevo Vindicatus*". In A. A. Kazmi (ed.), *Meaning and Reference*, Canadian Journal of Philosophy, Supp. Vol. 23: 25–65.

Cameron, R. P. (2010), "The Grounds of Necessity". *Philosophy Compass* 5: 348–58.

Cameron, R. P. (2008), "Recombination and Intrinsicality". *Ratio* 21: 1–12.

Campbell, J. K., M. O'Rourke, and M. Slater (eds) (2011), *Carving Nature at Its Joints. Natural Kinds in Metaphysics and Science*. Cambridge, MA: MIT Press.

Campbell, R. (1964), "Modality 'De Dicto'; and 'De Re'". *Australasian Journal of Philosophy* 42: 345–58.

Carey, S. (2009), *The Origin of Concepts*. New York: Oxford University Press.

Carnap, R. (1947), *Meaning and Necessity*. Chicago: University of Chicago Press.

Carnap, R. (1946), "Modalities and Quantification". *Journal of Symbolic Logic* 11: 33–64.

Carnap, R. (1936), "Testability and Meaning I". *Philosophy of Science* 3: 420–71.

Carrara, M., R. Ciuni, and G. Lando (2011), *Composition, Counterfactuals, and Causation*. Special issue of *Humana.Mente*, 19.

Casullo, A. (2003), *A Priori Justification*. Oxford: Oxford University Press.

Chalmers, D. (2002), "Does Conceivability Entail Possibility?" In T. Gendler and J. O'Leary-Hawthorne (eds), *Conceivability and Possibility*. Oxford: Oxford University Press: 145–200.

Chase, J. and J. Reynolds (2010), *Analytic Versus Continental: Arguments on the Methods and Value of Philosophy*. New York: Acumen.

Chellas, B. (1980), *Modal Logic: An Introduction*. Cambridge: Cambridge University Press.

Chignell, A. (2012), "Kant, Real Possibility, and the Threat of Spinoza". *Mind* 121: 635–75.

Chihara, C. (1998), *The Worlds of Possibility. Modal Realism and the Semantics of Modal Logic*. Oxford University Press, Oxford.

Clark, M. and D. Ligging (2012), "Recent Work on Grounding". *Analysis* 72: 812–23.

Cohen, M. S. (2014), "Aristotle's Metaphysics". In E. N. Zalta (ed.), *The Stanford Encyclopedia of Philosophy* (Summer 2014). Available from <http://plato.stanford.edu/archives/sum2014/entries/aristotle-metaphysics/

Contessa, G. (2013), "Dispositions and Interferences". *Philosophical Studies* 165: 401–19.

Contessa, G. (2010), "Modal Truth-Makers and Two Varieties of Actualism". *Synthese* 174: 342–53.

Copeland, B. J. (2002), "The Genesis of Possibile Worlds Semantics". *Journal of Philosophical Logic* 31: 99–137.

Correia, F. (2012), "On the Reduction of Necessity to Essence". *Philosophy and Phenomenological Research* 84: 639–53.

Correia, F. (2010), "Grounding and Truth-Functions". *Logique et Analyse* 53: 251–79.

Correia, F. and B. Schnieder (eds) (2012), *Metaphysical Grounding: Understanding the Structure of Reality*. Cambridge: Cambridge University Press.

Corry, R. (2011), "Can Dispositional Essences Ground the Laws of Nature?" *Australasian Journal of Philosophy* 89: 263–75.

Craig, E. (2002), "The Idea of Necessary Connexion". In P. Millican (ed.), *Reading Hume on Human Understanding*. Oxford: Oxford University Press: 211–30.

Craig, W. L. (1988), *The Problem of Divine Foreknowledge and Future Contingents from Aristotle to Suárez*. Leiden: Brill.

Cresswell, M. J. (1972), "The World Is Everything That Is the Case". *Australasian Journal of Philosophy* 50: 1–13.

Cunning, D. (2014), "Descartes' Modal Metaphysics". In E. N. Zalta (ed.), *The Stanford Encyclopedia of Philosophy* (Spring 2014). Available from http://plato.stanford.edu/archives/spr2014/entries/descartes-modal/

Curley, E. (1984), "Descartes on the Creation of the Eternal Truths". *The Philosophical Review* 93: 569–97.

Curley, E. and G. Walski (1999), "Spinoza's Necessitarianism Reconsidered". In R. Gennaro and C. Huenemann (eds), *New Essays on the Rationalists*. Oxford: Oxford University Press: 241–62.

Darby, G. and D. Watson (2010), "Lewis's Principle of Recombination: Reply to Efird and Stoneham". *Dialectica* 64: 435–45.

Denby, D. A. (2008), "Generating Possibilities". *Philosophical Studies* 141: 191–207.

Denby, D. A. (2006), "In Defense of Magical Ersatzism". *The Philosophical Quarterly* 56: 161–74.

Denyer, N. and S. Makin (2000), "Aristotle on Modality". *Proceedings of the Aristotelian Society, Supplementary Volumes* 74: 143–61, 163–78.

De Pierris, G. and M. Friedman (2013), "Kant and Hume on Causality." In E. N. Zalta (ed.), *The Stanford Encyclopedia of Philosophy* (Winter 2013). Available from http://plato.stanford.edu/archives/win2013/entries/kant-hume-causality/>

Dever, J. (2003), "Modal Fictionalism and Compositionality". *Philosophical Studies* 114: 223–51.

Divers, J. (2014a), "An Inconvenient Modal Truth". *Analysis* 74: 575–7.

Divers, J. (2014b), "Mere Possibilities: Metaphysical Foundations for Modal Semantics." *Philosophical Quarterly* 64: 163–6.

Divers, J. (2014c), "The Modal Status of the Lewisian Analysis of Modality". *Mind* 123: 861–72.

Divers, J. (2014d), "Modal Reality and (Modal) Logical Space". *Philosophy and Phenomenological Research* 88: 726–33.

Divers, J. (2013), "The Analysis of Possibility and the Extent of Possibility." *Dialectica* 67: 183–200.

Divers, J. (2012), "Modal Reality and (Modal) Logical Space". *Philosophy and Phenomenological Research* 88: 726–33.

Divers, J. (2007), "Quinean Skepticism about De Re Modality after David Lewis". *European Journal of Philosophy* 15: 40–62.

Divers, J. (2004), "Agnosticism about Other Worlds: A New Antirealist Programme in Modality". *Philosophy and Phenomenological Research* 69: 660–85.

Divers, J. (2002), *Possible Worlds*. London and New York: Routledge.

Divers, J. (1999), "A Modal Fictionalist Result". *Noûs* 33: 317–46.

Divers, J. (1995), "Modal Fictionalism Cannot Deliver Possible Worlds Semantics". *Analysis* 55: 81–8.

Divers, J. and J. Hagen (2006), "The Modal Fictionalist's Predicament". In F. McBride (ed.), *Identity and Modality: New Essays in Metaphysics*. Oxford: Oxford University Press: 57–73.

Divers, J. and J. Melia (2003), "Genuine Modal Realism Limited." *Mind* 112: 83–6.

Divers, J. and J. Melia (2002), "The Analytic Limit of Genuine Modal Realism." *Mind* 111: 15–36.

Dorr, C. (2005), "Propositions and Counterpart Theory." *Analysis* 65: 210–18.

Drewery, A. (2005), "Essentialism and the Necessity of the Laws of Nature". *Synthese* 144: 381–96.

Dutihl Novaes, C. (2007), *Formalizing Medieval Logical Theories: Suppositio, Consequentiae and Obligationes*. Dordrecht: Springer.

Dutihl Novaes, C. and S. Read (forthcoming), *Cambridge Companion to Medieval Logic*. Cambridge: Cambridge University Press.

Eco, U. (1999), *Kant and the Platypus: Essays on Language and Cognition*. Orlando, FL: Harcourt.

Efird, D. (2010), "Is Timothy Williamson a Necessary Existent?" In B. Hale and A. Hoffmann (eds), *Modality. Metaphysics, Logic, and Epistemology*. Oxford: Oxford University Press: 97–108.

Efird, D. and T. Stoneham (2006), "Combinatorialism and the Possibility of Nothing." *Australasian Journal of Philosophy* 84: 269–80.

Eklund, M. (2007), "Fictionalism". In E. N. Zalta (ed.), *The Stanford Encyclopedia of Philosophy* (Summer 2007). Available from http://plato.stanford.edu/archives/sum2007/entries/fictionalism/

Ellis, B. (2002), *The Philosophy of Nature—A Guide to the New Essentialism*. Montreal: McGill-Queens University Press.

Ellis, B. (2001), *Scientific Essentialism*. Cambridge: Cambridge University Press.

Ellis, B. and C. Lierse (1994), "Dispositional Essentialism". *Australasian Journal of Philosophy* 72: 27–45.

Ereshefsky, M. (2010), "Microbiology and the Species Poblem". *Biology & Philosophy* 25: 553–68.

Fara, M. and T. Williamson (2005), "Counterparts and Actuality". *Mind* 114: 1–30.

Farrell, R. (1981), "Metaphysical Necessity Is Not Logical Necessity". *Philosophical Studies* 39: 141–53.

Feldman, R. (2002), *Epistemology*. Upper Saddle River, NJ: Pearson.

Field, H. (1989), *Realism, Mathematics and Modality*. Oxford: Blackwell.

Field, H. (1980), *Science Without Numbers*. Oxford: Blackwell.

Fine, K. (2012), "A Guide to Ground". In F. Correia and B. Schnieder (eds), *Metaphysical Grounding: Understanding the Structure of Reality*. Cambridge: Cambridge University Press: 37–80.

Fine, K. (2005), *Modality and Tense: Philosophical Papers*. Oxford: Oxford University Press.

Fine, K. (2002), "The Varieties of Necessity". In T. S. Gendler and O'Leary-Hawthorne (eds), *Conceivability and Possiblity*. Oxford: Oxford University Press: 253–81.

Fine, K. (2001), "The Question of Realism". *Philosopher's Imprint* 1: 1–30.

Fine, K. (1995), "The Logic of Essence". *Journal of Philosophical Logic* 24: 241–73.

Fine, K. (1994), "Essence and Modality". In J. Tomberlin (ed.), *Philosophical Perspectives 8: Logic and Language*. Atascadero: Ridgeview Publishing: 1–16.

Fine, K. (1985), "Plantinga on the Reduction of Possibilist Discourse". In J. Tomberlin and P. Van Inwagen (eds), *Alvin Plantinga*. Dordrecht: D. Reidel: 145–86.

Fine, K. (1974), "Model Theory for Modal Logic Part I: the 'De Re/De Dicto' Distinction". *Journal of Philosophical Logic* 7: 125–56.

Fitch, G. (1979), "Analyticity and Necessity in Leibniz". *Journal of the History of Philosophy* 17: 29–42.

Fitting, M. and R. L. Mendelsohn (1998), *First-Order Modal Logic*. Dordrecht: Kluwer Academic Publishers.

Føllesdal, D. (1961), *Referential Opacity and Modal Logic*. Ph.D. Dissertation, Harvard University, Cambridge, MA.

Forbes, G. (1992), "Melia on Modalism". *Philosophical Studies* 68: 57–63.

Forbes, G. (1989), *Languages of Possibility. An Essay in Philosophical Logic*. Oxford: Blackwell.

Forbes, G. (1985), *The Metaphysics of Modality*. Oxford: Oxford University Press.

Forbes, G. (1982), "Canonical Counterpart Theory". *Analysis* 42: 33–7.

Friedman, R. L. and L. O. Nielsen (eds) (2003), *The Medieval Heritage in Early Modern Metaphysics and Modal Theory*. Dordrecht: Kluwer.

Gabbay Dov, M. and J. Woods (eds) (2009), *Handbook of the History of Logic Volume 5. Logic from Russell to Church*. Amsterdam: Elsevier.

Gabbay Dov, M. and J. Woods (eds) (2008a), *Handbook of the History of Logic Vol. 2. Medieval and Renaissance Logic*. Amsterdam: Elsevier.

Gabbay Dov, M. and J. Woods (eds) (2008b), *Handbook of the History of Logic Vol. 4. British Logic in the Nineteenth Century*. Amsterdam: Elsevier.

Gabbay Dov, M. and J. Woods (eds) (2006), *Handbook of the History of Logic Vol. 7. Logic and the Modalities in Twentieth Century*. Amsterdam: Elsevier.

Gabbay Dov, M. and J. Woods (eds) (2004a), *Handbook of the History of Logic Vol. 1. Greek, Indian and Arabic Logic*. Amsterdam: Elsevier.

Gabbay Dov, M. and J. Woods (eds) (2004b), *Handbook of the History of Logic Vol. 3. The Rise of Modern Logic: Leibniz to Frege*. Amsterdam: Elsevier.

Garrett, D. (2001), "Spinoza"s Necessitarianism". In Y. Yovel (ed.), *God and Nature in Spinoza"s Metaphysics*. Leiden: E. J. Brill: 191–218.

Garrett, D. (1985), "Priority and Separability in Hume's Empiricism". *Archiv für Geschichte der Philosophie* 67: 270–88. Reprinted in D. W. D. Owen (ed.) (2000), *Hume: General Philosophy*, The International Library of Critical Essays in the History of Philosophy. Aldershot: Dartmouth Publishing Company: 71–89.

Garson, J. W. (2006), *Modal Logic for Philosophers*. Cambridge: Cambridge University Press.

Gaskin, R. (1995), *The Sea Battle and the Master Argument: Aristotle and Diodorus Cronus on the Metaphysics of the Future*. Berlin and New York: De Gruyter.

Geirsson, H. (2014), "Conceivability and Coherence: A Skeptical View of Zombies". *Erkenntnis* 79: 211–25.

Geirsson, H. (2005), "Conceivability and Defeasible Modal Justification". *Philosophical Studies* 122: 279–304.

Gendler, T. S. and J. O'Leary-Hawthorne (eds) (2002), *Conceivability and Possibility*. Oxford: Oxford University Press.

Gibbard, A. (2003), *Thinking How to Live*. Cambridge, MA: Harvard University Press.

Gibbard, A. (1990), *Wise Choices, Apt Feelings*. Cambridge, MA: Harvard University Press.

Girle (2003), *Possible Worlds*. Montreal: McGill–Queens University Press.

Girle (2000), *Modal Logics and Philosophy*. Teddington: Acumen.

Goble, L. (2006), "Paraconsistent Modal Logic". *Logique et Analyse* 193: 3–29.

Haack, S. (1978), *Philosophy of Logics*. Cambridge: Cambridge University Press.

Hacking, I. (2009), *The Social Construction of What?* Cambridge, MA: Harvard University Press.

Hale, B. (1995a), "A Desperate Fix". *Analysis* 55: 74–81.

Hale, B. (1995b), "Modal Fictionalism: A Simple Dilemma". *Analysis* 55: 63–7.

Hale, B. (1993), "Can There Be a Logic of Attitudes?". In J. Haldane and C. Wright (eds), *Reality, Representation and Projection*. Oxford: Oxford University Press: 337–63.

Hale, B. and A. Hoffman (eds) (2010), *Modality: Metaphysics, Logic, and Epistemology*. Oxford: Oxford University Press.

Harré, R. (1970), "Powers". *British Journal for the Philosophy of Science* 21: 81–101.

Hasle, P. and P. Øhrstrøm (2011), "Future Contingents". In E. N. Zalta (ed.), *The Stanford Encyclopedia of Philosophy* (Summer 2011). Available from http://plato.stanford.edu/archives/sum2011/entries/future–contingents/

Hawke, P. (2011), "Van Inwagen"s Modal Skepticism". *Philosophical Studies* 153: 351–64.

Heil, J. (2003), *From an Ontological Point of View*. Oxford: Oxford University Press.

Heller, M. (2005), "Anti–Essentialism and Counterpart Theory". *The Monist* 88: 600–18.

Heller, M. (2002), "Transworld Identity for the Ersatzist". *Philosophical Topics* 30: 77–102.

Heller, M. (1998), "Property Counterparts in Ersatz Worlds". *The Journal of Philosophy* 30: 293–316.

Heller, M. (1996), "Ersatz Worlds and Ontological Disagreement". *Acta Analytica* 15: 35–44.

Hendricks, V. F. and J. Symons (2005), *Formal Philosophy*. New York: Automatic Press/VIP.

Hintikka, J. (1975), "Impossible Possible Worlds Vindicated". *Journal of Philosophical Logic* 4: 475–84.

Hintikka, J. (1973), *Time and Necessity: Studies in Aristotle's Theory of Modality*. Oxford: Oxford University Press.

Hintikka, J. (1963), "The Modes of Modality". *Acta Philosophica Fennica* 16: 65–79.

Hintikka, J. (1961), "Modality and Quantification". *Theoria* 27: 119–28.

Hintikka, J., U. Remes, and S. Knuuttila (1977), *Aristotle on Modality and Determinism*. Amsterdam: North-Holland.

Hirsch, E. (2009), "Ontology and Alternative Languages". In D. J. Chalmers, D. Manley, and R. Wasserman (eds), *Metametaphysics. New Essays on the Foundations of Ontology*. Oxford: Oxford University Press: 231–58.

Hirsch, E. (1997), *Dividing Reality*. Oxford: Oxford University Press.

Hirsch, E. (1986), "Metaphysical Necessity and Conceptual Truth". *Midwest Studies in Philosophy* 11: 243–56.

Huggett, N. (2010), "Zeno's Paradoxes". In E. N. Zalta (ed.), *The Stanford Encyclopedia of Philosophy* (Winter 2010). Available from http://plato.stanford.edu/archives/win2010/entries/paradox-zeno/

Hughes, G. E. and M. J. Cresswell (1984), *A Companion to Modal Logic*. London: Methuen.

Hughes, G. E. and M. J. Cresswell (1968), *An Introduction to Modal Logic*. London: Methuen.

Humberstone, L. (2007), "Modal Logic for Other-World Agnostics: Neutrality and Halldén Incompleteness". *Journal of Philosophical Logic* 36: 1–32.

Hylton, P. (2007), *Quine*. New York: Routledge.

Ichikawa, J. and B. Jarvis (2012), "Rational Imagination and Modal Knowledge". *Noûs* 46: 127–58.

Jackson, F. and G. Priest (eds) (2004), *Lewisian Themes: The Philosophy of David K. Lewis*. Oxford: Clarendon Press.

Jacobs, J. D. (2010), "A Powers Theory of Modality: Or, How I Learned to Stop Worrying and Reject Possible Worlds". *Philosophical Studies* 151: 227–48.

Jago, M. (2014), *The Impossible. An Essay on Hyperintensionality*. Oxford: Oxford University Press.

Jago, M. (2013a), "Impossible Worlds". *Noûs* 47: 713–28.

Jago, M. (2013b), "Against Yagisawa's Modal Realism". *Analysis* 73: 10–17.

Jauernig, A. (2008), "The Modal Strength of Leibniz's Principle of the Identity of Indiscernibles". *Oxford Studies in Early Modern Philosophy* 4: 191–225.

Jenkins, C. S. (2010), "Concepts, Experience and Modal Knowledge". *Philosophical Perspectives* 24: 255–79.

Jubien, M. (2009), *Possibility*. Oxford: Oxford University Press.

Jubien, M. (2007), "Analyzing Modality". *Oxford Studies in Metaphysics* 3: 99–139.

Kail, P. (2003), "Conceivability and Modality in Hume. A Lemma in an Argument in Defense of Skeptical Realism". *Hume Studies* 29: 43–61.

Kalderon, M. (ed.) (2005), *Fictionalism in Metaphysics*. Oxford: Clarendon Press.

Kane, R. (ed.) (2002), *The Oxford Handbook of Free Will*. Oxford: Oxford University Press.

Keskinen, A. (2012), "Quine on Objects and *De* Re Modality". *European Journal of Analytic Philosophy* 8: 4–17.

Keskinen, A. (2010), *Quine's Critique of Modal Logic and His Conception of Objects*. Tampere: Tampere University Press.

Khalidi, M. A. (2013), *Natural Categories and Human Kinds. Classification in the Natural and Social Sciences*. Cambridge: Cambridge University Press.

Kim, S. (2005), "Modal Fictionalism and Analysis". In M. Kalderon (ed.), *Fictionalism in Metaphysics*. Oxford: Clarendon Press: 116–33.

Kim, S. (2002), "Modal Fictionalism Generalized and Defended". *Philosophical Studies* 111: 121–46.

Kim, S. (1986), "Possible Worlds and Armstrong's Combinatorialism". *Canadian Journal of Philosophy* 16: 595–612.

Kistler, M. (2002), "The Causal Criterion of Reality and the Necessity of Laws of Nature". *Metaphysica* 3: 57–86.

Kitcher, P. (2000), "A Priori Knowledge Revisited". In P. Boghossian and C. Peacocke (eds), *New Essays on the A Priori*. Oxford: Oxford University Press: 65–91.

Kitcher, P. (1980), "A Priori Knowledge". *The Philosophical Review* 79: 3–23.

Klima, G. (2009), *John Buridan*. Oxford: Oxford University Press.

Kment, B. (2012), "Varieties of Modality". In E. N. Zalta (ed.), *The Stanford Encyclopedia of Philosophy* (Winter 2012). Available from http://plato.stanford.edu/archives/win2012/entries/modality-varieties/

Kment, B. (2006), "Counterfactuals and the Analysis of Necessity". *Philosophical Perspectives* 20: 237–302.

Kneale, W. and M. Kneale (1962), *The Development of Logic*. Oxford: Oxford University Press.

Knuuttila, S. (2014), "Medieval Theories of Future Contingents". In E. N. Zalta (ed.), *The Stanford Encyclopedia of Philosophy* (Spring 2014). Available from http://plato.stanford.edu/archives/spr2014/entries/medieval-futcont/

Knuuttila, S. (2013), "Medieval Theories of Modality". In E. N. Zalta (ed.), *The Stanford Encyclopedia of Philosophy* (Fall 2013). Available from http://plato.stanford.edu/archives/fall2013/entries/modality-medieval/>

Knuuttila, S. (2008), "Medieval Modal Theories and Modal Logic". In D. M. Gabbay and J. Woods (eds), *Handbook of the History of Logic Vol. 2. Medieval and Renaissance Logic*. Amsterdam: Elsevier: 505–78.

Knuuttila, S. (ed.) (1998), *Modern Modalities. Studies of the History of Modal Theories from Medieval Nominalism to Logical Positivism*. Synthese Historical Library 33: Dordrecht: Kluwer.

Knuuttila, S. and T. Kukkonen (2011), "Thought Experiment and Indirect Proof in Averroes, Aquinas, and Buridan". In K. Ierodiakonou and S. Roux (eds), *Thought Experiments In Methodological and Historical Perspectives*. Leiden: Brill: 83–99.

Koistinen, O. (2003), "Spinoza's Proof of Necessitarianism". *Philosophy and Phenomenological Research* 67: 283–310.

Krakauer, B. (2013), "What are Impossible Worlds?" *Philosophical Studies* 165: 989–1007.

Kripke, S. (1980), *Naming and Necessity*. Oxford: Blackwell.

Kripke, S. (1963), "Semantical Considerations on Modal Logics". *Acta Philosophical Fennica* 16: 83–94.

Kripke, S. (1959), "A Completeness Theorem in Modal Logics". *Journal of Symbolic Logic* 24: 1–14.

Kukkonen, T. (2005), "Possible Worlds in the *Tahâfut al-falâsifa*. Al-Gazâli on Creation and Contingency". *Journal of the History of Philosophy* 38: 479–502.

Kukkonen, T. (2000), "The Impossible insofar as it is Possible: Ibn Rushd and Jean Buridan on Logic and Natural Theology". In D. Perler and U. Rudolph (eds), *Logik und Theologie. Das Organon im arabischen und lateinischen Mittelalter*, Studien und Texte zur Geistesgeschichte des Mittelalters 84. Leiden: Brill: 447–67.

Kung, P. (2011), "On the Possibility of Skeptical Scenarios". *European Journal of Philosophy* 19: 387–407.

Kung, P. (2010), "Imagining as a Guide to Possibility". *Philosophy and Phenomenological Research* 81: 620–63.

Lagerlund, H. (2000), *Modal Syllogistics in the Middle Ages*. Leiden: Brill.

Laporte, J. (2009), *Natural Kinds and Conceptual Change*. Cambridge: Cambridge University Press.

Lewis, C. I. (1918), *A Survey of Symbolic Logic*. Berkeley, CA: University of California Press. (Reprinted by Dover Publications: New York, 1960, with the omission of Chapters 5 and 6.)

Lewis, C. I. and C. H. Langford (1932), *Symbolic Logic*. New York: Century Company. (Reprinted by Dover Publications, New York, 1959, 2nd edn with an Appendix III by C. I. Lewis.)

Lewis, F. A. (2009), "Parmenides's Modal Fallacy". *Phronesis* 54: 1–8.

Lewis, D. K. (1992), "Armstrong on Combinatorial Possibility". *Australasian Journal of Philosophy* 70: 211–224.

Lewis, D. K. (1991), *Parts of Classes*. Oxford: Basil Blackwell.

Lewis, D. K. (1986), *On The Plurality of Worlds*. Oxford: Clarendon Press.

Lewis, D. K. (1983), *Philosophical Papers Vol. 1*. Oxford: Clarendon Press.

Lewis, D. K. (1979), "Attitudes *De Dicto* and *De se*". *The Philosophical Review* 88: 513–43.

Lewis, D. K. (1973), *Counterfactuals*. Oxford: Basil Blackwell.

Lewis, D. K. (1970), "Anselm and Actuality". *Noûs* 4: 175–88.

Lewis, D. K. (1968), "Counterpart Theory and Quantified Modal Logic". *Journal of Philosophy* 65: 113–26.

Liggins, D. (2008), "Modal Fictionalism and Possible-Worlds Discourse". *Philosophical Studies* 138: 151–60.

Lin, M. (2012), "Rationalism and Necessitarianism". *Noûs* 46: 418–48.

Linsky, B. (1991), "Is Lewis a Meinongian?" *Australasian Journal of Philosophy* 69: 438–53.

Linsky, B. (ed.) (1974), *Reference and Modality*. Oxford: Oxford University Press.

Linsky, B. and E. Zalta (1996), "In Defense of the Contingently Nonconcrete". *Philosophical Studies* 84: 283–94.

Linsky, B. and E. Zalta (1994), "In Defense of the Simplest Quantified Modal Logic". In J. Tomberlin (ed.), *Philosophical Perspectives 8: Logic and Language*. Atascadero: Ridgeview: 431–58.

Loewer, B. and J. Schaffer (2015), "A Companion to David Lewis". Oxford: Blackwell Publishers.

Look, B. C. (2013), "Leibniz's Modal Metaphysics". In E. N. Zalta (ed.), *The Stanford Encyclopedia of Philosophy* (Spring 2013). Available from http://plato.stanford.edu/archives/spr2013/entries/leibniz-modal/

Loux, M. J. (2006), *Metaphysics: A Contemporary Introduction*, 3rd edn. New York: Routledge.

Loux, M. J. (ed.) (1979), *The Possible and the Actual. Readings in the Metaphysics of Modality*. Ithaca, NY: Cornell University Press.

Lowe, E. J. (2012), "What is the Source of our Knowledge of Modal Truths?" *Mind* 121: 919–50.

Lowe, E. J. (2006), *The Four-Category Ontology: A Metaphysical Foundation for Natural Science*. Oxford: Oxford University Press.

Lycan, W. (1979), "The Trouble With Possibile Worlds". In M. J. Loux (ed.), *The Possible and the Actual Readings in the Metaphysics of Modality*. Ithaca, NY: Cornell University Press: 274–316.

Machiavelli, N. (1513), *The Prince*. Trans. by H. C. Mansfield. Chicago: University of Chicago Press, 1985.

Mackie, P. (2006), *How Things Might Have Been: Individuals, Kinds, and Essential Properties*. Oxford: Oxford University Press.

Malink, M. (2006), "A Reconstruction of Aristotle's Modal Syllogistic". *History and Philosophy of Logic* 27: 95–141.

Manley, D. and R. Wasserman (2011), "Dispositions, Conditionals, and Counterexamples". *Mind* 120: 1191–227.

Manley, D. and R. Wasserman (2008), "On Linking Dispositions and Conditionals". *Mind* 117: 59–84.

Marcus, R. B. (1993), *Modalities: Philosophical Essays*. Oxford: Oxford University Press.

Marek, J. (2013), "Alexius Meinong". In E. N. Zalta (ed.), *The Stanford Encyclopedia of Philosophy* (Fall 2013). Available from http://plato.stanford.edu/archives/fall2013/entries/meinong/

Marmodoro, A. (2015), "Potentiality in Aristotle's Metaphysics". In K. Engelhard and M. Quante (eds), *The Handbook of Potentiality*. Dordrecht: Springer: forthcoming.

Martin, C. (2010), "A New Challenge to the Necessitarian Reading of Spinoza". *Oxford Studies in Early Modern Philosophy* 5: 25–70.

Martin, C. B. (1994), "Dispositions and Conditionals". *The Philosophical Quarterly* 44: 1–8.

Martin, C. B. and J. Heil (1999), "The Ontological Turn". *Midwest Studies in Philosophy* 23: 34–60.

Mates, B. (1986), *The Philosophy of Leibniz. Metaphysics and Language*. Oxford: Oxford University Press.

Mates, B. (1972), "Leibniz on Possible Worlds". In H. Frankfurt (ed.), *Leibniz. A Collection of Critical Essays*. New York: Doubleday: 335–64.

McDaniel, K. (2006), "Modal Realism". *Philosophical Perspectives: Metaphysics* 20: 303–31.

McDaniel, K. (2004), "Modal Realism with Overlap". *Australasian Journal of Philosophy* 82: 137–52.

McMichael, A. (1983), "A Problem for Actualism about Possible Worlds". *The Philosophical Review* 92: 49–66.

Meinong, A. (1904), "On Object Theory". In R. Chisholm (ed.), *Realism and the Background of Phenomenology*. Glencoe: The Free Press, 1960; translation of "Über Gegenstandstheorie". In A. Meinong (ed.), *Untersuchungen zur Gegenstandstheorie und Psychologie*. Leipzig: Barth.

Melia, J. (2005), "Truthmaking Without Truthmakers". In H. Beebee and J. Dodd (eds), *Truthmakers: The Contemporary Debate*. Oxford: Oxford University Press: 21–46.

Melia, J. (2003), *Modality*. Montreal and Kingston: McGill-Queen's University Press.

Melia, J. (2000), "Review of Charles S. Chihara, *The Worlds of Possibility*". *British Journal for the Philosophy of Science* 51: 333–7.

Melia, J. (1992), "Against Modalism". *Philosophical Studies* 68: 35–56.

Mellor, D. H. (1974), "In Defense of Dispositions". *The Philosophical Review* 83: 157–81.

Menzel, C. (2015), "Possible Worlds". In E. N. Zalta (ed.), *The Stanford Encyclopedia of Philosophy* (Spring 2015). Available from http://plato.stanford.edu/archives/spr2015/entries/possible-worlds/

Menzies, P. and P. Pettit (1994), "In Defence of Fictionalism about Possible Worlds". *Analysis* 54: 27–36.

Merricks, T. (2003), "The End of Counterpart Theory". *Journal of Philosophy* 100: 521–49.

Merricks, T. (1999), "Composition as Identity, Mereological Essentialism, and Counterpart Theory". *Australasian Journal of Philosophy* 77: 192–5.

Mignucci, M. (1989), "Truth and Modality in Late Antiquity: Boethius on Future Contingent Propositions". In G. Corsi, C. Mangione and M. Mugnai (eds), *Atti del Convegno internazionale di storia della logica: le teorie delle modalità*. Bologna: CLUEB: 47–78.

Miller, J. A. (2001), "Spinoza's Possibilities". *Review of Metaphysics* 54: 779–815.

Molnar, G. (2003), *Powers*. Oxford: Oxford University Press.

Mondadori, F. (1985), "Understanding Superessentialism". *Studia Leibnitiana* 17: 162–90.

Mondadori, F. (1983), "Counterpartese, Counterpartese*, Counterpartese$_D$". *Histoire, Epistémologie, Langage* 5: 69–94.

Mondadori, F. and A. Morton (1976), "Modal Realism. The Poisoned Pawn". *The Philosophical Review* 85: 3–20.

Morato, V. (2006), "Propositions and Necessary Existents". *Grazer Philosophische Studien* 72: 211–31.

Morgan, C. G. (1973), "Systems of Modal Logic for Impossible Worlds" *Inquiry* 16: 280–9.

Mortensen, C. (1989), "Anything is Possible". *Erkenntnis* 30: 319–37.

Mumford, S. (1998), *Dispositions*. Oxford: Oxford University Press.

Mumford, S. and R. Anjum (2011), *Getting Causes from Powers*. Oxford: Oxford University Press.

Naylor, M. (1986), "A Note on David Lewis's Realism about Possible Worlds". *Analysis* 46: 28–9.

Neale, S. (2000), "On a Milestone of Empiricism". In P. Kotatko and A. Orenstein (eds), *Knowledge, Language and Logic: Questions for Quine*. Dordrecht: Kluwer: 237–346.

Nelson, M. (2012), "Existence". In E. N. Zalta (ed.), *The Stanford Encyclopedia of Philosophy* (Winter 2012). Available from http://plato.stanford.edu/archives/win2012/entries/existence/

Newlands, S. (2013), "Leibniz and the Ground of Possibility". *The Philosophical Review* 122: 155–87.

Nolan, D. (2015), "Noncausal Dispositions". *Noûs* 49: 425–39.

Nolan, D. (2013), "Impossible Worlds". *Philosophy Compass* 8: 360–72.

Nolan, D. (2011), "The Extent of Metaphysical Necessity". *Philosophical Perspectives* 25: 313–39.

Nolan, D. (2007), "Modal Fictionalism". In E. N. Zalta (ed.), *The Stanford Encyclopedia of Philosophy* (Winter 2007). Available from http://plato.stanford.edu/archives/win2007/entries/fictionalism–modal/

Nolan, D. (2005), *David Lewis*. Montreal and Kingston: McGill–Queen's University Press.

Nolan, D. (1997), "Three Problems for 'Strong' Modal Fictionalism". *Philosophical Studies* 87: 259–75.

Nolan, D. and J. O'Leary-Hawthorne (1996), "Reflexive Fictionalisms". *Analysis* 56: 26–32.

Nolt, J. (1986), "What are Possible Worlds?". *Mind* 95: 432–45.

Noonan, H. (1994), "In Defence of the Letter of Fictionalism". *Analysis* 54: 133–9.

Normore, C. (1991), "Descartes's Possibilities". In G. J. D. Moyal (ed.), *René Descartes: Critical Assessments* (Volume III). London and New York: Routledge: 68–83.

Normore, C. (1982), "Future Contingents". In N. Kretzmann, A. Kenny, and J. Pinborg (eds), *The Cambridge History of Later Medieval Philosophy*. Cambridge: Cambridge University Press: 358–81.

Palmer, J. (2012a), "Parmenides". In E. N. Zalta (ed.), *The Stanford Encyclopedia of Philosophy* (Summer 2012). Available from http://plato.stanford.edu/archives/sum2012/entries/parmenides/

Palmer, J. (2012b), "Zeno of Elea". In E. N. Zalta (ed.), *The Stanford Encyclopedia of Philosophy* (Spring 2012). Available from http://plato.stanford.edu/archives/spr2012/entries/zeno-elea/

Palmer, J. (2009), *Parmenides and the Presocratic Philosophy*, Oxford: Oxford University Press.

Parsons, T. (1980), *Nonexistent Objects*. New Haven: Yale University Press.

Parsons, T. (1979), "The Methodology of Nonexistence". *The Journal of Philosophy* 76: 649–62.

Parsons, T. (1969), "Essentialism and Quantified Modal Logic". *The Philosophical Review* 78: 35–52.

Parsons, T. (1967), "Grades of Essentialism in Quantified Modal Logic". *Noûs* 1: 181–91.

Patterson, R. (1995), *Aristotle"s Modal Logic. Essence and Entailment in the Organon*. Cambridge: Cambridge University Press.

Peacocke, C. (1999), *Being Known*. Oxford: Oxford University Press.

Peacocke, C. (1997), "Metaphysical Necessity: Understanding, Truth, Epistemology". *Mind* 106: 521–74.

Pike, N. (1977), "Divine Foreknowledge, Human Freedom, and Possible Worlds". *The Philosophical Review* 86: 209–16.

Plantinga, A. (2003), *Essays in the Metaphysics of Modality*. Oxford: Oxford University Press.

Plantinga, A. (1992), *The Nature of Necessity*. Oxford: Clarendon Press.

Plantinga, A. (1985), "Reply to Kit Fine". In J. Tomberlin and P. Van Inwagen (eds), *Alvin Plantinga: A Profile*. Dordrecht: Reidel: 341–9.

Plantinga, A. (1983), "On Existentialism". *Philosophical Studies* 44: 1–20.

Plantinga, A. (1974a), *The Nature of Necessity*. Oxford: Clarendon Press.

Plantinga, A. (1974b), *God, Freedom, and Evil*. New York: Harper & Row.

Popper, K. (1990), *A World of Propensities*. Bristol: Thoemmes.

Preyer, G. and F. Siebelt (eds) (2001), *Reality and Humean Supervenience: Essays on the Philosophy of David Lewis*. Lanham, MD: Rowman and Littlefield.

Price, H. (2004), "Naturalism Without Representationalism". In M. De Caro and D. Macarthur (eds), *Naturalism in Question*. Cambridge, MA: Harvard University Press: 71–88.

Priest, G. (2005), *Towards Non-Being. The Logic and Metaphysics of Intentionality*. Oxford: Oxford University Press.

Priest, G. (ed.) (1997), "Impossible Worlds". Special issue of the *Notre Dame Journal of Formal Logic* 38: 481–660.

Priest, G. and F. Berto (2013), "Dialetheism". In E. N. Zalta (ed.), *The Stanford Encyclopedia of Philosophy* (Summer 2013). Available from http://plato.stanford.edu/archives/sum2013/entries/dialetheism/

Prior, A. N. (1957), *Time and Modality*. Oxford: Oxford University Press.

Prior, A. N. and K. Fine (1977), *Worlds, Times and Selves*. London: Duckworth.

Pruss, A. R. (2011), *Actuality, Possibility, and Worlds*. New York: Continuum.

Pruss, A. R. (2002), "The Actual and the Possible". In R. M. Gale (ed.), *Blackwell Guide to Metaphysics*. Oxford: Blackwell: 317–33.

Pruss, A. R. and J. Rasmussen (2015), *Necessary Existence*. Oxford: Oxford University Press.

Quine, W. V. O. (1976), "Worlds Away". *The Journal of Philosophy* 22: 859–63.

Quine, W. V. O. (1974), *Roots of Reference*. La Salle: Open Court.

Quine, W. V. O. (1953a), "Three Grades of Modal Involvement". *Proceedings of the XIth International Congress of Philosophy*, Vol. 11. Amsterdam: North-Holland: 65–81.

Quine, W. V. O. (1953b), "Reference and Modality". In W. V. O. Quine, *From a Logical Point of View*. Cambridge, MA: Harvard University Press, 1980: 139–59.

Quine, W. V. O. (1947), "The Problem of Interpreting Modal Logic". *Journal of Symbolic Logic* 12: 43–8.

Rasmussen, J. (2013), "From Necessary Truth to Necessary Existence". *Polish Journal of Philosophy* 7: 19–30.

Raven, M. (2015), "Ground". *Philosophy Compass* 10: 322–3.

Ray, G. (2000), "*De Re* Modality: Lessons from Quine". In A. Orenstein A. and P. Kotatko (eds), *Knowledge, Language and Logic: Questions for Quine*, Boston Studies in the History and Philosophy of Science, Vol. 210. Dordrecht: Kluwer Academic: 347–67.

Read, S. (forthcoming), "Logic in the XIVth Century". In C. Dutilh Novaes and S. Read (eds), *Cambridge Companion to Medieval Logic*. Cambridge: Cambridge University Press.

Rescher, N., R. Manor, A. Vander Nat, and Z. Parks (eds) (1974), *Studies in Modality*. Oxford: Blackwell.

Rini, A. (2010), *Aristotle's Modal Proofs: Prior Analytics A 8-22 in Predicate Logic*, The New Synthese Historical Library 68. Dordrecht: Springer.

Robertson, T. and P. Atkins (2013), "Essential vs. Accidental Properties". In E. N. Zalta (ed.), *The Stanford Encyclopedia of Philosophy* (Winter 2013). Available from http://plato.stanford.edu/archives/win2013/entries/essential–accidental/

Roca–Royes, S. (2011), "Conceivability and De Re Modal Knowledge". *Noûs* 45: 22–49.

Rorabiji, R. (1980), *Necessity, Cause and Blame. Perspectives on Aristotle's Theory*. Ithaca, NY: Cornell University Press.

Rosen, G. (1995), "Modal Fictionalism Fixed". *Analysis* 55: 67–73.

Rosen, G. (1993), "A Problem for Fictionalism about Possible Worlds". *Analysis* 53: 71–81.

Rosen, G. (1990), "Modal Fictionalism". *Mind* 99: 327–54.

Routley, R. (1980), *Exploring Meinong's Jungle and Beyond*. Canberra: Australian National University Press.

Roy, T. (1995), "In Defense of Linguistic Ersatzism". *Philosophical Studies* 80: 217–42.

Rudder Beker, L. (1985), "Was Leibniz Entitled to Possible Worlds?" *Canadian Journal of Philosophy* 15: 57–74.

Rumfitt, I. (2003), "Contingent Existents". *Philosophy* 78: 461–81.

Russell, B. (2014), "*A Priori* Justification and Knowledge". In E. N. Zalta (ed.) *The Stanford Encyclopedia of Philosophy* (Summer 2014). Available from http://plato.stanford.edu/archives/sum2014/entries/apriori/

Ryle, G. (1949), *The Concept of Mind*. London: Hutchinson.

Sauchelli, A. (2013), "Modal Fictionalism, Possible Worlds, and Artificiality". *Acta Analytica* 28: 411–21.

Schrenk, M. (2010), "The Powerlessness of Necessity". *Noûs* 44: 725–39.

Schrenk, M. (2009), "Hic Rhodos, Hic Salta: From Reductionist Semantics to a Realist Ontology of Forceful Dispositions". In G. Damschen, R. Schnepf, and K. Stueber (eds), *Debating Dispositions: Issues in Metaphysics, Epistemology, and Philosophy of Mind*. Berlin: De Gruyter: 145–67.

Shalkowski, S. (1994), "The Ontological Ground of the Alethic Modality". *The Philosophical Review* 103: 669–88.

Shoemaker, S. (1998), "Causal and Metaphysical Necessity". *Pacific Philosophical Quarterly* 79: 59–77.

Shoemaker, S. (1980), "Causality and Properties". In P. Van Inwagen (ed.), *Time and Cause: Essays Presented to Richard Taylor*. Dordrecht: D. Reidel Publishing: 109–36.

Shroeder, M. (2010), *Noncognitivism in Ethics*. London: Routledge.

Shroeder, M. (2008a), "Expression For Expressivists". *Philosophy and Phenomenological Research* 76: 86–116.

Shroeder, M. (2008b), "How Expressivists Can and Should Solve their Problem with Negation". *Noûs* 42: 573–99.

Sidelle, A. (2009), "Conventionalism and the Contingency of Conventions". *Noûs* 43: 224–41.

Sidelle, A. (2002), "On the Metaphysical Contingency of Laws of Nature". In

T. Gendler and J. O'Leary-Hawthorne (eds), *Conceivability and Possibility*. Oxford: Oxford University Press: 309–36.

Sidelle, A. (1989), *Necessity, Essence, and Individuation*. Ithaca, NY: Cornell University Press.

Sider, T. (2009), "Williamson's Many Necessary Existents". *Analysis* 69: 250–8.

Sider, T. (2006), "Beyond the Humphrey Objection", ms. Available from http://tedsider.org/papers/counterpart_theory.pdf.

Sider, T. (2005), "Another Look at Armstrong's Combinatorialism". *Noûs* 39: 680–96.

Sider, T. (2003), "Reductive Theories of Modality". In M. J. Loux and D. Zimmerman (eds), *The Oxford Handbook of Metaphysics*. Oxford: Oxford University Press: 180–208.

Sider, T. (2002), "The Ersatz Pluriverse". *The Journal of Philosophy* 99: 279–315.

Sider, T. (2001), "Review of Charles S. Chihara, *The Worlds of Possibility*". *The Philosophical Review* 110: 88–91.

Siderits, M. and J. D. O'Brien (1976), "Zeno and on Nāgārjuna on Motion". *Philosophy East and West* 26: 281–99.

Skyrms, B. (1981), "Tractarian Nominalism". *Philosophical Studies* 40: 199–206.

Skyrms, B. (1976), "Impossible Worlds, Physics and Metaphysics". *Philosophical Studies* 30: 323–32.

Smith, R. (2014), "Aristotle's Logic". In E. N. Zalta, *The Stanford Encyclopedia of Philosophy* (Spring 2014). Available from http://plato.stanford.edu/archives/spr2014/entries/aristotle-logic/

Smullyan, A. F. (1948), "Modality and Description". *Journal of Symbolic Logic* 13: 31–7.

Soames, S. (2010), *Philosophy of Language*. Princeton, NJ: Princeton University Press.

Sosa, E. (2000), "Modal and Other *A Priori* Epistemology: How Can We Know What is Possible and What is Impossible?". *The Southern Journal of Philosophy* XXXVIII (Supplement): 1–16.

Spade, P. V. (ed.) (1999), *The Cambridge Companion to Ockham*. Cambridge: Cambridge University Press.

Spade, P. V. and C. Panaccio (2011), "William of Ockham". In E. N. Zalta (ed.), *The Stanford Encyclopedia of Philosophy* (Fall 2011). Available from http://plato.stanford.edu/archives/fall2011/entries/ockham/

Speaks, J. (2012), "On Possibly Nonexistent Propositions". *Philosophy and Phenomenological Research* 85: 528–62.

Stalnaker, R. (2012), *Mere Possibilities. Metaphysical Foundations of Modal Metaphysics*. Princeton, NJ: Princeton University Press.

Stalnaker, R. (2010), "Merely Possible Propositions". In B. Hale and A. Hoffman eds, *Modality: Metaphysics, Logic, and Epistemology*. Oxford: Oxford University Press: 21–32.

Stalnaker, R. (2003), *Ways a World Might Be. Metaphysical and Anti-Metaphysical Essays*. Oxford: Oxford University Press.

Stalnaker, R. (1996), "Impossibilities". *Philosophical Topics* 24: 193–204.

Stalnaker, R. (1984), *Inquiry*. Cambridge, MA: MIT Press.

Strawson, G. (2000), "David Hume: Objects and Power". In R. Read and K. A. Richman (eds), *The New Hume Debate*. New York: Routledge: 31–51.

Strawson, G. (1989), *The Secret Connexion: Causation, Realism and David Hume*. Oxford: Clarendon Press.

Swoyer, C. (1982), "The Nature of Natural Laws". *Australasian Journal of Philosophy* 60: 203–23.

Thom, P. (2003), *Medieval Modal Systems. Problems and Concepts*. Ashgate Studies in Medieval Philosophy, Aldershot Ashgate.

Thomas, H. G. (1996), "Combinatorialism and Primitive Modality". *Philosophical Studies* 83: 231–22.

Thomasson, A. (2010), "Modal Expressivism and the Methods of Metaphysics". *Philosophical Topics* 35: 135–60.

Torza, A. (2015), "Speaking of Essence". *The Philosophical Quarterly* 65: 211–31.

Torza, A. (2011), "Models for Counterparts", *Axiomathes* 21: 553–79.

Trogdon, K. (2013), "An Introduction to Grounding". In M. Hoeltje, B. Schnieder, and A. Steinberg (eds), *Varieties of Dependence. Ontological Dependence, Grounding, Supervenience, Response-Dependence*. München: Philosophia: 97–122.

Vacek, M. (2013), "Concrete Impossible Worlds". *Filozofia* 68: 523–29.

Van Fraassen, B. C. (1980), *The Scientific Image*. Oxford: Clarendon Press.

Van Fraassen, B. C. (1977), "The Only Necessity is Verbal Necessity". *Journal of Philosophy* 74: 71–85.

Van Inwagen, P. (1998), "Modal Epistemology". *Philosophical Studies* 92: 67–84.

Van Inwagen, P. (1986), "Two Concepts of Possible Worlds". In P. A. French, T. E. Uehling, and H. K. Wettstein, Jr. (eds), *Midwest Studies in Philosophy, XI: Studies in Essentialism*. Minneapolis: University of Minnesota Press: 185–213.

Van Inwagen, P. (1985), "Plantinga on Trans-World Identity". In J. Tomberlin and P. Van Inwagen (eds), *Alvin Plantinga: A Profile*. Dordrecht: Reidel: 101–20.

Van Inwagen, P. (1983), *An Essay on Free Will*. Oxford: Clarendon Press.

Van Inwagen, P. (1980), "Indexicality and Actuality". *The Philosophical Review* 89: 403–26.

Van Rijen, J. (1989), *Aspects of Aristotle's Logic of Modalities*. Synthese Historical Library 35. Dordrecht: Kluwer.

Van Roojen, M. (2014), "Moral Cognitivism vs. Non-Cognitivism". *Stanford Encyclopedia of Philosophy (Fall 2014)*. Available from http://plato.stanford.edu/archives/fall2014/entries/moral–cognitivism/

Vance, C. (2014), "Dispositional Modal Truthmakers and the Necessary Origin". *Philosophia* 42: 1111–27.

Varzi, A. C. (2002), "Words and Objects". In A. Bottani, M. Carrara, and D. Giaretta (eds), *Individuals, Essence, and Identity. Themes of Analytic Metaphysics*. Dordrecht: Kluwer: 49–75.

Varzi, A. C. (2001), "Parts, Counterparts, and Modal Occurrents". *Travaux de Logique* 14: 151–71.

Vetter, B. (2015), *Potentiality. From Dispositions to Modality*. Oxford: Oxford University Press.

Vetter, B. (2014), "Dispositions without Conditionals". *Mind* 123: 129–56.

Vetter, B. (2013a). "<<Can>>" without Possible Worlds: Semantics for Anti-Humeans". *Philosopher's Imprint* 13: 1–27.

Vetter, B. (2013b), "Multi-track Dispositions". *Philosophical Quarterly* 63: 330–52.

Vetter, B. (2011a), "Recent Work: Modality without Possible Worlds". *Analysis* 71: 742–54.

Vetter, B. (2011b), "On Linking Dispositions and Which Conditionals?". *Mind* 120: 1173–89.

Vihvelin, K. (1988), "The Modal Argument for Incompatibilism". *Philosophical Studies* 53: 227–44.

Von Wright, G. (1951), *An Essay in Modal Logic*. Amsterdam: North-Holland.

Wang, J. (2015), "The Modal Limits of Dispositionalism". *Noûs* 49: 454–69.

Wang, J. (2013), "From Combinatorialism to Primitivism". *Australasian Journal of Philosophy* 91: 535–54.

Waterloo, S. (1982), *Passage and Possibility. A Study of Aristotle's Modal Concepts*. Oxford: Oxford University Press.

Weatherson, B. and D. Marshall (2012), "Intrinsic vs. Extrinsic Properties". In E. N. Zalta (ed.), *The Stanford Encyclopedia of Philosophy* (Fall 2014). Available from http://plato.stanford.edu/archives/fall2014/entries/intrinsic-extrinsic/

Wee, C. (2006), "Descartes and Leibniz on Human Free Will and the Human Ability to Do Otherwise". *Canadian Journal of Philosophy* 36: 387–414.

Wiggins, D. (2003), "Existence and Contingency: A Note". *Philosophy* 78: 483–94.

Wiggins, D. (1980), *Sameness and Substance*. Oxford: Basil Blackwell.

Williamson, T. (2013), *Modal Logic as Metaphysics*. Oxford: Oxford University Press.

Williamson, T. (2010), "Modal Logic within Counterfactual Logic". In B. Hale and A. Hoffman (eds), *Modality: Metaphysics, Logic, and Epistemology*. Oxford: Oxford University Press: 81–96.

Williamson, T. (2007a), *The Philosophy of Philosophy*. Oxford: Basil Blackwell.

Williamson, T. (2007b), "Philosophical Knowledge and Knowledge of Counterfactuals". *Grazer Philosophische Studien* 74: 89–123.

Williamson, T. (2005), "Armchair Philosophy: Metaphysical Modality and Counterfactual Thinking". *Proceedings of the Aristotelian Society* 105: 1–23.

Williamson, T. (2002), "Necessary Existents". In A. O'Hear (ed.), *Royal Institute of Philosophy Supplement*. Cambridge: Cambridge University Press: 269–87.

Williamson, T. (2000), "The Necessary Framework of Objects". *Topoi* 19: 201–8.

Williamson, T. (1998), "Bare Possibilia". *Erkenntnis* 48: 257–73.

Williamson, T. (1990), "Necessary Identity and Necessary Existence". In R. Haller and J. Brandl (eds), *Wittgenstein—Towards a Re-evaluation. Proceedings of the 14th International Wittgenstein Symposium*, Vol. 1. Vienna: Hoder-Pichler-Tempsky: 168–75.

Wilson, C. (2000), "Plenitude and Compossibility in Leibniz". *The Leibniz Review* 10: 1–20.

Wittgenstein, L. (1953), *Philosophical Investigations*. Oxford: Basil Blackwell.

Wittgenstein, L. (1921), "Logisch–philosophische Abhandlung". In *Annalen der Naturphilosophie* 14: 185–262; revised English edition, *Tractatus Logico-Philosophicus*. London: Kegan Paul, Trench, Trubner & Co.

Woodward, R. (2012), "Fictionalism and Incompleteness". *Noûs* 46: 781–90.

Woodward, R. (2011), "Is Modal Fictionalism Artificial?" *Pacific Philosophical Quarterly* 92: 535–50.

Woodward, R. (2008), "Why Modal Fictionalism is Not Self-Defeating". *Philosophical Studies* 139: 273–88.

Wright, C. (1980), *Wittgenstein on the Foundations of Mathematics*. London: Duckworth.

Yablo, S. (2001), "Go Figure: A Path Through Fictionalism". *Midwest Studies in Philosophy* 25: 72–102.

Yablo, S. (1994), "Is Conceivability a Guide to Possibility?". *Philosophy and Phenomenological Research* 53: 1–42.

Yagisawa, T. (2010), *Worlds and Individuals. Possible and Otherwise*. Oxford: Oxford University Press.

Yagisawa, T. (1988), "Beyond Possible Worlds". *Philosophical Studies* 53: 175–204.

Yates, D. (2015), "Dispositionalism and the Modal Operators." *Philosophy and Phenomenological Research* 91: 411–24.

Zalta, E. N., (2010), "Logic and Metaphysics". *Journal of Indian Council of Philosophical Research* 27: 155–84.

Zalta, E. N. (2006), "Essence and Modality". *Mind* 115: 659–93.

Zalta, E. N. (1988), *Intentional Logic and the Metaphysics of Intentionality*. Cambridge, MA: MIT Press.

Zalta, E. N. (1983), *Abstract Objects. An Introduction to Axiomatic Metaphysics*. Cambridge, MA: MIT Press.

Zupko, J. (2014), "John Buridan". In E. N. Zalta (ed.), *The Stanford Encyclopedia of Philosophy* (Spring 2014). Available from http://plato.stanford.edu/archives/spr2014/entries/buridan/

Index of Names

Index of Terms